Business Environment

Managing in a strategic context

John Kew and John Stredwick

The Chartered Institute of Personnel and Development

Published by the Chartered Institute of Personnel and Development
151 The Broadway, London, SW19 1JQ

First published 2005
Reprinted 2006

Typeset by Ferdinand Page Design, Surrey
Printed in Great Britain by The Cromwell Press, Trowbridge, Wiltshire

British Library Cataloguing in Publication Data
A catalogue of this publication is available from the British Library

ISBN-1 84398 079 7
ISBN-13 978 184398 079 7

The views expressed in this book are the authors' own and may not necessarily reflect those of the CIPD.

Chartered Institute of Personnel and Development, CIPD House,
151 The Broadway, London, SW19 1JQ
Tel: 020 8612 6204
Email: cipd@cipd.co.uk   Website: www.cipd.co.uk
Incorporated by Royal Charter   Registered Charity No. 1079797

Business Environment

Managing in a strategic context

2⌐

John Kew was Principal Lecturer in Management Studies and Head of the Business School at Harlow College until 1993, teaching Business Environment and Strategic Management on CIPD and DMS programmes. Since 1993 he has been an educational consultant, and has also written Flexible Learning material for the CIPD's Professional Development Scheme.

John Stredwick spent 25 years as a Human Resource Practitioner in publishing and shipbuilding before joining Everest Double Glazing for 11 years as Head of Personnel. In 1992, he joined Luton University as Senior Lecturer and has directed the CIPD programmes since that time. *Business Environment* is his sixth book with the CIPD including *Flexible Working* (2nd edition, 2005). He is a national moderator for the CIPD and has run several CIPD short courses on reward management.

The CIPD would like to thank the following members of the CIPD Publishing Editorial Board for their help and advice:

- Pauline Dibben, Middlesex University Business School
- Edwina Hollings, Staffordshire University Business School
- Caroline Hook, Huddersfield University Business School
- Vincenza Priola, Wolverhampton Business School
- John Sinclair, Napier University Business School

The Chartered Institute of Personnel and Development is the leading publisher of books and reports for personnel and training professionals, students, and all those concerned with the effective management and development of people at work. For details of all our titles, please contact the publishing department:
Tel: 020 8612 6204
E-mail: publish@cipd.co.uk
The catalogue of all CIPD titles can be viewed on the CIPD website:
www.cipd.co.uk/bookstore

CONTENTS

Preface

The worldwide interest in business grows at an extraordinary pace, fuelled by the burgeoning power and influence of Far Eastern economies and especially by the growth of China. An understanding of the business environment is therefore vital for students who wish to gain a fuller understanding of both the context in which business decisions are taken and the major influences in those decisions. As the context becomes more turbulent and unpredictable, the more important it becomes to grasp the complexity of the many issues presented and the strategic options that can be followed.

This publication follows closely the CIPD standards for Managing in a Strategic Business context but is suitable for students at all levels whose syllabus includes a module in Business Environment, as it covers all the standard subjects normally included in such modules. The emphasis is very much on developing the knowledge and understanding of students, while the main aim has been to make the text accessible and encourage students to follow up key issues by linking the text with up-to-date cases, activities and associated reading.

The edition will be supported by a tutor support site at www.cipd.co.uk/tss. The information contained on this site is available free of charge to tutors, but tutors will need to register to gain access to the material. Visit www.cipd.co.uk/tss to complete the online registration form. The site contains links to general business sites and advice to lecturers who adopt the text on how to use the book as part of a planned series of lectures. Powerpoint presentations will be available to accompany each chapter and there will be suggested feedback for Activities, as well as additional Activities.

A summary of the book's contents is as follows.

Chapter 1 sets the scene for business in its environment, explaining how the environment influences business decisions while, in turn, decisions by business help to shape the contexts within which businesses operate. The STEEPLE model is utilised to illustrate this process.

Chapter 2 introduces students to the principles of market economies, reveals theories on sources of competitive advantage, discusses the roles of players in the economic and ethical scene, such as trade unions and professional associations and illustrates how different competitive strategies have implications for human resource activity.

Chapter 3 discusses the role and function of the European Union and debates major issues around integration and enlargement. The causes, extent and desirability of the globalisation process then follows, together with the range of responses by governments, and its impact on the markets for goods, services and labour. The attempts by international bodies to support and regulate trading behaviour are also examined.

Chapter 4 analyses the roles and functions of government in the fields of economics, industry, education and social policy with their implications for employment markets. International variations in government policy are set out with particular reference to the European Union. The chapter ends with an examination of the ways that organisations seek to influence the development of government policy through the operation of variants of pressure groups.

Chapter 5 examines a wide range of legal and regulatory aspects, starting with an essential summary of the UK legal system and the way that the regulation has developed in the fields of employment, health and safety, consumer and commercial law. The impact of regulation on particular sectors is discussed and the direction of regulation is debated.

Chapter 6 summarises the startling changes in demography in recent years both in the UK and worldwide, discussing the major implications of an ageing population in the advanced economies and a still rapidly rising population growth in the developing countries. There is a debate about the natural flow of migrants from one grouping to the other. The influence on markets for goods and services and the challenges and opportunities in the employment field are considered in detail, together with government initiatives in key areas, such as pensions and migration.

Chapter 7 focuses on the major social trends and attitudes alongside the changing social structure. The causes of major social problems, such as the increase in criminal behaviour, are debated and the implications for employment and labour markets are examined. How organisations can react to the changes and the options available are considered.

Chapter 8 presents an analysis on technological change and its substantial influence on the business environment, especially in the fields of information and communication technology. The opportunities in the labour markets that technology offers, such as teleworking and online recruitment, are discussed together with the benefits and difficulties associated with such techniques. The reasons why there is considerable resistance to technology in certain quarters are examined.

Chapter 9 focuses on the application of social responsibility and ethics to the business community, examining stakeholder models and issues of accountability and professionalism. The nature and extent of corporate social responsibility and the systems of ethical responses to developments in the competitive environment are debated, together with issues arising from environmental developments, such as global warming and sustainability. The role of human resources in these issues is examined.

Chapter 10 brings together all the major strands covered earlier to examine the effects upon constructing and developing business strategy. This includes the major tools and techniques in environmental analysis, the various approaches to strategy-making and the constraints that the environment imposes upon strategy formation and implementation. The chapter includes debates on project and risk management and the major principles in effective strategic leadership, change formulation and management.

Chapter 11 concludes the book with two extended business case studies.

We would like to acknowledge the help and encouragement we have received from colleagues and friends in writing the text but special thanks are extended to our families for their support and forbearance over an extended period.

For those tutors and students using this text to support the CIPD Leadership and Management module 'Managing in a Strategic Business Context', a table is provided on the next page detailing how the content of the text fits with the indicative content of the CIPD module.

CIPD Leadership and Management Standards: managing in a strategic business context

The indicative content of the standards is covered as follows:

CIPD Leadership and Management Standards   **Business Environment chapters**

	CIPD Leadership and Management Standards		Business Environment chapters
1	The Competitive Environment	Chapter 2	The Competitive Environment
2	The Technological Context	Chapter 8	Technology
3	Globalisation	Chapter 3	The European Union and Globalisation
4	Demographic Trends	Chapter 6	Demography
5	Social Trends	Chapter 7	Social Trends
6	Government Policy	Chapter 4	Government policy
7	Regulation	Chapter 5	Regulation
8	Developing Strategy	Chapter 10	Strategic Management
9	Social Responsibility and Ethics	Chapter 9	Social Responsibility and Ethics

National Occupational Standards: Management and Leadership Standards

The knowledge and understanding of the standards are covered as follows:

B2 *Map the environment in which your organisation operates*

Chapter 1	Organisations and their Environments
Chapter 2	The Competitive Environment
Chapter 3	The International Scene: the European Union and Globalisation
Chapter 4	Government Policy
Chapter 6	Demography
Chapter 7	Social Trends
Chapter 8	Technology

B3 *Develop a strategic business plan for your organisation*

Chapter 10	Strategic Management
Chapter 11	Managing in a Strategic Business Context – an Integrative Case Study

B4 *Put the strategic business plan into action*

Chapter 10	Strategic Management

B8 *Ensure compliance with legal, regulatory, ethical and social requirements*

Chapter 5	Regulation
Chapter 7	Social Trends
Chapter 9	Social Responsibility and Ethics

C4 *Lead change (part)*

Chapter 10	Strategic Management

C5 *Plan change (part)*

Chapter 10	Strategic Management

C6 *Implement change (part)*

Chapter 10	Strategic Management

Organisations and Their Environments

CHAPTER 1

OBJECTIVES

By the end of this chapter, readers should be able to understand, explain and critically evaluate:

- **the distinction between the general and the task environment**
- **the STEEPLE model of environmental analysis**
- **the difference between placid, dynamic and turbulent environments, and their impact on organisations**
- **the identification of key environmental factors**
- **the use of SWOT analysis**
- **the Miles and Snow classification of environmental responses.**

WHAT IS THE ENVIRONMENT?

At its simplest, the environment is anything outside an organisation which may affect an organisation's present or future activities. Thus the environment is situational – it is unique to each organisation. As a result, we must always bear in mind the interaction between a particular organisation, and its particular environment.

It is useful to think of the environment on two levels. One is the general environment (also known as the societal environment, the far environment or the macro environment). The other is the task environment (or the specific environment, the near environment or the micro environment).

Forces in the general environment have a major impact at the level of the industry. These forces include national culture, including historical background, ideologies and values; scientific and technological developments; the level of education; legal and political processes; demographic factors; available resources, the international environment; and the general economic, social and industrial structure of the country.

The task environment covers the forces relevant to an individual organisation within an industry. These include customers, suppliers, competitors, regulators, the local labour market, and specific technologies.

The distinction between general and task environments is not a static one. Elements in the general environment are continually breaking through to the task environment, and impacting on individual organisations.

A different but complementary approach is to see the organisation as an open system, which interacts in two main ways with its task environment. It takes in resources from the environment, converts them into goods and/or services, and returns outputs to the environment in order to satisfy some need (Fig. 1.1).

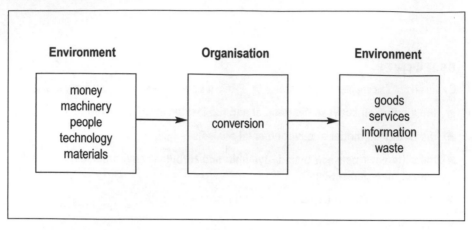

Figure 1.1 *A systems model of the organisation and its environment*

In order to function effectively in such a system, the organisation must fully understand both its input and its output environments.

A more complex variation is to add a third element – that of regulations which control the conversion process. The three elements (inputs, outputs and regulations) provide the organisation with both opportunities and constraints. All three elements are also subject to the influences of the general environment.

ACTIVITY 1.1

The systems approach

Identify inputs, outputs, regulators and the conversion process in:

1   a manufacturer of baked beans

2   a trade union

3   your own organisation.

ANALYSING THE ENVIRONMENT

Most organisations will not have a great deal of problems in analysing their task environment. They know who their customers, suppliers, competitors, etc. are. Analysing the general environment is more complex. The first step will probably be to brainstorm a list of various environmental factors which seem to impact on the organisation. This is a start, but to progress further, it will be necessary to classify these influences.

One widely used tool for classification is PEST analysis and its derivatives. PEST analysis breaks down environmental influences into four categories:

Political/legal	Taxation policy, European Union directives, trade regulations, geopolitical factors like the 'war on terror', government stability, employment law, contract law, competition law, etc.
Economic	Business cycles, economic growth, interest rates, supply and demand factors, competition factors, public spending, money supply, inflation, unemployment, disposable income
Socio-cultural	Demographic trends, income distribution. Social mobility, lifestyle, attitudes to work and leisure, levels of education
Technological	Research and development, new inventions or innovations, speed of technology transfer, rates of obsolescence, development of systems.

PEST analysis was widely used during the 1980s and early 1990s. By the mid-1990s, it was becoming more common to talk of PESTLE analysis. Political and Legal were split from each other, and an extra factor, Environment, was added. This reflected a growing awareness of environmental factors, and the first concerns about global warming.

By the early 2000s, PESTLE had evolved into STEEPLE, with the addition of Ethics, reflecting the development of concern for corporate social responsibility and business ethics. The classification currently used is thus:

S	Social
T	Technological
E	Economic
E	Environmental
P	Political
L	Legal
E	Ethical.

The STEEPLE model forms the structure of this book. We will be examining each of the STEEPLE elements in turn (although not in this order), and we will conclude by bringing everything together in an analysis of strategy formation.

ACTIVITY 1.2
The Post Office

Mr and Mrs Fletcher have owned the sub post office and only shop in a medium-sized village (600 inhabitants) in central Wales for two years. The village is 60 per cent Welsh-speaking, but the Fletchers, who originally came from Birmingham, do not speak Welsh. The sub post office is operated under licence from the Post Office. The post office business has shown a slow rate of increase over the last 10 years, but this now seems to be levelling off. They also sell basic groceries, sweets, tobacco, soft drinks, childrens' toys, and stationery. The village still has an agricultural sector in farming and food processing, although this was hard hit by foot and mouth disease in 2001. The population of the village has declined by about 100 in the past 20 years, and a number of houses are now weekend holiday cottages, mainly owned by people from the West Midlands. About a third of the village population are retired.

There are three small towns (population 5,000–10,000) within 20 miles. There are weekly bus services from the village to each of these towns. Some inhabitants of the village work in light industry in these towns, each of which has at least one small supermarket. There is a local farmer with a milk round in the village. He has recently started carrying groceries on his round.

The village is on a holiday route to the Welsh coastal resorts, and there is a certain amount of passing trade. There is also a well-known pub and a stately home in the village. When the Fletchers bought the shop, they found that the business was about breaking even, but that its turnover had declined in the previous three years as their predecessors had deliberately cut down on their range of groceries, partly because of their own increasing age, and partly because of difficulties which they had encountered with efficient stock-keeping.

The Fletchers manage all the work themselves, except for employing one part-time assistant for two mornings a week – Saturday to cope with the passing trade, and Tuesday, when George Fletcher goes to the cash-and-carry for supplies.

Using the STEEPLE model, analyse the general environmental factors which could impinge on the shop.

WHY DO WE NEED TO UNDERSTAND AND MANAGE THE ENVIRONMENT?

Organisations have a choice in how they manage their relationships with their environment. They can sit back and wait for the environment to change, without attempting to predict its behaviour, and then react to changes as they happen. Here they are being reactive – constantly fire-fighting immediate problems. Or they can identify and foresee changes in the environment, and plan their responses before these changes happen. They are being proactive – planning for the future. A few organisations are in the fortunate position of being able to go even further and manage the environment in their own interests – at different times since 1900, Ford, IBM, Sony, McDonalds and Microsoft have done this.

The nature of the environment is also significant. Some organisations have static or placid environments, where it is reasonable to suppose that the future will be a continuation of the past. For example, this was true of many UK nationalised industries before privatisation. An organisation in this happy situation can afford to limit its analysis of its environment to past history. However, such an organisation is likely to be caught totally unawares if the nature of its environment does change rapidly. For example, many airlines in continental Europe were either owned by, or heavily protected by, their home governments. This cosy relationship was totally disrupted by the events of September 11th 2001, with the resultant rapid collapse of two national airlines, Swissair and Sabena.

Other organisations face turbulent environments, because the environment is either dynamic or in a state of rapid change, for example the pharmaceutical industry or the defence industry; or because the environment is complex, and thus difficult to analyse, for example a multinational company with interests in many countries or industries. Turbulent environments are uncertain. If the environment facing an organisation is dynamic, the organisation will need to have procedures for sensing future environmental changes, and contingency plans for dealing with a range of possible changes. This involves the technique known as scenario building. An organisation with a complex environment may need to break down the complexity, so that environmental analysis is decentralised to product groups or countries within the organisation.

The most difficult situation of all, of course, is where the environment is both dynamic and complex. Here the organisation may have to recognise that it cannot predict its environment, and what is important is to foster a culture in the organisation that welcomes and is able to cope with radical change. The organisation must learn to live with chaos. One definition of a learning organisation is an organisation which has developed systematic procedures to ensure that it can learn from its environment.

ACTIVITY 1.3

Turbulent environments

In what ways have the environments of local authorities become more turbulent in recent years?

Johnson, Scholes and Whittington (2004) propose a five-stage model in analysing the environment as follows.

Stage 1 Audit of environmental influences

Stage 2 Assessment of nature of the environment

Stage 3 Identification of key environmental factors

Stage 4 Identification of the competitive position

Stage 5 Identification of the principal opportunities and threats.

Strategic position

Stage 1 involves the preparation of a STEEPLE analysis. Stage 2 builds on the placid/dynamic/turbulent classification of environments discussed above. Stage 3 involves a more sophisticated analysis which may include the following.

- Identifying a smaller number of key environmental influences. For example, for the NHS these might be demographic trends (ageing population), technological developments in health care, and implementation of government policy (public-private partnerships).

- Identifying long-term drivers of change. For example, the increasing globalisation of markets for some products, eg consumer electronics, cars and pharmaceuticals.

The key principle here is that not all environmental influences are equally important. The analysis in Stage 3 involves identifying those that are most important.

Stage 4 (identifying the organisation's competitive position) will be tackled in the next chapter, using techniques such as Porter's Five Forces (Porter 1980).

Stage 5 (identifying principal opportunities and threats) involves another well-known technique, SWOT analysis.

SWOT stands for:

Strengths

Weaknesses

Opportunities

Threats.

Strengths and Weaknesses are inward-looking, and particularly concerned with the resources of the organisation. Opportunities and Threats are outward-looking and involve the analysis of environmental factors. The organisation should ensure that its Strengths (or core competencies) are appropriate ones to exploit Opportunities or to counter Threats.

Both Opportunities and Threats can be analysed using matrices. Opportunities can be assessed according to their attractiveness and the organisation's probability of success.

		Probability of success	
		High	Low
Attractiveness	High	1	2
	Low	3	4

Figure 1.2 *An attractiveness–success matrix*

Opportunities in cell 1 offer the greatest scope, and organisations should concentrate on these. Cell 4 represents opportunities which in practice can be ignored. Cells 2 and 3 may be worth investigating further.

Threats can be assessed on the basis of their seriousness and their probability of occurrence.

		Impact	
		High	Low
Probability of occurrence	High	1	2
	Low	3	4

Figure 1.3 *An impact–probability matrix*

A threat which has a high probability of happening, and the likelihood of a considerable impact on the organisation (cell 1), will be a key factor which must be a driver of the organisation's strategy, and for which detailed contingency plans must be prepared. At the other extreme (cell 4), a threat which has little likelihood of happening, and little impact if it does happen, can be largely ignored. The threats in cells 2 and 3 should be carefully monitored in case they become critical.

It should be remembered that opportunities and threats are rarely mutually exclusive. Many factors can be both. For example, the technological development of EFTPOS (Electronic Funds Transfer at Point of Sale) money transfer systems (using debit and credit cards) can be a threat to small retailers, as their use by competitors may give the latter a competitive edge, but can also be an opportunity, because they lessen the amount of cash likely to be in tills, and so make the shop less attractive to thieves.

ACTIVITY 1.4

The Hospital

How would you classify the following factors on a probability/seriousness matrix for a Hospital Trust. What contingency planning should the Trust make?

1 a serious accident on the local railway line, casing scores of deaths and injuries
2 an ageing local population
3 a leakage of radioactive material at a nuclear power station 200 miles (downwind) away.

Managing the environment

Miles and Snow (1978) suggest four main ways in which organisations can cope with and manage their environments. These involve an interaction between the organisation's strategy, its culture, and its environment. They can be as follows.

Defenders	They operate in generally placid environments. They do not actively search for new opportunities, but concentrate on maximising the efficiency of their existing operations. They are very vulnerable to a sudden shift in their environment.
Prospectors	They are attracted to turbulent environments. They are constantly experimenting with novel responses to the environment. They thrive on change and uncertainty, but pay little attention to efficiency. They are thus vulnerable if the environment settles down.
Analysers	They are successful poachers. They watch competitors for new ideas, and adopt the successful ones. Their approach to the environment is therefore second-hand, and they let the prospectors make the mistakes. A classic example of the analyser strategy is the video-recorder war. Sony pioneered the industry with the Betamax format, but was eventually defeated by Matsushita and its VHS format.
Reactors	They make adjustments to their strategy when forced to do so by environmental pressures. Unlike the defenders, they are prepared to change, but they are even more market followers than the analysers.

Figure 1.4 *The Miles and Snow classification of responses to the environment*

Organisations must recognise that a strategy which suited them very well in the past may no longer be appropriate if the nature of the environment which faces them has changed.

SUMMARY AND CONCLUSIONS

This Chapter has analysed the nature of environments, ways in which they can be analysed, and responses which organisations can make to them. Key Learning Points are as follows.

KEY LEARNING POINTS

- The general environment consists of factors which impact at an industry-wide level, while the task environment is primarily concerned with the immediate environment which impacts on an individual organisation within an industry.
- Organisations can be seen as open systems which interact with their environments.
- The STEEPLE model lists and classifies the major general environmental factors which impact on organisations.
- The main point of STEEPLE analysis is to identify key environmental drivers.
- Opportunities and Threats to the organisation can be classified according to probability of success and attractiveness; and probability of occurrence and impact respectively.
- Miles and Snow (1978) have identified four different ways in which organisations react to their environments.

FURTHER READING

No specific further reading is recommended for this introductory chapter.

The Competitive Environment

OBJECTIVES

By the end of this chapter, readers should be able to understand, explain and critically evaluate:

- the fundamental economic problem of scarcity and choice, and the ways in which this problem is tackled by market and mixed economies

- determinants of supply and demand

- the main types of market structure, including perfect and monopolistic competition, monopoly and oligopoly, and their implications for price and output

- Michael Porter's Five Forces model of competitive structure

- portfolio approaches to Strategic Business Unit (SBU) analysis, including the Boston Matrix and the Shell Directional Policy Matrix

- the effect of environmental pressures on the public and voluntary sectors

- HR implications of responses to environmental change

- strategic responses to environmental change.

ECONOMIC SYSTEMS

Different types of societies have organised their economies in different ways, but all have to produce answers to the same questions, whatever their economic system.

ACTIVITY 2.1

Scarcity and choice

Economists often say that economics is about scarcity and choice. What do you think they mean by this? What problems are caused by the conflict of scarcity and choice?

Three main models have emerged:

1 The command economy
2 The market economy
3 The mixed economy.

Of these we will consider the market and mixed economies in some depth. The command economy we can dismiss quite quickly, as it no longer exists in any real sense, except perhaps in North Korea. Here all economic decisions are made by the state, or rather by a central planning authority acting on the state's behalf, which decides what will be produced, by whom and who gets it.

The market economy

Here economic decisions are taken on the basis of prices. There are no central planners, and decisions are taken by millions of individual consumers and producers. Producers produce only what they can sell to consumers; workers sell their services to producers and receive income, which they use to buy goods and services from the producers. In the last resort it is therefore the consumers who decide what is produced (consumer sovereignty), and the economy is a closed two-player system (Fig. 2.1).

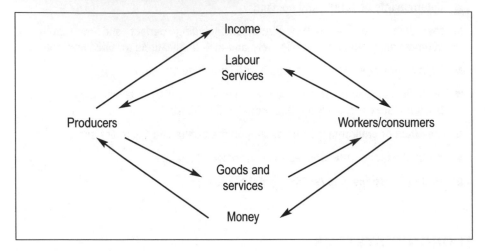

Figure 2.1 *Flows in the market economy*

Our core economic problems are thus answered as follows.

- What is going to be produced? Anything which consumers are prepared to buy (demand in the jargon).
- How is it going to be produced? In the most efficient way. If a producer is not efficient, he will be driven out of business by an efficient one.
- Who is going to get it? Anyone who is prepared to pay for it.

ACTIVITY 2.2

Market economies

1 What would you say are the strengths and weaknesses of the market system?
2 Can you think of any examples of pure market economies?

Mixed economies

In practice all economies are mixed to a greater or lesser extent. Command elements commonly include:

- a framework of law – the law of contract, company law
- publicly provided social goods like defence, police, education, welfare and health
- publicly owned industries – the BBC in the UK, Amtrak in the USA, Electricité de France in France
- state regulation of the level of economic activity
- control of economic behaviour – employment law, anti-trust law, anti-discrimination law, etc.
- often the use of taxation to redistribute income as well as to raise revenue for public services.

Throughout the rest of this chapter, we will be analysing the working of the mixed economy, with particular reference to the UK.

MARKET STRUCTURES

Economists classify market structures by the number of firms within the market (and to a lesser extent the number of purchasers).

The main classifications are:

- perfect competition
- monopolistic competition
- monopoly
- oligopoly.

There are also two other less commonly found firms.

1 monopsony
2 bilateral monopoly.

Perfect competition

This is a market where no one producer has an advantage over any other producer. There are many producers, none of whom has a sufficient share of the market to be able to influence the market price. They are known as price-takers. Similarly, there are a large number of buyers, who are also price takers. The price in the market is set by supply and demand.

Demand measures the amount of the good or service which buyers are willing to buy at a given price (note not the amount they need – demand is based on willingness to pay). Broadly speaking the lower the price the greater the quantity which buyers will demand. This enables us to plot a demand curve – in practice plotted as a straight line (Fig. 2.2).

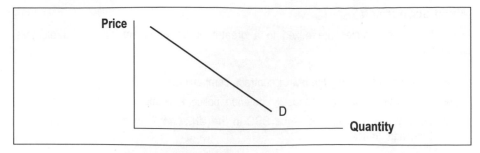

Figure 2.2 *A typical demand curve*

If the price rises, the quantity which buyers are prepared to buy will fall. This is known as a fall in quantity demanded. On the other hand, some external event may mean that buyers are prepared to buy more of the product at all prices – perhaps their incomes have increased. This is known as a rise in demand, and is illustrated in our diagram by a shift of the demand curve to the right (Fig. 2.3). Similarly, a fall in demand is shown by a shift of the curve to the left.

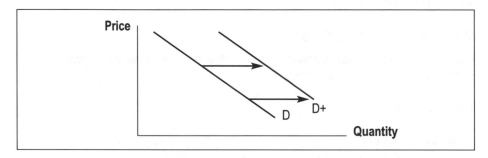

Figure 2.3 *An increase in demand*

The same principles apply to supply. Broadly speaking, the quantity of a good which producers are prepared to supply is higher the higher the price, producing a supply curve (Fig. 2.4). Again, a movement along this line is known as a change in quantity supplied; a shift to of the curve rightwards or leftwards is known as an increase or decrease in supply.

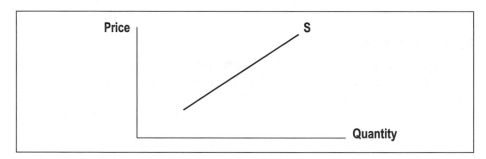

Figure 2.4 *The supply curve*

If we put together the supply curve and the demand curve, the result is Figure 2.5. This shows that there is one unique combination of price and quantity where the two lines intersect (point E).

This sets the price that will be charged in that market, and the quantity which will be bought and sold, and crucially this is an outcome which is equally acceptable to both buyers and sellers.

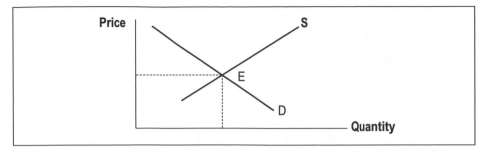

Figure 2.5 *Supply, demand and equilibrium*

The product sold in a perfectly competitive market is assumed to be identical – thus there is no reason to favour one seller over another on grounds of quality or special features or service. It is also assumed that all players in the market are extremely well informed, and capable of reacting very quickly to any changes. There is thus no point in advertising – all products are identical and buyers know them to be identical. Buyers will react very quickly to any change in price, while sellers will very rapidly copy any innovation introduced by one of their rivals. Entry to the market is also completely free – anyone can enter or leave the market at any time.

Because of the nature of the market, there is no incentive for any one seller to cut his price – remember he can sell as much as he likes at the current market price. Conversely, if he raises his price even a fraction above the market level, he will sell nothing, because there is no incentive for his customers to stay loyal.

Economists freely admit that perfect competition is extremely unlikely to exist in the real world – its assumptions are too restrictive. Why spend so much space describing it, you may say. The reason is that it is a classic example of an economic model – it is a stylised attempt to explain behaviour, rather than a prescription for managers who want to make sound decisions. Models simplify the real world, and cut it down to its bare essentials, and on the basis of these bare essentials they make logical predictions. Thus the essence of the perfect competition model is to say that if the real world was like this, certain predictions would logically follow from it.

One consequence of the model is that it would lead to an efficient use of resources in the economy. Market forces would push production costs down to the minimum, and ensure that the most efficient production methods are used. Any firm which did not use them would be forced out of business. Profits would also be forced down to the minimum level required to keep firms in business. Any firm which made more profits than the minimum in the short term would be unable to sustain this position in the long term. Unfortunately this also writes economic progress out of the model. There is no incentive to innovate or develop new products, because any advantage will be immediately wiped out through perfect knowledge.

It is also possible to apply the perfect competition model to labour markets. The lower the wage, the higher the number of workers which will be demanded by employers, while the higher the wage the greater the incentive to work in that industry. The only difference is that people's labour services are being sold, rather than, say, apples. Again, the result will be a market equilibrium – exactly the number of workers who are prepared to work for the equilibrium wage will be employed.

ACTIVITY 2.3

Perfect competition

1 How far do you think that the market for Tesco shares on the Stock Exchange meets the requirements of perfect competition?

2 Until the early nineteenth century, farm labourers in England were hired on an annual basis at hiring fairs, where large numbers of labourers and prospective employers would turn up in the local market town and negotiate contracts. How far do you think this system meets the requirements of perfect competition?

Monopolistic competition

Rather more likely is that many firms will compete in a market, but each will sell a slightly different product. This type of market is classified as monopolistic competition. As the product is differentiated, the firms in the market have slightly more freedom in setting their prices. They can decide to charge a slightly higher price and sell a slightly lower volume of goods, and vice versa. To a small extent they are price makers. They can build up customer loyalty, and loyal customers will be prepared to pay a higher price for what they perceive as higher quality, or a closer match with their precise requirements, either in the product itself, or in the services which surround its delivery. Each firm is thus seeking to obtain a mini-monopoly for its product.

Note that a real difference in product is not necessary – what is required is that consumers perceive there to be a difference. Firms in monopolistic competition frequently advertise in order to differentiate their product, while firms in perfect competition do not, as they can sell all they wish anyway.

ACTIVITY 2.4

Monopolistic competition

Can you identify any real-world examples of monopolistic competition?

Monopoly

Theoretically, a firm has a monopoly if it is the only firm supplying a market – ie it has 100 per cent of the market. This is very rare in practice, particularly if one defines a market widely. The Post Office has a monopoly in the UK for delivery of letters of a certain weight, but we also need to include close substitutes for letters in our definition of this market. Once we do this, it is clear that the Post Office faces competition in information transfer from a host of organisations and services, including e-mail, faxes and courier services. Virtually the only organisation with anything approaching a world-wide monopoly is Microsoft, whose operating systems have about 90 per cent of the PC market. Even here, in practice the monopoly is weakened by software piracy, with some estimates saying that half of all software in the UK is illegally copied.

In practice, economists tend to define monopoly functionally – a firm is in a monopoly position if it is able to control the market price of the product it produces. This depends on the size of the firm relative to that of other firms in the industry. If firms in the industry tend to be large, the market leader may need to have perhaps half the market in order to dominate, but in an industry characterised by very small firms, 20 per cent of the market may be enough.

Because it has some control over price, a monopoly can manipulate the price and the quantity which it produces in order to maximise its own profit. Thus price will tend to be higher and quantity produced lower than in a competitive market. This does not necessarily mean that a monopoly will make an excessive profit. If no one wants to buy the product sold by the monopoly, there will be no excessive profit. Being the only producer of horse-drawn hansom cabs is not the best short cut to a fortune!

However, monopoly does have a tendency to excess profit, as well as other disadvantages. It encourages inefficiency in management and production, as there is no competition to force efficiency, and, most crucially, monopoly leads to a misallocation of resources in the economy as a whole. This would tend to suggest that monopoly will not be in the best interests of consumers, and therefore should be at worst controlled, at best banned. This is broadly the approach taken by anti-trust legislation in the USA.

In practice things are not so simple. Often monopolists can gain significant cost advantages (economies of scale) purely because they are big, and the end result might be both higher profits for the monopolist, and a lower price for the consumer. As we will see later, this argument is put forward by supermarkets in the UK. This argument (the natural monopoly argument) has been put forward to oppose the break-up of British Rail at privatisation. Similarly, it may be judged desirable for a company to have a monopoly in the UK market, if the result is that it is big enough to compete efficiently on the world market. As a an example, the Monopolies Commission in the 1970s and 1980s was prepared to tolerate both British Airways' dominant position in the UK market, and its takeover of competitors like British Caledonian and Dan-Air.

There is also a view that monopolies and monopoly profits may well be a necessary part of the competitive process (Schumpeter 1950). Entrepreneurs are continually trying to exploit new opportunities. If they do so, they will achieve a temporary monopoly. Unless this monopoly arises from the sole ownership of a resource for which there is no substitute, the monopoly will be temporary because other firms will recognise the opportunity and enter the market, or they will devise substitute products. Schumpeter called this process 'creative destruction'.

Profits may thus be true monopoly profits, based on ability to restrict entry to the industry; windfall profits, based on short-term fluctuations in the environment and which in different circumstances could be windfall losses, and entrepreneurial profits, based on superior foresight or management, exploiting opportunities which were open to all. This view is supported by the law on patents. Anyone may invent a new process or product, but the reward for doing so is to be granted a temporary monopoly by the state, in return for the entrepreneurial risk and research and development expenses which have been incurred. Patent protection is the driving force behind industries like pharmaceuticals.

Following this view, the key element in assessing monopoly power is not market share but barriers to entry. This has led to the development of the concept of contestable markets

(Lipsey and Chrystal 1999). Markets are contestable if entry is easy; entrants can compete on equal terms with incumbents, and they are not deterred by the threat of retaliatory price cutting by incumbents. The threat of entry to the market can be as effective as actual entry.

Oligopoly

An oligopoly exists when a few large producers control a market between them. The number of firms may vary between two (a duopoly) and about a dozen, and the products can be homogeneous or diversified. Oligopolies are also known as complex monopolies, and it is the latter term which is used by the UK competition authorities. In all cases, the firms in the industry are interdependent. The performance of each firm depends not only on its own actions, but on the actions of the other firms in the industry. Thus, for example, before an oligopoly takes the decision to raise its prices, it must decide whether the other firms are likely to follow, or to keep their prices down and aggressively push to increase their market shares.

Oligopoly is extremely common in the UK. Indeed, think of any major consumer good or service, and it will almost certainly be supplied by oligopoly firms – cars, petrol, banks, cigarettes, soap powder, instant coffee, chocolate, baked beans, etc.

One way of measuring oligopoly is by calculation of the Five Firm Concentration ratio. This is simply the share of the market in percentage terms held by the five largest firms. The higher this figure, the higher the degree of oligopoly (Table 2.1).

Table 2.1 *UK concentration ratios 1990*

Industry	Concentration ratio
Tobacco	99.3
Motor vehicles	87.7
Ice-cream and sweets	58.8
Pharmaceuticals	55.8
Toys and sports goods	24.7
Leather goods	12.4

Source: Census of Production 1990; Business Monitor PA 1002

Remember that these figures only cover UK producers. As a result of globalisation, all manufacturers are subject to increasingly greater international competition, and only in tobacco and pharmaceuticals of the industries listed above can the UK be considered world class. Real oligopoly power is higher in services, where there is less chance of competition from imports. The five firm ratio in food retailing in 2003 was 75, and this has become a four firm ratio since the takeover of firm number 4 (Safeway) by Morrison (number 5). In the case of food production and retailing we have a bilateral oligopoly. Many branded goods are produced by oligopolies, and then sold through oligopolies.

Firms in an oligopoly market have a choice between a number of broad types of behaviour, as follows.

Collusion

One possible outcome is that the firms in the industry join together and collectively behave as if they were a monopolist. They can then collectively exploit any monopoly profits which are available. An extreme form of this type of behaviour is a cartel or price ring like OPEC (the Organisation of Petroleum Exporting Countries). Unfortunately from the point of view of potential cartel members, in most countries cartels and other forms of collusive behaviour are illegal. Cartels also tend to be unstable. They must have some mechanism for dividing up production and market quotas among their members, and this is fraught with difficulty. There is also a great temptation for individual members to cheat on their quotas. The cartel may be undercut by new producers (like UK oil in the 1970s), or new substitutes may be developed (as happened to a limited extent after the oil price hikes of 1973 and 1979).

Price war

An opposite possibility may be a price war, with the aim of driving the competition out of business, and eventually emerging with a single firm monopoly, which can then be exploited. The enormous risk, of course, is that you might lose, and be forced out of business yourself. In nearly all cases, the stakes are simply too high, and the risks too great. Indeed, in many cases it is only the market leader which can afford the risk of a price war, and it is the market leader which has the least need of one. In practice, most apparent price wars are extremely limited, and are used by the market leader as a sharp shock to the rest of the industry to stay in line.

Non-price competition

Rather than risk an all-out price war, firms will frequently engage in non-price competition – they will compete on everything except price. This might include competitions, quality, individual features or BOGOF (buy one get one free – for a limited period). The aim is not to drive the competition out of business, but to gain a marginal increase in market share. All participants understand the rules of the game, and know very well that the war is limited not total. Another possible form of non-price competition is complexity. In the old days, there was one mortgage rate, charged by all mortgage lenders on all mortgages. Now there are a multiplicity of different types of mortgage, each with its own terms and conditions, with the result that it is almost impossible to compare rates. The same thing has happened with utility pricing.

CASE STUDY 2.1

The cut-price airline industry

The cut-price airline industry has developed in the UK since the mid-1990s, on the lines pioneered in the USA by South West Airlines. It is based on providing a no-frills service at low cost. It is dominated by two firms, Ryanair and easyJet. Both Ryanair and easyJet are constantly engaged in sniping at each other, with each claiming that it has the lowest fares, and that the other is inefficient, incompetent or worse. There appears to be every sign of a constant price war, with both companies sometimes in effect offering free flights. However, appearances can be deceptive. Neither has the serious intention of driving the other out of business. Direct competition between them (in the sense of flights to and from the same airport) is limited. The 'price war' is aimed much more at deterring new entrants to the industry (both Ryanair and easyJet have taken over one of their competitors, Buzz in the case of Ryanair, and Go in the case of easyJet), and squeezing better terms out of airports (who gain from a big throughput of passengers).

Price leadership

Here one firm within the industry is regarded unofficially as the price leader. If the leader changes its prices, the other firms in the industry are likely to follow suit. In order to be legal, it is essential that there is no collusion between the firms.

Game theory

Here the firm makes assumptions about the nature of the environment and the behaviour of competitors. Game theory is a huge area, but two simple strategies which can be followed are *maximax*, where the firm assumes that the best possible combination of circumstances will happen, and chooses the strategy which will maximise its position in this favourable set of circumstances, and *maximin*, where the firm assumes that the worst will happen, and chooses the best (or least bad) strategy on these pessimistic assumptions.

Monopsony and bilateral monopoly

Monopsony is a market form where there is a monopoly buyer. Normally the monopsonist is the Government or one of its agencies. For example, for all practical purposes the NHS is a monopsony buyer of pharmaceuticals in the UK. If we have a market where a monopoly is selling to a monopsony, we have a bilateral monopoly. This applies where the NHS buys a particular patented drug from one pharmaceutical company.

CASE STUDY 2.2

Supermarkets: an oligopolistic industry

Introduction

The supermarket industry has come a long way since Sainsbury's opened the first self-service supermarket in the UK in 1951. Until the 1970s, the industry was fragmented, with a large number of supermarket groups mostly operating small stores, and over 100,000 independent grocery outlets of various types. Economies of scale were low, with deliveries being made direct by wholesalers or manufacturers to individual stores. Supermarkets were in town centres, and most people shopped regularly several times a week.

By the late 1970s, two leaders had emerged from the pack – Sainsbury's and Tesco. Sainsbury's was a private family company until 1973. It was concentrated in London and the South East, with a mainly middle class clientele. Tesco was a much younger company, founded by Jack (later Lord) Cohen, who was responsible for the notorious slogan 'pile 'em high, sell em' cheap'. In the late 1970s, Tesco began the slow and at times painful move upmarket that has continued ever since. The two firms were neck and neck in the market until 1995, when Tesco took the lead for the first time.

Tesco is now way out in front, with a market share of 28 per cent in August 2004 (Finch 2004). Sainsbury's has fallen back to third place, with 15 per cent, behind Asda, which was a northern-based also-ran until it was taken over by the biggest grocer in the world, Wal-Mart of the USA, in June 1999. It now has 17 per cent of the market. In fourth place is Morrison's, which again was a long-established northern chain which came from nowhere to take over the struggling but larger Safeway group in 2004. It has 14 per cent of the market, but is having trouble in digesting its prey.

Superstores

In the late 1970s, the UK supermarket groups started to adopt the French concept of hypermarkets, huge out-of-town stores. In the UK they became known as superstores. A superstore was defined as a store with at least 25,000 square feet of selling space, at least 20 check-outs and selling at least 16,000 lines. In theory, a superstore can be located anywhere, but increasingly they came to be purpose-built buildings on green or brownfield sites either on the edge of towns or out of town, with their own extensive and normally free car parking. Increasingly, they also included a petrol station selling cut-price petrol, rapidly making the supermarket chains the biggest retailers of petrol in the UK. Evidence suggested that people were prepared to drive up to 10 miles to visit a superstore. By 1993 there were 750 superstores, taking half of all grocery sales. Superstores yielded very high economies of scale. They were supplied from huge centralised depots, which minimised distribution costs, and the huge superstore buildings were very cheap to maintain. Increasingly the big groups used new technology to improve efficiency and lower costs. Electronic point of sale (EPOS) was used by all the big groups. This enabled the store to re-order automatically from the till, to minimise on warehousing, to maximise use of shelf space as less stock needed to be on the shelves, and to react almost instantaneously to changed circumstances. Combined with EFTPOS (Electronic Funds Transfer at Point of Sale), transaction costs were lowered. Both EPOS and EFTPOS, although very cost-effective, were extremely expensive to install, and stretched the financial resources of the smaller groups.

By the mid-1990s, the explosive growth period of superstores was over. Most of the best sites had gone, and the Government was tightening up the planning controls on new development. The response of the supermarkets, particularly Tesco, was fourfold.

■ Opening hours were extended. Many of the larger stores are now open 24 hours a day, and only close (very reluctantly) on Christmas Day.
■ There was a move into e-commerce, with grocery deliveries co-ordinated from the local store.
■ There was a move back into town centres. Tesco started to develop its Tesco Metro chain, and Sainsbury's started Sainsbury's Central. Both aimed particularly at lunchtime and commuter shoppers, selling a more restricted range of convenience goods.
■ New services were introduced, such as pharmacies and film processing and, in some cases, dry cleaning.

Diversification

Another growth route for the supermarkets was diversification. Both Tesco and Sainsbury accelerated their movement into the convenience store market through takeovers. Tesco took over T&S Stores, and Sainsbury's took over Jacksons Stores (Wheatcroft 2004). Even the Co-op got into the act, taking over Alldays. The big groups also moved heavily into non-food sales, which now make up more than 10 per cent of their total sales (Hiscott 2004). One pound in every eight spent in the UK goes to Tesco. It sells more DVDs than HMV and more shampoo than Boots (Purvis 2004). In the summer of 2004, it was reported that Asda had become the UK's biggest clothing retailer, overtaking Marks & Spencer. Sainsbury's for a long time owned the DIY store Homebase.

Diversification has also been global, particularly by Tesco. They have moved into France, Hungary, Poland and Thailand, and are poised to move into China. They are thus excellently positioned to exploit the expansion of EU membership into central Europe in May 2004. Sainsbury's has made less-good strategic decisions by opting for expansion in the USA, a saturated market. Asda has gone the other way. It has been expanded into by Wal-Mart, with its huge purchasing power, which gives Asda a bigger influence on the market than its market share would suggest.

Price wars

Supermarkets are notorious for their price wars. These are launched by all the groups at regular intervals with a fanfare of publicity. The reaction of customers to price wars tends, probably rightly, to be cynical. Market research in the summer of 1993, during a particularly intense period of price cutting, showed that more than half of shoppers regarded price cuts as gimmicks; 20 per cent said they took no notice of these cuts, and only 22 per cent believed they were genuine. Price cuts always tend to be concentrated on Known Value Items (KVIs) – the 200 or so items, such as tea, butter and coffee, for which customers remember prices. The great bulk of the 20,000 lines stocked by the average superstore are not affected by price cuts. The analysts Smith New Court estimated that the 1993–94 price war would have saved on average 1.5p on a £100 shopping trolley. Remember also that in the main it is not the supermarkets who pay for the price cuts – it is the suppliers. After an investigation of the industry, the Office of Fair Trading brought in a 'voluntary' code of practice governing how supermarkets treat their suppliers, particularly farmers, and there was some evidence in the summer of 2004 that this was about to be tightened up (Eaglesham 2004).

Competition

In the mid-1990s, supermarkets appeared for the first time to be facing serious new competition. On the one hand this came from the American warehouse club operation Costco, a giant cash-and-carry, which opened its first store in the UK in 1993. Tesco, Sainsbury's, and the then number three in the market, Argyll, brought a joint High Court action, claiming that Costco was really a retailer not a wholesaler, and so should have been subject to the tougher retail planning controls. They lost, in a welter of bad publicity (Cohen 1993). However, the warehouse club concept failed to take off in the UK.

The other new competition came from the entry into the market of discount stores from the continent, particularly Aldi and Netto, which had been very successful in Germany and the Netherlands. They stocked a very limited range, mainly of tertiary brands (brands which no one had ever heard of), and at rock-bottom prices. Although much feared at the time, they seem only to have affected the bottom end of the market, particularly Kwik Save (now part of Somerfield).

Questions

1 Why do you think the competition authorities allowed Tesco to take over T&S Stores, even though Tesco had a market share over the 25 per cent which would make it a monopoly under UK law?

2 In what ways does the behaviour of the supermarkets fit with the theory of oligopoly?

More questions will be set on this case study later in this chapter.

COMPETITIVE STRUCTURE

Michael Porter's Five Forces model

The economic theory of market structure, distinguishing perfect and monopolistic competition, monopoly and oligopoly, provides a powerful but inevitably simplified model. The real industrial world is much more complex. One important model which attempts to match this complexity is Michael Porter's Five Forces model of competitive rivalry (Porter 1980).

According to the model, the structure of competition in an industry can be described in terms of five major forces. These are:

1 the threat of entry of new firms
2 the power of buyers
3 the power of suppliers
4 the power of substitutes
5 the intensity of rivalry among existing forms.

Each of the five forces is itself determined by a number of different factors. When the five forces are completely analysed, this determines how attractive the industry is to firms within it, and those who might wish to enter it.

Unlike economic models, the value of this model lies not in its predictive ability, but in the way in which it provides a checklist whereby particular firms can clearly analyse and define their own position in relation to their own industry. It is a tool which can be used as the first stage of strategic analysis.

The threat of entry
The threat of entry of new firms to an industry depends on the extent of barriers to entry. These include the following.

- Economies of scale

    Some industries have very high economies of scale – unit costs of output fall considerably as output increases, as in the car industry or the aircraft industry. Others have very low economies of scale, for example estate agencies. A new firm seeking to enter an industry with big economies of scale must either buy a high market share on entry or suffer a cost disadvantage. Economies of scale are measured by the concept of Minimum Efficient Scale (MES), or the market share which is necessary to compete at minimum unit cost. It is also possible to calculate the cost penalty incurred by producing at below this volume. However, note first that globalisation has meant increasingly that what is significant is not share of the UK market, but share of a world market and, secondly, that lean production and flexible manufacturing techniques like 'Just in Time' have somewhat reduced the importance of economies of scale.

CASE STUDY 2.3
Economies of scale in the aircraft industry

The aircraft industry is an extreme example of economies of scale. The MES for the aircraft industry is more than 100 per cent of the UK market, and there is a considerable increase in cost for a firm operating below MES. This means that it is not economic for a UK company to compete on its own in the mass market airliner industry. BAe Systems, the UK's only mainstream aircraft producer, has put its airliner manufacturing activities into joint ventures, particularly the European-based Airbus Industrie, in order to keep a foothold in a world market which can only accommodate two manufacturers, Boeing of the USA and Airbus.

- Capital requirements

  Capital-intensive industries like the car industry have a very high cost of entry, while an online consultancy operating from home has a very low cost of entry.

- Access to distribution channels

  A new entrant must establish its own distribution channels. For example, it is difficult to persuade supermarkets to stock new products in competition with existing brands. Reforms in the tied house system, and the spread of the concept of guest beers, have made it easier for small real ale brewers to gain a foothold in the beer market.

- Absolute cost advantages

  Established firms in an industry frequently gain from a learning curve effect, which gives them a cost advantage over new entrants. In other cases incumbents may use a technology or process which is protected by patents.

- Expected retaliation

  The likely reaction of existing firms is key. If incumbents are expected to retaliate to defend their markets, entry becomes more difficult.

- Government policy

  In some cases, the Government might restrict entry (commercial television and radio). In other cases, government policy might open up a market to competition (eg the telephone directory enquiries service).

- Differentiation

  If existing operators have established a strong brand image for their products or services, this effectively deters new entrants. Existing operators often produce a wide range of brands to plug all possible niches in the market.

- Switching costs for buyers

  If it is very expensive for buyers to switch to a new supplier, this will deter new entrants to the market. For example, if you have a gas central heating system, it is very expensive for you to switch to electricity, but very cheap to switch to a new gas supplier.

The power of buyers

Buyer power will depend on the following.

- Concentration of buyers

  If there is only a small number of buyers, buyer power will be high, particularly if the volume purchases of the buyers are high. For example, although cola drinks are sold through a multiplicity of outlets, high volume sales are dependent on the big supermarket chains, and even Coca-Cola does not have the muscle to dictate terms to them.

- Alternative sources of supply

  If the buyer is able to shop around, this will increase his power. This may come about because deregulation of markets has produced new competitors. For example, when the gas industry was privatised and deregulated, consumers became able to buy gas from a large number of possible suppliers, not just British Gas. Similarly, the ending of pre-entry trade union closed shops has helped buyers of labour such as the newspaper industry.

- Component cost as a percentage of total cost

  If materials form a high percentage of the total cost of a finished product, there is a greater incentive for buyers to shop around. Thus the provision of power to a steelworks forms a high percentage of cost, while the provision of paper clips to a management consultancy forms a very low percentage.

- Possibility of backward integration

  If there is a risk that the buyer may be in a position to set up his own supply operation, this increases the buyer's power.

Power relationships between buyers and suppliers can be changed as a result of deliberate strategic decisions. For example, car manufacturers since the 1980s have followed a deliberate strategy of reducing the number of their suppliers. Suppliers have gained bigger orders and greater security, but at the cost of strict adherence to quality and JIT requirements

Power of sellers

Seller power will depend on the following.

- Number of suppliers

  The smaller the number of suppliers, the greater their power, as in any other monopoly or oligopoly situation.

- Switching costs

  If switching costs to another supplier are high, this will increase seller power, particularly in a situation where the product supplied is highly specialised, and the supplier is integrated into the production process, for example in a JIT environment.

- Brand power

  If the supplier's brand is powerful, this will give it more bargaining power. For example, Heinz or Kelloggs, who do not produce own brands, can exercise influence over supermarkets, who have to stock the brand leader.

■ Possibility of forward integration

If there is a risk that the seller may be in a position to set up its own distribution operation, this increases the seller's power.

■ Dependence on customer

If the supplier is not dependent on selling a high volume of output to a particular customer, and his individual customers are generally small, this will increase seller power.

Threat of substitutes

The threat of substitution can take many forms. There could be technological substitution of one product for another – the fax for the letter, then the e-mail for the fax. In the last resort all goods are substitutes for each other, because they are all competing for consumer spending. This is particularly true of non-essential goods, where there is the ultimate substitute of doing without.

Key questions that need to be addressed are as follows.

■ Relative price and performance of substitutes

If substitutes are available that offer similar performance at comparable prices, the threat of substitution is very strong and limits are put on the ability to charge high prices – for example brands of pet food.

■ Switching costs

The cheaper it is for consumers to switch to other products, the higher the threat of substitutes. Switching costs for pet food appear to be zero, so long as the pet is prepared to eat the substitute!

■ Buyers' willingness to substitute

If an article is both low-cost and an infrequent purchase, little effort is likely to be put into shopping around. No one shops around for the best value box of matches.

Competitive rivalry

Competitive rivalry is to some extent a function of the other factors. However, there are the following special factors to be taken into account.

■ Industry growth

If the industry is growing rapidly, there is plenty in the cake for everyone so competition does not need to be intense. As an industry moves into the maturity phase of its life cycle, competition will become more intense.

■ High fixed costs

This is likely to lead to a high break-even point, and the likelihood of price wars in times of depression to maintain turnover. See for example the steel wars of the late 1990s, when the USA and the EU each accused the other of dumping steel on export markets.

■ Volatile demand

This is likely to lead to intermittent over-capacity, with resultant price wars – steel again.

■ Product differentiation

The more homogeneous the product, the more intense the rivalry – steel yet again.

■ Extra capacity in large increments

The competitor making such an addition is likely to create at least short-term over-capacity. For example in the late 1980s, the Japanese car firms Nissan, Toyota and Honda all built new car assembly plants in the UK.

■ Balance of firms

If the number of firms is large and/or firms are of a similar size, the risks of aggression may appear acceptable, and rivalry will be intense, although probably not lethal. Conversely, a clear market leader can enforce discipline in the industry.

■ High exit barriers

If there are high exit barriers, excess capacity is likely to persist and rivalry to be intense. This would apply, for example, if there were high pollution clean-up costs associated with decommissioning a plant.

ACTIVITY 2.5

A Five Forces analysis of the UK supermarket industry

Refer back to the supermarkets case study (Case Study 2.2).

Carry out a Five Forces analysis of the UK supermarket industry.

Bear in mind when using Five Forces that it is an analytical technique, which can tell you where you are now, and probably why you are there, but not how to get where you want to get. There is also a danger is carrying out more and more detailed analysis – paralysis by analysis!

PORTFOLIO ANALYSIS

In the 1970s and early 1980s, strategic emphasis was on organisations building up a balanced portfolio of activities, or strategic business units (SBUs). Several techniques were developed to assist with analysis of portfolios of SBUs.

Boston Matrix

This technique was developed in the 1970s by the Boston Consulting Group, and plots SBUs according to their rate of market growth and their market share.

Market growth rate is arbitrarily divided into high growth and low growth, ranging between 0 and 20 per cent per annum. Market share is assessed as share relative to that of the largest competitor, with a high of ten times that of the nearest rival, and a low of one-tenth. SBUs are plotted on the matrix, with their precise position within a cell depending on their exact market share and market growth rate.

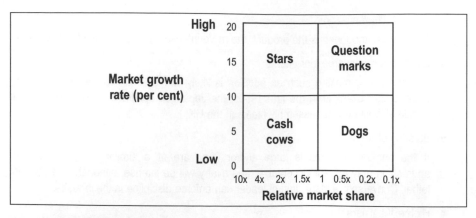

Figure 2.6 *The Boston Matrix*

The significance of the Boston Matrix is that an SBU's position on the matrix has an impact in its profits and its cash flow. One of the main selling points of the technique consists in the colourful names attached to the various cells (Joyce and Woods 1996).

Dogs	They have a weak market share in a low-growth market. They generate a very low profit or even a loss, and also may well have negative cash flow. They absorb management resources, and the organisation must decide whether they are worth keeping in the long term, closed down or sold off.
Stars	They have a high market share in a high growth market. Production will be at relatively low cost because of economies of scale, and profits are likely to be sound. However, because the market is growing rapidly, heavy investment will be needed to sustain market share. Cash flow is therefore likely to be at best neutral.
Question marks	They have a low market share in a high growth market. This means that like the stars they need heavy investment, but as they are not the market leader they cannot fully exploit economies of scale. Cash flow is likely to be negative, but profits may well be positive. Management has to take hard decisions – either close down (on the assumption that the question marks may turn into a dog) or sit it out (on the assumption that it will turn into a cash cow).
Cash cows	They have high market share in a low growth mature market. In the short and medium term this is an ideal position. Because the product is a market leader, it will be low cost, and it does not need heavy investment to cope with market growth. It is therefore likely to produce both profits and positive cash flow, which can be milked.

Figure 2.7 *The Boston Matrix (continued)*

Two further types have also been identified off the bottom of the matrix. These are *war horses* (high market share and negative growth – a cash cow on its last legs), and *dodos* (low market share and negative growth – dead dogs!)

The strategic implication is that an organisation should aim for a balanced portfolio of SBUs, which should include products which can evolve through the sequence of question mark – star – cash cow. Some organisations, particularly at the height of the popularity of conglomerates in the 1980s, became extremely successful by identifying and exploiting cash cows. One such was Hanson Group, whose strategy was to purchase cash cow products/companies (Imperial Tobacco – cigarettes, London Brick – bricks, Ever Ready – batteries), put in the minimum level of new investment, and exploit the cash-generating potential of the products.

There are, however, some weaknesses in the Boston Matrix approach. One is that there is no clear-cut way to define markets. If the market is defined too narrowly, the organisation will over-state its market strength, and so tend to ignore 'over the horizon' competitors, who may be quietly building up their strength in a related market. Possibly more serious is that the matrix ignores any synergy factors. Synergy is defined as the way in which the whole organisation is greater than the sum of its parts. SBUs are not totally self-contained – they often provide each other with benefits, such as sharing production processes or distribution channels, or being part of a balanced catalogue of products. As a result, if an organisation decides to kill off a dog product, this may have adverse impacts on its other products. A final weakness is that it assumes a simple relationship between market leadership and profitability. This ignores the way in which many organisations have prospered long term by exploiting small niche markets. Despite these weaknesses, however, the Boston Matrix has been used successfully by a number of companies, including Black and Decker Europe, although alongside other techniques (Walker 1990).

Shell Directional Policy Matrix

This technique, developed by the Shell Chemical Company, meets some of the criticisms of the Boston Matrix. Rather than using market share as a variable, it uses the enterprise's competitive capabilities, assessed as weak, average or strong. This can take into account factors such as managerial skills, possession of appropriate technology and competencies, etc. as well as market share. Market growth rate is replaced by prospects for sector profitability, which again can include other factors. Finally, the analysis is made more discriminating by being based on a 3,x,3 matrix rather than the Boston Matrix's 2,x,2.

Enterprise's competitive capabilities		Prospects for sector profitability		
		Unattractive	Average	Attractive
	Weak	Disinvest	Phased withdrawal	Double or quits
	Average	Phased withdrawal	Custodial growth	Try harder
	Strong	Cash generation	Growth leader	Leader

Figure 2.8 *The Shell Directional Policy Matrix*

ACTIVITY 2.6

Killing the dog

The board at Gamma Manufacturing was deeply divided. Under discussion was Product X, which had been a source of argument within the company for years past. The finance director wanted Product X dropped. He argued that it had absorbed considerable development funds over the years, but had never fulfilled its original promise. It tied up valuable production capacity in the factory, and wasted a lot of management time. 'It's a dog,' he said. 'We should put it out of its misery now.'

The marketing director disagreed. She argued that a lot of time, energy and money had been put into the product, and it would be a shame to waste all this just at the point when it might be about to take off. She also made the point that it filled a hole in the product mix. With some customers, it was important to be able to offer a complete product line, including Product X. 'If we haven't got X, I can name at least two big customers who will go straight to the competition,' she said.

If you were the managing director, how would you evaluate the arguments put forward by the finance and marketing directors?

THE PUBLIC AND VOLUNTARY SECTORS

Broadly speaking, three types of organisation operate in the UK today – businesses, which produce goods and services which the aim of making a profit, the public sector, which supplies goods and services which cannot be supplied at a profit, public goods (where the whole of society benefits from a service such as public health, whether they pay for it or not) and some natural monopolies. The voluntary sector meets the needs of its members (clubs, mutual organisations or professions) and its clients (charities), or campaigns on issues (Greenpeace, RSPB).

Unfortunately, these distinctions are not as watertight as they were 30 years ago. Some public goods and natural monopolies are now supplied by privatised businesses. The private and voluntary sectors provide some services, such as refuse collection and welfare services, on behalf of the public sector. Many public sector and voluntary bodies have commercial arms (like BBC Enterprises and CIPD Enterprises) which operate in competition with the private sector. One organisation, Railtrack, has changed in a 5-year period from being part of a nationalised industry (British Rail), to being a privately-owned company on privatisation, and then to a non profit-making trust (Network Rail) when Railtrack collapsed in 2001.

The three sectors also have more similarities than differences in how they are managed. They:

- spend money
- need income to carry out their activities
- produce a product or service
- have consumers of their good or service (whether or not the consumers directly pay for this)

- need people to staff their operations
- use the same range of management services – accounting, IT, personnel, etc.

This all suggests a convergence. This view would be supported by the Prime Minister, Tony Blair. His Third Way philosophy argues that what is important is not ownership (public or private), but how efficiently services are delivered, along with accountability.

Lawton and Rose (1994) distinguish the following four different cultures which they see as prevalent in the public sector.

1 *Political culture*: Particularly prevalent in local government, where council officers are in almost day to day contact with the politicians to whom they are answerable. Also true in the sense that the whole of the public sector is ultimately politically directed.

2 *Legal culture*: Public bodies are only permitted to do what is specifically allowed to them by statute. Any other action is *ultra vires* (beyond their powers), and is subject to judicial review. Private sector companies are in theory limited in their activities by their Articles and Memoranda of Association, but the control is much less strict.

3 *Administrative culture*: Concerned with rules, roles, and authority – the 1960s and 1970s caricature of the local authority 'jobsworth'.

4 *Market culture*: Where public sector organisations are exposed to the market through competitive tendering, best value, contracting out, internal markets, etc.

They argue that the last of these, the market culture, is becoming predominant, and that as a result, running the public sector is becoming much more an issue of management, and much less an issue of administration.

The distinction between the sectors is becoming more and more blurred.

- Many local authority services which may previously have been free, are now charged for, and often contracted-out to the private sector (leisure centres, for example). This has involved the development and application of legal systems such as Tupe.
- Much of the long-term finance for the public sector is now provided by the public sector, through the Private Finance Initiative and public–private partnerships. The biggest of these is London Underground, where train services continue to be provided by the public sector, but where all the maintenance of and investment in improving the lines is carried out by three private sector consortia.
- There is a growing realisation that the private sector, almost as much as the public sector, operates in a political environment, and that the activities of the private sector are heavily constrained by the legal environment.
- The Government is keen to increase the involvement of the voluntary sector in the delivery of public services, partly to move the debate away from a head-to-head clash between the public and private sectors (Ward 2001). Not-for-profit trusts are the Government's preferred option for failing public services. They can borrow private cash without this counting as public borrowing, and they can also reinvest any surpluses into service improvement (Weaver 2001).

CASE STUDY 2.4

The two-tier workforce

Under the EU Acquired Rights Directive, implemented in the UK through the Transfer of Undertakings (Protection of Employment Regulations) (Tupe), 1981 onwards, workers who are transferred from the public to the private sector as a result of contracting out of a public service to the private sector, have their wage level and terms and conditions of employment protected (although not their pension arrangements). However, no protection was afforded to new recruits who were subsequently taken on by the transferee. This resulted in a two-tier workforce, where two workers could be doing exactly the same job, but under different wages, terms and conditions.

The trade unions have long campaigned against this, and in 2002 it was agreed that the two-tier workforce in local government would be abolished. The agreement, which came into effect in 2003, was originally proposed by the CBI, and involved detailed negotiation over the precise wording of the protection to be offered. The unions called for 'no less favourable terms and conditions' for new recruits, while the CBI offered 'broadly comparable' terms and conditions. In the first year of the agreement, the unions raised no disputes, which suggests either that workers are broadly satisfied with the deal, or that companies are in practice simply replicating local authority employment conditions.

In July 2004, the CBI agreed to end the two-tier workforce across the public sector, an offer which was taken up by the Labour Party and the unions in late-night negotiations to agree the terms of the Labour manifesto for the next election. The unions and Labour also agreed that pensions should be protected on transfer (Wintour 2004a,b).

HR IMPLICATIONS OF RESPONSE TO CHANGES IN THE ENVIRONMENT

We illustrate this section with an Activity which analyses several examples where environmental change had to be met with HR responses.

ACTIVITY 2.7

HR implications

After privatisation in the 1980s, British Airways was extremely successful under the leadership of Sir Collin (later Lord) Marshall. Marshall's strategy was to emphasise customer care and employee empowerment in a (largely successful) attempt to build the 'World's Favourite Airline'. He shed the airline's previous quasi-RAF culture, and ensured that the old nickname of 'Bloody Awful' became a thing of the past.

In 1996, Marshal became chairman, and was replaced as chief executive by Bob Ayling, who had a very different vision. He saw BA as over-staffed and bloated, with an excessive cost base. Although profits were still high, as a result of the airline boom which followed the recovery from the first Gulf War in 1991, he initiated an ambitious cost-cutting programme, which inevitably involved redundancies.

In practice, few redundancies were actually carried through, but the result was labour unrest in 1997 which cost BA £130m. By 2000, BA had slumped into a loss, and morale was at rock bottom. In March 2000, Ayling was sacked, and replaced by the Australian Rod Eddington, who had previously run Qantas.

Before Eddington could impose his own personality on the company, BA, like other world airlines, was hit by the hammer blow of the September 11th, 2001 attacks. BA reacted very quickly, and announced 12,000 redundancies, (about 20 per cent of staff). Twenty per cent of all BA flights from Heathrow were scrapped.

The recovery from September 11th was slow but, by 2004, BA was back in profit. It was then hit by the side effects of the redundancy programme. It found itself understaffed, particularly among check-in staff. The result was long waits for check-in, rising tempers among customers, stress for staff, and a soaring absenteeism rate. Over the August Bank Holiday, BA was forced to cancel many flights, leading to furious travellers and much adverse publicity (Harper 2000; Gillan 2001; Kim and Mauborgne 2001).

Questions

Given that the cost-cutting programme was necessary:

■ What steps should BA have taken to ensure that it was carried out more effectively? Could the crisis in 2004 have been avoided?

■ What do you feel are the HR implications of the introduction of a more market-orientated culture in the public services?

STRATEGIC RESPONSES

A later chapter on developing and implementing strategy will consider this issue in greater depth, but here we will consider strategic responses in more general terms. Basically, an organisation can make only two responses if it is in an industry where it does not have monopoly or oligopoly power, and so is not in a position to manage its competition and its environment. It can opt for low price, or it can opt for differentiation. In the supermarket industry, Aldi and Netto have opted for low price, albeit at the cost of low perceived quality, and have seized a somewhat precarious niche by doing so. Differentiation could include high quality, innovation or specialisation. The next activity examines other strategies adopted in the supermarket industry

ACTIVITY 2.8

Strategies in the supermarket industry

What successful strategies have been pursued by

1 Marks & Spencer (food)
2 Waitrose
3 Budgens.

A firm in an oligopoly market has more freedom of manoeuvre, but it is constrained by the need to consider how its competitors will react to a change in its tactics. If it increases its price, and its competitors follow, the chances are that all firms in the industry will increase their profits, although if there is a suspicion of collusion, the competition authorities may intervene. However, if our firm increases its price, and the competition does not follow, our firm will lose sales, and almost certainly lose profit, while the competition will gain. A monopoly has a simpler decision to make. In principle it can choose whatever combination of price and quantity produced and sold which will maximise its profits, although in practice its ability to do this is constrained by the ability of new firms to enter the market (contestability).

SUMMARY AND CONCLUSIONS

This chapter has analysed the nature of the competitive environment, explored various models that can be used, and examined the responses which organisations can make to the competitive environment. Key Learning Points are as follows.

KEY LEARNING POINTS

- The fundamental economic problem is how to reconcile scarcity and choice. Market and mixed economies tackle these problems in slightly different ways.

- Market economies are underpinned by the concepts of supply and demand, and their interaction to create equilibrium.

- Perfect competition is an unrealistic but ideal model. Other models of the market are measured by their deviation from perfect competition.

- The extent of monopoly power can be measured either by market share or by the degree of contestability of the market in which they operate.

- Performance in oligopoly markets depends on an interaction between the firms operating in the market.

- Porter's Five Forces model is a powerful way of analysing the competitive forces operating in an industry.

- Portfolio analyses, including the Boston Matrix and the Shell Directional Policy Matrix, are valuable but must be used with care.

- There is growing convergence between the market, public and voluntary sectors.

- A variety of strategic responses can be made to changes in the competitive environment, and these have implications for HR.

FURTHER READING

The theoretical background to this chapter is covered in any good economics textbook, such as Lipsey and Chrystal's *Principles of Economics* (Oxford University Press). However, as a manager you need to be able to apply the theory to contemporary examples and situations. The best way to do this is to make sure that you regularly read *The Economist*, and at least one of the quality broadsheet newspapers – preferably two, one broadly liberal, like the *Guardian* or the *Independent*, and one broadly conservative, like *The Times* or the *Daily Telegraph*.

The International Scene: the European Union and Globalisation

OBJECTIVES

By the end of this chapter, readers should be able to understand, explain and critically evaluate:

- the role and function of the European Union and its major institutions

- debates about the evolution of the European Union (integration and enlargement)

- major international bodies which impact on the business environment of organisations (IMF, World Bank, WTO)

- the causes and extent of globalisation processes

- major debates about the significance and desirability of globalisation

- the response of governmental organisation to globalisation processes

- the impact of globalisation on markets for goods and services

- the impact of globalisation on employment and labour markets.

Should the UK ratify the new European Union constitution? Is globalisation good or bad for the developing world? These are the kinds of issues which will be explored in this chapter on the international economy.

Since the end of the Second World War, the world economy has become more and more integrated. Partly this has been a deliberate, planned development. The International Monetary Fund, the World Bank and the General Agreement on Tariffs and Trade were set up to regulate the world economy, and to ensure that the world did not suffer from a recurrence of the Great Depression of the 1930s. The European Economic Community, the predecessor of the European Union, was set up partly to ensure that France and Germany could never again go to war with each other. Other developments were only made possible as a result of technological developments in communication and transport which enabled the growth of globalisation.

THE EUROPEAN UNION

The historical background to the European Union

The origins of the European Union go back to the period just after the Second World War, when there was a strong desire in Continental Europe (particularly France and West Germany) to ensure that a further war would be impossible. One way to achieve this was to integrate the economies of Europe, thereby limiting the ability of an individual country to wage war. The result was the European Coal and Steel Community, set up by the Treaty of Paris in 1951. The European Economic Community and Euratom followed with the signing of the Treaty of Rome on 25 March 1957.

The founding states of the three Communities were France, West Germany, Italy, Belgium, the Netherlands and Luxembourg. Britain declined an invitation to join, seeing its economic interests as lying much more with the USA and the Commonwealth.

The UK, Ireland and Denmark joined on 1 January 1973, Greece on 1 January 1981, Spain and Portugal on 1 January 1986, and Sweden, Austria and Finland on 1 January 1995. The former East Germany automatically joined on German reunification in 1990. Norway twice negotiated entry, but on each occasion that was rejected by a referendum. Switzerland did not apply to join, citing its long-standing policy of strict neutrality (it has only very recently become a member of the United Nations), but it has close economic relations with the EU.

In 1976 the three Communities were merged, and designated the European Community, and the Maastricht Treaty of 1992 adopted the name European Union from 1 January 1993.

Up to the end of the twentieth century, the EU was very much a Western European club. With the exception of Greece, Spain and Portugal, which had recent histories of Fascist rule, all the members were long-standing stable, prosperous and democratic countries. This changed fundamentally with the next enlargement, from 15 to 25 members on 1 May 2004. This came about with the accession of five post-Communist central European states (Poland, Hungary, the Czech Republic, Slovakia and Slovenia), the three Baltic states of Estonia, Latvia and Lithuania, which had previously been republics within the USSR, and two small Mediterranean islands (Malta and Cyprus). The implications of this expansion for the EU will be considered below.

The aims of the EU

The European Union has a number of general aims. These include:

- upholding peace in Europe by integrating national economies
- increasing prosperity by developing a single market
- easing inequalities between people and regions
- pooling the energies of member states for technological and industrial development
- developing an effective means of resolving political disputes
- implementing a Union-wide social policy
- implementing European Monetary Union
- assisting people of the Third World.

These aims reflect a number of different perceptions concerning the future development of the Union (Morris and Willey 1996).

Single market ('European single market')
This sees the EU in economic terms, and concentrates on removal of national restrictions which limit the free movement of labour, capital, goods and services. In effect, the EU is seen as

solely a free trade area, without a political dimension. Common political institutions should be minimal, and so should the structure of EU law, which should be limited to that necessary to ensuring that the single market functions effectively. The single market concept underpinned the early development of the European Community, and reached its fullest expression in the Single European Act 1986, which led to the setting up of the Single European Market in 1993. At least in theory, this ensured the free movement of labour, capital, goods and services. However, this does not fully work in practice. For example, the Schengen Agreement in 1990 eliminated internal border controls within the EU, meaning that travel within the EU was possible without a passport, but the agreement has never been implemented by the UK and Ireland.

Federalist ('United States of Europe')

Here the EU is seen as having the structure of a federal state like the USA or Germany – a central, or federal government which sets the general direction of policy, and local governments (states in the USA, *Länder* in Germany, nation states in the EU) which are responsible for the practical administration of policy. Some political mechanism is needed at the centre to decide on overall policy, but this should be kept to a minimum. The function of EU law is to settle disputes between the central authority and the member states. Central to this perspective is the concept of subsidiarity, which says that as a matter of principle, decision-making in the EU should be taken at the lowest possible level.

Integrationist ('Europe')

The aim here is ultimately a long-term shift of power from member states to EU-wide institutions. The classic example of this is Economic and Monetary Union (discussed in detail in a later chapter), which led to a single currency, the Euro, and to control of EU monetary policy passing from member states to the European Central Bank. Subsidiarity may still apply, but the member states would only have those powers specifically delegated to them by the central government. EU law would not only settle disputes between member states and the centre, but would directly impinge on EU citizens.

The issue of how far to move towards the integrationist model underpins the ongoing argument about an EU constitution, which has occupied much of the EU's efforts since the Nice Summit in 2000, and is discussed in detail below.

ACTIVITY 3.1

Models of the EU

1 Which of the models of EU organisation (single market, federalist, integrationist) would best describe the view of the following political parties in the UK?

- New Labour
- Conservative
- Liberal Democrat
- UK Independence Party.

2 Why do the other members of the EU feel that true implementation of the Single Market also requires harmonisation of taxation, and why does the UK oppose this?

THE INSTITUTIONS OF THE EU

In this section, we examine the institutions of the European Union as they were just before the massive changes made in mid-2004 – the EU enlargement of May 2004, from 15 to 25 members, and the agreement on the EU Constitution in June 2004. In later sections, we will look at the impact of the enlargement and of the Constitution.

Responsibility for achieving the aims of the EU rests with four institutions:

1   the Commission
2   the Council of Ministers
3   the European Parliament
4   the Court of Justice.

and two auxiliary bodies:

1   the European Central Bank
2   the Economic and Social Committee.

The Commission

The Commission is the executive of the EU. It is responsible both for proposing policy and legislation, and for implementing policy after it has been agreed. It is completely independent of member states, even though its members are appointed by the member states.

Before the 2004 enlargement, the Commission had 20 members, two each from France, Germany, the UK, Italy and Spain, and one from each of the other member states. Each commissioner is responsible for an area of EU policy. This was already causing some problems, as it was generally felt that there were not enough real areas of policy available to keep every commissioner fully occupied. The Commission is headed by a president, appointed by the Council of Ministers. The president is usually a powerful figure in his own right. The president until October 2004 was Romano Prodi, ex-prime minister of Italy, and from late 2004, Jose Manuel Durao Barroso, ex-prime minister of Portugal.

The responsibilities of the Commission are laid down by the various EU treaties (Rome, Maastricht, Amsterdam, Nice, etc.). They include:

- initiating legislation (The Commission tables proposals to the Council of Ministers after wide-ranging consultation with interested parties.)
- guardian of the treaties (The Commission has to ensure that the treaties and EU legislation are properly implemented.)
- implementing policy (The Commission either directly implements policy itself, or supervises programmes administered by member states under the principle of subsidiarity, which we looked at earlier.)

The Commission is collectively answerable to the European Parliament, and can be removed by a vote of censure carried by a two-thirds majority – although there is no procedure for removing individual Commissioners. In early 1999, after a report which criticised the then President, Jacques Santer, and several individual commissioners, and a series of debates in the European Parliament, the whole Commission resigned, and Santer was replaced by Romano Prodi.

The Council of Ministers

The Council is the final decision-making body of the EU. It consists of representatives of the governments of the member states. In practice, the Council is really a series of specialist bodies, dealing with particular areas of policy, and attended by the appropriate ministers from the member states. When the Heads of State or Government meet, the Council is referred to as the European Council, which meets twice a year. Each member state in turn acts as President of the Council for six months. Council meetings are attended by the President of the Commission, who has a full right to take part in discussions, but who does not have a vote.

Until 1986, decisions in the Council of Ministers were taken by unanimity, which meant that each member state had an absolute veto. This was becoming unworkable, and would clearly become more so as more countries joined the EU. The Single European Act in 1986 introduced the concept of qualified majority voting (QMV), under which decisions in clearly specified areas could be taken by a majority vote. In practice, this gave the Big Four states a collective veto, but meant that they could not force a proposal through unless they obtained the support of several of the smaller states.

DEFINITION

Qualified Majority Voting

With a simple majority voting system, decisions are taken on the basis of half the votes cast plus one. With a qualified majority voting system, as used by the EU, additional conditions are introduced into the decision process. Prior to the new EU constitution of 2004, votes of member states were weighted roughly according to population, with Germany, France, Italy and the UK having 10 votes each, down to Luxembourg with two votes. A qualified majority was 62 votes out of an available 87.

The European Parliament

The European Parliament is directly elected by all member states for five years. The most recent elections were held in June 2004. Its powers are mainly budgetary. It has the final say on all 'non-compulsory' spending (any spending which is not the inevitable consequence of EU legislation, making up 25 per cent of the budget). It can also reject the budget in total, and did so in 1979 and 1984.

The Parliament has a right to debate all EU issues, and the Council can reject its views only by a unanimous vote. It cannot initiate legislation (the responsibility of the Commission), not does it have the final say in passing law (the responsibility of the Council of Ministers), but it can reject measures which were passed by the Council of Ministers through QMV. In October 2004, it came very close to rejecting the whole of the new Commission proposed by the new president, Jose Manuel Barosso, because of the illiberal views held by the Italian nominee. The crisis was only defused at the last minute when Barosso withdrew his whole Commission for reconsideration, and the Italian Government withdrew its nominee.

The European Court of Justice (ECJ)

The ECJ rules on the interpretation and application of EU rules, and on disputes between the Commission and member states. Its decisions apply directly in the member states. It consists of judges appointed by the member states.

The Economic and Social Committee

This is a consultative body made up of representatives of employers (UNICE – the Union of Industrial and Employers' Confederations of Europe, and CEEP – the European Centre of Enterprises with Public Participation), trade unions (ETUC – the European Trades Union Confederation), and special interest groups (collectively known as the 'social partners'). It must be formally consulted by the Commission on economic and social proposals.

The European Central Bank (ECB)

The ECB was set up in 1999 to administer Economic and Monetary Union (EMU) (which will be discussed in detail in Chapter 4). It has sole responsibility for setting interest rates in the euro zone. It is headed by a president appointed by the Council of Ministers, and representatives from each member of EMU (which does not include the UK).

ACTIVITY 3.2

EU institutions and power

1   Why do you think that ultimate power in the EU lies with the Council of Ministers rather than the Commission?

2   You work for an FTSE-100 company. Your company is concerned about a possible change in EU social policy which could lead to legislation in the next few years. How can your company influence forthcoming EU decisions on this change?

CASE STUDY 3.1

The Stability and Growth Pact

In 1996, as part of the preparations for the launch of the single currency, Germany called for a Stability and Growth Pact which would impose financial discipline on members of the euro zone. One crucial element of this was that no member of the euro zone would be permitted a budget deficit greater than 3 per cent of their GDP. Any member which breached this limit would be subject to a fine of up to 0.5 per cent of the GDP (ie billions of euros). The Stability and Growth Pact was agreed as part of the Amsterdam Summit in June 1997, and incorporated in the Amsterdam Treaty. This gave it the force of EU law. There was a let-out clause, but only if a member state's GDP fell by 0.75 per cent.

By 2003, both France and Germany were in breach of the 3 per cent limit. The Commission therefore called on the Council of Ministers (technically ECOFIN, the Council of Economic and Finance Ministers) to impose the financial sanctions. Despite opposition from countries such as the Netherlands and Portugal, ECOFIN refused to do so. The Commission took ECOFIN to the European Court of Justice.

The ECJ produced its judgement in July 2004. The judgement was not completely clear cut, but its key point was that ECOFIN was acting illegally in refusing to apply sanctions. EU law, as expressed in the treaties, was binding not only on member states but on the Council of Ministers.

This case throws some interesting light on who has the final say in the EU. It is not the Commission or the Council of Ministers, but the law, as expressed in the treaties and interpreted by the ECJ. The treaties, right back to the Treaty of Rome, have in effect always been the EU's written Constitution.

EU ENLARGEMENT

The enlargement of the EU which took place on 1 May 2004, from 15 to 25 members, increased the population of the EU by 74 million, ranging from 38 million in Poland to 400,000 in Malta. This enlargement was qualitatively different from any which had gone before.

- The sheer number of new entrants was larger than any before. This in itself will put new strains on the EU's institutions, and increased pressure for speedy agreement on the new Constitution.
- Some of the new entrants – Latvia, Lithuania and Slovakia for example – are far poorer than any previous entrant. GDP per head of the new entrants is about 15 per cent of the old EU average.
- The biggest new entrant, Poland, has a massive and underdeveloped agricultural sector.
- There are fears in some quarters that enlargement will release a flood of immigrants from the new to the old EU states.
- Eight of the new entrants are ex-communist, and three, the Baltic states, were once part of the USSR. Russia will inevitably feel threatened by this, particularly as an outlying part of its territory, Kaliningrad, is now completely surrounded by EU territory (Poland and Lithuania).
- One new entrant, Cyprus, is divided between an officially recognised Greek state, which is in the EU, and a non-recognised Turkish state, which is not.
- Further expansion is inevitable. The accession of Bulgaria and Romania has been agreed in principle and is likely to take place in 2007. These countries are even poorer than the 2004 entrants.

There are three requirements for new entrants to the EU:

1 Each applicant must show that it is in sympathy with the fundamental ethos of the EU, by demonstrating that it practises liberty, democracy, respect for human rights and fundamental freedoms, and the rule of law.

2 Each applicant must comply with the body of EU laws and standards (the *acquis communitaire*) – which is 80,000 pages long!

3 The applicant must be part of Europe.

It is interesting to consider how well Turkey, one of the outstanding applicants for membership, fits these criteria. Negotiations with Turkey are at an advanced stage, and entry is almost certain at some stage in the future. Turkey is a long-standing democratic country, but does have a history of military coups, and a dubious human rights record in relation to its treatment of its Kurdish minority. There is some opposition to Turkish entry on the grounds that its 65 million predominantly Muslim population would upset the religious and cultural balance of the EU.

However, Turkey is a fiercely secular state, not an Islamic one, and to say that we don't want Muslims in Europe is an insult to the Muslim minorities in the UK, France, Germany and Spain. Only a small part of Turkey (Thrace) is technically within geographical Europe, with the rest (Anatolia) being in Asia, but Turkey has always seen itself as part of Europe.

ACTIVITY 3.3

EU expansion

What do you think is the likely impact of EU expansion on your own organisation or sector?

THE EU CONSTITUTION

By the late 1990s, it was clear that the EU was about to undergo a dramatic enlargement, and equally clear that the existing structure of EU institutions would not be able to cope with a greatly increased membership; hence the move towards an EU Constitution to modernise the EU's structure. A first attempt at modernisation was made at the Nice Summit in 2000, but the arrangements agreed there really satisfied no-one. A Convention under the former French President, Giscard D'Estaing, produced a draft Constitution, and, eventually, after much haggling and amendment, a new Constitution was agreed in June 2004.

The main points of the Constitution were:

- The Council President
  The European Council (the heads of state or government of member states) will elect a president of the Council, by qualified majority, for a term of two-and-a-half years, renewable once. The president would have to be approved by the European Parliament. The idea here was to give greater continuity. At present, the presidency rotates through the member states every six months.

- The Foreign Minister
  The European Council would appoint a Foreign Minister, by qualified majority. That individual would speak for the EU on foreign policy. This new post effectively combines two existing posts. However, the Foreign Minister will not decide policy, and will only be able to speak for the EU where the European Council has decided on policy. Most importantly, foreign policy is one of the three areas (the others being defence and taxation), where each member state still has a veto.

- The Commission
  From November 2004, each member state will appoint one commissioner. This means that the big powers (Germany, France, the UK and Italy) would lose one of their commissioners, as already agreed at Nice. However, it was agreed that by 2014 the

size of the Commission will be reduced to two-thirds of the number of member states, although the precise mechanism for doing this has still to be negotiated.

- The Parliament
  The powers of the Parliament are being significantly increased. It will have powers of 'co-decision' with the Council of Ministers for those policies requiring a decision by qualified majority. This means that the Parliament will effectively have the right to veto proposed legislation, a very real increase in power.

- Qualified majority voting
  There are two significant changes to the system of qualified majority voting in the Council of Ministers. First, more areas will now be subject to majority voting. These include asylum and immigration policy, and cross-border crime. As we saw above, only foreign affairs, defence and taxation are still subject to veto. Secondly, the procedure of qualified majority voting will change. Gone is the system where member states had different numbers of votes. Now all will have one vote, but a qualified majority is defined as 'at least 55 per cent of the members of the Council, comprising at least 15 of them and representing member states comprising at least 65 per cent of the population of the Union.'

Several points are of interest here.

- The Constitution already makes provision for some limited expansion (presumably the accession of Bulgaria and Romania). At present, 15 members represent 60 per cent of membership, not 55 per cent.

- By setting a population threshold, the Constitution gives considerable power to the big states, particularly to Germany, which on its own has 18 per cent of the EU's population. Together, Germany, France and either Italy or the UK would have a blocking minority.

- Charter of Fundamental Rights.
  This sets out key 'rights, freedoms and principles'. These include the right to life and liberty, and the right to strike. This could affect existing UK industrial relations law, but the UK Government feels that national laws on industrial relations will not be affected. This has yet to be tested by the European Court of Justice.

The fact that the member states have agreed on the Constitution does not mean that it immediately comes into force. The Constitution has to be ratified by each of the 25 member states, and, in the case of the UK, this will only be after a referendum, likely to be held in late 2006. Final ratification of the Constitution is unlikely before 2007.

ACTIVITY 3.4

The EU Constitution

The first opinion polls after the announcement of agreement on the Constitution suggested that there would be a two-to-one majority against it in a UK referendum. Why do you think this is so?

THE EU AND OTHER REGIONAL BLOCS

The EU is not the only major regional trading group in the world. The North American Free Trade Agreement (NAFTA) covers the USA, Canada and Mexico, while the Association of

South East Asian Nations (ASEAN) includes the Asian tiger states of Indonesia, Malaysia, the Philippines, Singapore and Thailand, as well as states including Vietnam and Myanmar, with China, India, Japan and Australia as Dialogue Partners. Both NAFTA and ASEAN are primarily free trade area agreements, with thus much narrower scope than the EU.

All three encourage trade within their own area, and thus may indirectly discourage trade between the three blocs. Those of you who have read George Orwell's *1984* may see parallels with his three competing blocs of Eurasia, Eastasia and Oceania, who divided up the world between them!

In 2000, the so-called Triad of the USA, the EU and Japan received 71 per cent of total world inward direct investment, and was responsible for 82 per cent of outward direct investment (Williams 2001).

INTERNATIONAL FINANCIAL INSTITUTIONS
The Bretton Woods Conference
In 1944, the wartime Western Allies held a conference at Bretton Woods in New Hampshire which was to shape the economic future of the international economy. Their prime aim was to prevent a repetition of the competitive devaluations and protectionism which had followed the Wall Street crash in 1929, and which had made the ensuing Great Depression even more severe in its impact. The idea was to impose strict controls on the ability of each country to follow beggar-my-neighbour policies, and to force international economic co-operation.

Out of Bretton Woods came three great international institutions, the International Monetary Fund (the IMF), the International Bank for Reconstruction and Development (the World Bank), and the General Agreement on Tariffs and Trade (GATT).

The IMF
The main plank of the IMF regime was a system of fixed exchange rates, which all member countries agreed to maintain. In practice this meant that each member state fixed the value of its currency in terms of the US dollar, while the US dollar itself was linked to gold. It was recognised that members might experience problems with their balance of payments in the short term (an excess of imports over exports). In such a situation, the IMF agreed to make hard currency available to them on a short-term basis, to allow the member a breathing space to adjust its economy. Only if the balance of payments problem was long term was the member state permitted to devalue its currency. The system was financed by subscriptions from member countries, with by far the largest contribution coming from the USA.

The system worked reasonably smoothly for nearly 30 years, although there were still balance of payments crises, and occasional devaluations (most notably in the UK, France, and Italy). Most lending was to developed countries, and the IMF had little involvement with the Third World. However, the world economic structure changed fundamentally in the early 1970s. Now it was the USA which experienced a balance of payments crisis. The IMF system could not cope with this – the absolute stability of the dollar was fundamental. Eventually, President Nixon abandoned the fixed price link between the US dollar and gold – in effect devaluing the dollar. As a result, fixed exchange rates were abandoned, and have never been restored on a world level.

The floating exchange rate regime immediately removed the IMF's major role. It still carries out its role of alleviating short-term financial crises, but almost always with developing rather than developed economies – the Asian tiger economies (Thailand, South Korea, Indonesia) in 1997, Russia in 1998, Brazil in 1999 and Argentina in 2001 – but the IMF also started to develop a wider role of encouraging structural reform in member states (often known as 'mission creep' – a typical example of an organisation broadening its original aims beyond all recognition). An early example of this was the loan to the UK in 1976, which was made conditional on the (Labour) Government cutting public spending and adopting monetarist policies. This process has now gone much further, and, from the 1980s onwards, the IMF has followed a policy of imposing Thatcherite, free-market neo-liberal requirements (particularly privatisation) conditional to its support, particularly in relation to Third World countries. The list below provides some examples.

- Tanzania was forced to charge for hospital visits and schooling.
- Ecuador was forced to sell its water system to foreigners and to increase the price of cooking oil by 80 per cent.
- Malawi was told to sell off its strategic reserves of maize, two years before the country was hit by famine.
- Guyana was told to privatise its sugar industry.
- Zambia was told to privatise its banks (Mathiason 2003).

Should the IMF try to impose long-term neo-liberal reform in the Third World, rather than concentrating on lending money to countries in short-term financial difficulties?

There are three main arguments in favour of this policy.

1 State-run sectors in Third World countries tend to be inefficient and corrupt devourers of resources, and they discourage foreign investment. The state may also spend wastefully and not in the best long-term interests of its population – for instance by excess spending on arms.

2 Moral hazard – the concept that because countries expect to be bailed out if they get into difficulties, they will be reckless in their behaviour, because they know they will never really be called to account for their actions. For example, Brazil has defaulted on its debts five times, and Venezuela nine times. In essence, this is the same argument that says that insurance companies should carry out very strict checks before they pay out on policies, in order to discourage fraudulent claims.

3 Short-term intervention tends by definition to treat short-term symptoms rather than the long-term illness. The only way to tackle long-term problems is through long-term reform.

There are two counter-arguments:

1 While the above may be true in the long run, the short-term effect of privatisation and liberalisation is to increase poverty and inequality in the Third World.

2 By concentrating on the long term rather than the short term, the IMF is moving into areas which should more appropriately be the responsibility of the World Bank.

The current consensus seems to be that the IMF should concentrate on macroeconomic factors such as budget deficits and inflation, rather than trying to micro-manage the economies of clients. Charles Wyplosz, professor of economics at the Institute of International Studies in Geneva, was quoted in *The Financial Times* in May 2004 as saying,

'When firemen come to your house to put out a blaze, you would not expect them to meddle in your marriage' (Swann 2004).

The World Bank

Like the IMF, the World Bank was set up at Bretton Woods, and nearly all countries in the world are members. Unlike the IMF, its main role is to provide access to capital for long-term development, particularly in the Third World. It does this partly through direct lending through a number of its own agencies, some of it interest-free, and partly by leveraging investment from the private sector.

It also has a wider social remit than the IMF. It emphasises social services, the environment and gender equality as well as economic growth. However, like the IMF it has been criticised for the neo-liberal conditions which it tends to attach to its loans, and also for over-lending to relatively advanced developing countries like Brazil and particularly China, which have sufficient clout to be able to borrow to finance their development on a commercial basis.

One proposal that has been put forward is that the IMF and the World Bank should merge. There is clear overlap – in practice if not in theory – between the activities of the IMF and the World Bank, although in principle their functions are distinct. A merger might therefore seem logical, and it might help to prevent mission creep. However, if the IMF had a dominant role in the merged organisation, its neo-liberal agenda might swamp the wider social and environmental principles of the World Bank

International trade and comparative advantage

Very few countries are self-sufficient, in the sense that they produce everything which they need within their own boundaries. Ever since the Stone Age, societies have traded with each other. The most obvious reason for a country to trade is to obtain something which it is incapable of producing for itself. For example, until the discovery of North Sea oil, the UK had to import oil. However, strictly speaking this only applies to extractive industries. Anything else could be made or grown, at a price. There is nothing to stop the UK growing its own bananas in greenhouses (except common sense!). It is a much more efficient use of resources for countries to concentrate on what they are best at producing, and to import other goods. For example, if we compare the UK and the Windward Islands, the UK has an *absolute advantage* in the production of pharmaceuticals, while the Windwards have an *absolute advantage* in the production of bananas. It therefore makes sense for the UK to specialise in pharmaceuticals, and to export these to the Windwards, while the Windwards should export bananas to the UK. (As we will see later when we look at the banana war, the real world is a lot more complicated than this simple example suggests.)

Even if one country is better at producing everything than another country, international trade will still benefit both sides. For example, let's stretch our banana example even further. Assume that the UK is four times as efficient as the Windwards at producing pharmaceuticals, and twice as efficient at producing bananas. In this case, the UK has a *comparative advantage* in the production of pharmaceuticals, and the Windwards a *comparative advantage* in bananas. Both sides would benefit if the UK specialised in pharmaceuticals, and the Windwards in bananas. The mathematics to prove this can be found in any textbook on international economics.

For comparative advantage to work, however, it is essential that there are no restrictions on trade between the countries involved, ie that there is *free trade*. For example, assume that the UK has a banana industry which is struggling to cope with competition from Windwards bananas, and then assume that the UK banana industry persuades the UK Government to place either quotas (restrictions on quantity) or tariffs (taxation) on imports of Windwards bananas. People working in the UK banana industry would benefit, but everyone else in both economies would lose.

If you think that this example seems totally unrealistic, you are probably right, but bear in mind that Japan, for example, protects its rice growers with a 500 per cent tariff on imported rice.

ACTIVITY 3.5

Is comparative advantage good for you?

The theory of comparative advantage suggests that everyone gains from free trade. Why then do so many countries protect their own domestic industries?

The World Trade Organisation (WTO)

After the Second World War, the Allies set up the General Agreement on Tariffs on Trade (GATT), whose remit was to encourage free trade, and prevent the destructive protectionism that had blighted the world economy in the 1930s. Its objectives were to:

- eliminate existing trade barriers
- deter the formation of new barriers
- eliminate all forms of trade discrimination.

In 1995, GATT was absorbed into a new body, the WTO, with wider objectives. Its membership now includes virtually the whole world, following the accession of China and Taiwan in the early 2000s. The WTO continues the process of liberalising world trade, but its powers also extend to trade in services as well as goods, and also the regulation of intellectual property rights such as patents and copyright. It also has the power to adjudicate on disputes between members, with the right to impose financial penalties.

The working of the WTO

The WTO (and its predecessor GATT) works in a series of long trade rounds, initiated at a major conference, and then negotiated and implemented over a long period. The Uruguay Round in the 1990s was primarily concerned with textiles, where the developing world had a comparative advantage, but where the developed countries maintained protection of their own textile industries. The developed Western countries agreed to eliminate protection, but only over a 10-year period, with most of the concessions coming in the last year! This tends to be the pattern – the West speaks the language of free trade, is keen to impose free trade on the developing world, but drags its heels when it comes to its own concessions.

Larry Elliott in *The Guardian* in 2004 drew a telling parallel with medieval Europe, where in theory all states owed spiritual allegiance to the papacy and the universal values of the Church, but in practice spent most of their time at war with each other (Elliott 2004).

The current round, the Doha Round, concentrates on the even more sensitive subject of agricultural products, in which the Third World has a clear comparative advantage, but where

CASE STUDY 3.1

The Banana War

The banana war was one of the most bitter trade disputes of the 1990s, and one of a number of disputes between the two dominant trading blocs, the EU and the USA. The key to the dispute was the preference that the EU gave to bananas from ex-British and ex-French colonies in Africa, the Pacific and the Caribbean (the APC countries). The EU argument was that, without protection, the banana industries in these areas, particularly in the Caribbean, would collapse, devastating the local economies, and perhaps pushing producers to alternative and less desirable crops like cannabis or coca. They pointed out that the WTO had an objective to assist developing and transition economies.

The USA responded that the EU action was a gross breach of WTO rules. Three US companies – Chiquita, Dole and Del Monte – control two thirds of world trade in bananas from their huge plantations in Central America (the APC has 4 per cent of the world market).

Legally, the USA had an unanswerable case, but it weakened its moral position by imposing punitive import tariffs in 1998 on a range of EU exports to the USA in retaliation, before the WTO delivered its judgement. Worse, this was announced shortly after Chiquita gave a big donation to the ruling US Democratic Party.

The WTO ruled in favour of the USA, and ordered the EU to abolish its protective quotas on APC bananas by 2005. The effects on the Caribbean have been predictably devastating. Between 1993 and 2000, two thirds of the banana growers in the Windward Islands went out of business, while exports of bananas from St Vincent and the Grenadines fell from $120m to $50m (Ryle 2002).

the EU, the USA and Japan give massive protection to their own farmers. In Geneva in August 2004, the WTO agreed that export subsidies should be abolished, but no starting date or timetable has been agreed. The developing world should not expect quick results!

Debt relief

One of the most pressing problems of the world economy is the crushing burden of Third World debt. The 52 most indebted countries, mostly in Africa, have debts of $375 billion, most of it unpayable, but on which interest still has to be paid. In 1998, it cost these countries $23.4bn to service their debt, mostly owed to Western governments, the IMF or the World Bank. In many countries, debt repayment dwarfs welfare budgets. Mauritania pays $63m to service its debt, but only $51m on education, and $17m on health (Madeley 2001).

Much of the debt is a product of the Cold War period, when the West was keen to tie the Third World to its side, and much of the money was wasted, either going on armaments, or disappearing through corruption, by the likes of the late unlamented presidents Amin and Mobutu.

Many arguments can be advanced for relieving at least some of this burden of debt. These range from the moral, that debt is denying the inhabitants of these countries the human rights of decent education and health, the economic, that money being spent on debt repayment is not being spent on imports from the West, and the geopolitical, that poverty and discontent create an environment conducive to terrorism.

An international campaign for debt relief was launched in 1996 by the pressure group Jubilee 2000, which has produced some results. The IMF and the World Bank have set up the Heavily Indebted Poor Countries (HIPC) initiative to administer debt relief to the 52 poorest states, the G7 promised the cancellation of $110bn of debt, while the UK Government agreed to hold debt repayments in a trust for poverty relief, to be released when each country agreed a poverty reduction plan (Madeley 2001).

However, progress has been limited. By the end of the Jubilee 2000 campaign in December 2000, only one country, Uganda, had had debt cancelled, with reductions agreed for another 21, and in line with normal IMF/World Bank policy, stringent conditions were attached. HIPCs are still expected to pay 20–25 per cent of their export earnings towards debt service (Sassen 2001). However, some progress has been made. In a sample of 10 HIPC countries, education spending rose by 50 per cent between 1998 and 2002, from less than the 10 states were spending on debt relief in 1998, to almost double the amount in 2002 (Stewart 2002).

ACTIVITY 3.6

Debt relief

Can you put forward any arguments against either the principle or the practice of debt relief for the Third World?

GLOBALISATION

Globalisation is an emotive word. It has inspired violent demonstrations all over the world, and also vehement defence. But what *is* globalisation? This is no single clear definition. John Gray sees its key features as free mobility of capital and free trade (Gray 1995). Ngaire Woods sees globalisation as much wider, and political and social as well as economic. She distinguishes the following three elements (Woods 2000):

- The expansion of markets
  Technological changes like the mobile phone and above all the Internet have speeded up communications to the extent that both financial and physical transactions can be carried out instantaneously, while improvements in transport permit goods to shipped quickly and relatively cheaply anywhere in the world. (Think of the universal availability in the UK of asparagus from Peru and French beans from Kenya.) At the same time, governments throughout the world have been deregulating, and reducing their control over their economies, at the same time as the growth of e-commerce has started to erode their control of their tax base. The result has been the spread of transnational enterprises and global brands, leading to what Kenichi Ohmae, the Japanese management guru and one of the early proponents of globalisation, called 'The Borderless World' (Ohmae 1990).
  The knowledge economy also creates a borderless world. Knowledge is not dependent on possession of natural resources, and can instantaneously be transmitted via the Internet. As Lester Thurow says, 'knowledge is the new basis for wealth' (Thurow 1999). Hence the outflow of call centre and data handling jobs from the UK to India.

- The transformation of politics
  Free movement of capital has produced a world financial market which has the potential to swamp any single economy. At the same time, transnational issues have become of

increasing importance: global warming, human rights, drugs, world poverty, immigration and terrorism. Increasingly, in order to have any influence, nation states have to join together in regional groupings. The European Union is the best known, but there are other important groupings like the North Atlantic Free Trade Area and ASEAN. Just as nation states are handing over power to regional groupings, they are also devolving power internally to regional entities – Scotland and Wales in the UK, Catalonia in Spain.

■ The emergence of new social and political movements
A global (or American) culture has developed, with US corporations like McDonalds, CNN, Disney and Nike setting trends across the world. At the same time, counter-movements have developed, ranging from the anti-globalisation movement to militant Islam.

Globalisation is nothing new. An early example came with the Opium Wars in the 1840s, when Great Britain forced China to open its borders to imports of opium in order to finance the early Victorians' obsession with China tea. It has often been argued that the golden age of globalisation was the period 1880–1914, when the world economy was regulated by the universal use of the Gold Standard, there was almost universal free trade, and free movement of capital. Indeed, this period had one element of globalisation which does not apply today – free movement of people. Not only could an individual travel without a passport; there was free movement of labour, and very little control on international migration – this is the period when the Statue of Liberty was erected in New York. One commentator even said in 1911 that a major war was now impossible, as the world had become so interdependent (Micklethwait and Wooldridge 2000).

Two dates mark the development of modern globalisation. One is 1973, and the first oil crisis. This led to two things – a realisation that the world economy was inextricably linked through its dependence on oil, and the collapse of the Bretton Woods system of fixed exchange rates, which ushered in a period when world financial markets became much more dominant.

The other is 1989. One factor here was the collapse of communism as a world ideology, and the triumph of the USA in the Cold War – what the US political scientist Francis Fukuyama called 'The End of History'. The other, much less noted at the time, but equally important, was the final bursting of the Japanese 'bubble economy'. Throughout the 1980s, it seems that globalisation was likely to be Japanese rather than US-dominated. Japanese industrial techniques were sweeping the world, and most of the world's biggest corporations were Japanese rather than US. The economic collapse of Japan ensured that globalisation would be US-dominated economically, as well as politically and culturally.

Drivers of globalisation

A number of drivers of globalisation have intensiifed in the last 20 years or so:

■ Technology
The most important developments here are in information and communication technology (ICT), particularly the mobile phone and the Internet. These have transformed the way in which particular industries operate. An example is the insurance industry, which traditionally was staid and conservative, but has been transformed by the application of new technology, which has led to a wave of mergers.

- Cultural homogenisation
  The universal availability of television, and the global audiences for international sporting events like the World Cup and the Olympic Games, combined with the explosion in overseas travel, has led to a homogenisation of international culture, which permits the development of global brands. However, global brands like McDonalds still have to be responsive to local cultural differences – no traditional beef Big Macs in India, for example.

- Economies of scale
  Developments in manufacturing techniques have meant that the minimum efficient scale of operations in many industries has become a significant percentage of the available world market. The most extreme example is the aircraft industry, where the total world market is barely big enough to support two firms (Boeing and Airbus Industrie).

- Deregulation
  Deregulation has been driven by bodies such as the WTO and the EU. It reduces the costs of cross-border trade, and so promotes the development of global companies.

- Competition
  If one firm in an industry globalises, it will gain a competitive advantage. In order to stay in touch, its competitors will also be forced to globalise (Segal-Horn 2002).

Multinational and transnational corporations

Multinational corporations (MNCs) are companies producing or distributing goods or services in two or more countries. A transnational corporation is an MNC with more than two thirds of its activities outside its home country. Such companies can locate different activities in parts of the world where they reap the biggest comparative advantage. Thus Rupert Murdoch's News Corporation is controlled through holding companies in the Cayman Islands, a notorious tax haven. The result is that News Corporation pays an average tax rate of 10 per cent.

In another example, the fall in the costs of air transport have led to the centralisation of the world flower industry in the Netherlands. Flowers are flown in from Kenya or India one day, sold at auction and then flown to customers in Europe or the USA the next day.

The best-known example of local advantage is low labour costs. This is most obvious in low-wage industries like textiles, but a high-tech example is that of the Brazilian manufacturer of regional jet airliners, Embraer. Its employment costs in 2002 were $26,000 per employee, as against $63,000 in the regional jet business of its major Canadian competitor, Bombardier (Ghemawat 2003).

In 2001, there were estimated to be 63,000 TNCs, which had 800,000 foreign affiliates, and which controlled two thirds of world trade. Of the top 100 non-financial TNCs, 91 were based in the USA, the EU or Japan (Unctad 2001)

ACTIVITY 3.7

Why do people hate the WTO and globalisation?

Throughout the West, there is deep suspicion, in many cases verging on hatred, of the progress of globalisation in general, and the activities of the WTO in particular. Why do you think this is?

CASE STUDIES 3.2 – GLOBALISATION

The Java furniture industry

The furniture industry in the Jepara region of central Java, Indonesia, is often cited as one of the success stories of globalisation. An article by Lienda Loebis and Hubert Schmitz for the Institute of Development Studies at the University of Sussex, examined the extent of this success (Loebis and Schmitz 2003). In particular, they examined two questions: Are the furniture companies and their workers winners from globalisation, and is their success sustainable?

There are two main ways in which local enterprises can compete in a global market. One is the race to the bottom – to aim to be the cheapest by paying low wages, disregarding environmental and employment standards, and avoiding taxes. The other is to compete by upgrading processes and standards. Loebis and Schmitz found examples of both in Java. Some big firms had long-standing contracts with Western customers. For example, Suwastama, employing 650 workers, supplied rattan furniture to IKEA. It had 350 sub-contractors, and supported a total of 7,000 workers. Working with both IKEA and its own suppliers, Suwastama had improved quality, and could guarantee timely delivery.

At the other extreme there were hundreds of small businesses employing a few workers, without direct access to Western buyers or Western know-how. The only way in which they could remain competitive was to use illegally logged timber, especially teak, which is considerably cheaper than legal timber.

Loebis and Schmitz concluded that the furniture industry was successful, and that on balance companies and workers were benefiting from globalisation. Part of their evidence for this was the motorcycle test – in the Jepara region the number of motorbikes registered increased by 50 per cent between 1998 and 2001, which they saw as clear evidence of growing prosperity.

As to the second question, they concluded that the success of the industry was probably not sustainable in the long term. Indonesia is running out of hardwood, a problem made worse by illegal felling, which tends to take immature trees. The industry had also received a short-term boost from the collapse of the Indonesian rupiah after the Asian financial crisis of 1997, and this may not last. Finally, the focus of the furniture industry was already starting to move to Vietnam and China, which could beat Indonesia on price.

This case illustrates the following general points about globalisation.

- Western buyers, often portrayed as one of the villains of globalisation, can often play a positive role by providing technical advice and long-term contracts.
- Third World gainers from globalisation are frequently large companies and their employees, who can take a value-added approach.
- In the race to the bottom, there are no long-term winners.

The Mozambique sugar industry

Mozambique was ranked as the poorest country in the world in the 1990s. It is slowly recovering from a ruinous civil war. Under the Portuguese colonial administration, sugar had been one of the country's key industries, but the infrastructure was devastated during the civil war. After peace was signed in 1992, the Government saw sugar as a way of creating thousands of new jobs (Macmullan 2004).

The world sugar trade is heavily distorted. Sugar can be produced either from beet, grown in rich northern hemisphere countries and expensive to produce, and cane, grown in the poor south, and cheap to produce. To protect their own industries, wealthy countries, especially the EU, heavily subsidise their sugar beet production and protect their markets from imports. The world price is thus held artificially low. In addition, surpluses are generally dumped anywhere where there is a market, frequently at prices below that of the most efficient producers.

Mozambique thus faced a problem in developing its sugar industry: How to protect its own market? They decided to impose import duties, based on a complex reference price. Unfortunately, this fell foul of the IMF, which in 2000 argued that Mozambique should open its market to international competition, thus reducing prices for consumers.

The Mozambican Government admitted that it was true that in theory liberalisation should mean lower prices for consumers. However, there was no guarantee traders would pass on low import prices to their customers, and Mozambique's huge size and poor communications would make it difficult for imported sugar to reach consumers. On the other hand, liberalisation would destroy many jobs in a very poor country, and imports would also cost foreign exchange which Mozambique did not have.

After pressure from European donors and aid agencies, and, it is believed, the World Bank, the IMF was persuaded to change its mind, and the Mozambican sugar industry was saved. By 2004, it employed 20,000 workers, and produced a foreign exchange benefit for Mozambique of $25 million.

The lessons of this case seem to be as follows.

- The hypocritical approach of the West, including the EU, to globalisation. Liberalisation is fine for a country like Mozambique, but not for its own protected sugar beet farmers
- The hard line approach of the IMF to liberalisation, and the more pragmatic approach of the World Bank
- The law of comparative advantage. Under the logic of free trade, Mozambique should be exporting sugar to the West.

The horticultural industry in Chile

Globalisation has greatly expanded the world horticultural industry. The need for a year-round supply of crops in Europe has facilitated a year-round rotation of crops from developing countries. Chile has a suitable climate for horticulture, and the advantage that, being in the southern hemisphere, its seasons are the opposite of those of Western Europe. It specialises in grapes, apples and pears, and exports about 30 per cent of its harvest to Western Europe (Barrientos and Barrientos 2002).

The industry in Chile is controlled by about 20 large exporters, supplied by 8,000 producers, who are dependent on low-paid temporary workers, most of whom are women. Many of the workers are supplied to the growers by contractors, and the work is highly seasonal. It is also hazardous, because of the pesticides involved. Between 50 and 60 per cent of temporary workers are paid less than the Chilean minimum wage, and of course receive this for only part of the year.

The lessons of this case seem to be as follows.

■ The desire of consumers in the West to enjoy fresh fruit and vegetables out of season has led to the growth of major horticultural industries in the developing world, producing for the export market – a classic example of globalisation.

■ By its very nature, much of the work in horticulture is seasonal and low paid, providing a golden opportunity for local labour contractors, and often leading to exploitation of the mainly female labour force.

■ However, is employment in the seasonal horticulture industry better than no employment at all?

THE GLOBALISATION DEBATE

Aisbett (2003) identifies the following four main areas of concern over globalisation:

1 an objection not to globalisation in principle, but to the way in which it is skewed in favour of developed countries. This is exemplified by the protectionist agricultural policies of the USA and the EU

2 loss of sovereignty, to transnational corporations and to institutions like the IMF and the WTO

3 neo-liberal or 'Washington consensus' policies, as imposed by the IMF on debtor countries – privatisation, welfare cut-backs, etc.

4 the rise of big corporations. Of the 100 biggest economic units in the world, 52 are corporations. They can expand or contract their activities in particular countries in order to maximise their overall profit.

However, Aisbett points out that the debate is no longer between supporters and opponents of globalisation. The anti-capitalist protest movements of the late 1990s have run out of steam, and the main arguments are now between enthusiastic and cautious globalisers. Even Oxfam has recognised that globalisation can have some benefits. A similar point is made by Jacobs (2001).

Aisbett identifies areas of agreement between the enthusiastic and cautious globalisers. These include:

■ Trade is often a source of economic growth and growth is good for the poor (although the Green Party argues that local production may be more efficient – see the Mozambique sugar case study above) (Lucas 2001).

■ The USA and the EU should open their markets to the developing world.

- Safety nets should be provided for the losers from globalisation, and education, health and welfare in developing countries should be safeguarded.
- Income is an inadequate measure of poverty, and social factors should be taken into consideration.
- Excessive corporate power is a problem.
- Political reform is needed in many developing countries.

There are also important areas of difference remaining, including those shown in Table 3.1.

Table 3.1 *The globalisation debate: remaining areas of difference*

Issue	Enthusiastic view	Cautious view
Attitudes to poverty	Globalisation in all its forms is good for the poor, and reducing poverty is what matters, even at the cost of increased inequality.	Reducing inequality is equally important, and globalisation frequently increases it.
Trade liberalisation	Trade liberalisation is always beneficial.	Totally free trade will often have adverse social or environmental side effects. Decisions should be taken on a case-by-case basis – see Mozambican sugar again.
Transnational corporations	Their activities should be encouraged as they provide jobs and bring in new technologies.	Big corporations destroy indigenous producers, and the net effect may be negative.
Privatisation	Government provision of essential services in developing countries is invariably corrupt and/or inefficient, and therefore these services should be privatised.	Only government provision of essential services can ensure that they are available to the poor.
Competitiveness	Opening developing economies to foreign trade and investment improves competitiveness by destroying local monopolies.	Opening developing economies to foreign trade destroys indigenous producers whether or not they were monopolies and further increases the power of the transnational corporations.

The high point of globalisation came in the 1990s, in the euphoria which followed the collapse of communism, and 'the end of history'. This era of full-blooded, red- in-tooth-and-claw globalisation may have already passed. The onward march of e-commerce, and the idea that the world had entered a 'new economic paradigm' of endless economic growth, was shattered by the dot.com crash in 2000, and the collapse of giant new economy corporations like Enron and WorldCom. Just as the economic confidence of the USA was shaken, its sense of political and military invulnerability was shattered by the attacks of September 11th 2001.

Coupled with the US military response to 'the war on terror', there is a growing though implicit feeling that the war on terror will be lost unless the west wins the hearts and minds of the Third World. Hence the criticisms from both Left and Right of the aggressive neo-liberal policies of the IMF and the World Bank, and possibly a more caring approach to debt relief and aid.

At the same time there is a growing realisation that globalisation has not made the nation state redundant. The role of the nation state is to provide good governance. In an article previewing his new book, *State Building*, Francis Fukuyama of 'the end of history' quotes from the doyen of free-market economists, Milton Friedman, as saying that his advice to former communist countries 10 years ago had been to concentrate on privatisation. Now he feels that he was wrong. 'It turns out that the rule of law is probably more basic than privatisation' (Fukuyama 2004).

Globalisation and the labour market

Globalisation and the greater integration of world markets will inevitably have an impact on the UK labour market, as we will examine in the following Case study and Activity.

CASE STUDY 3.3

The outsourcing of call centres

The call centre industry in the UK is large, employing 867,000 people, or 3 per cent of the workforce, in 2004 (Shah 2004). It is also a new industry, having grown from almost nothing over the past 15 years. As a result, there has been considerable concern about the steady movement of call centre jobs, particularly in the financial services industry, to India, particularly to Mumbai and Bangalore. Opponents of globalisation see this as an example of the detrimental effect of globalisation on UK employment, while supporters see it as a positive development, lowering costs for UK industry, and so increasing national prosperity.

Both are right. The short-term effect is that the UK is losing jobs. Call centres in the UK were frequently set up in areas of high unemployment, and the loss of these jobs is disproportionately felt. On the other hand, if outsourcing increases the profits of UK companies, this should free up resources for future investment. A short-term loss must thus be set against a long-term gain.

The typical Indian call centre goes to great lengths to make their operators acceptable to UK consumers. The call centres operate on UK rather than Indian time, and operators are expected to keep themselves informed about the English weather, and the latest plot twists in *Eastenders*. However, there is some evidence that Indian call centres are less efficient than UK ones. One study claimed that UK operators answered 25 per cent more calls per hour, resolved 17 per cent more calls first time, and stayed with their company three times as long, although this is offset by average salaries in India of only 12 per cent of the UK level (Clennell 2004). This would suggest that UK companies which are more concerned with the quality of their customer service than with minimising their short-term costs should think very seriously before they outsource to India.

The long-run future of the call centre industry in the UK must lie with developing a more sophisticated knowledge-based, value-added service. Basic information giving services can be better performed in India, or over the Internet.

ACTIVITY 3.8

Globalisation and your organisation

What impact, if any, has globalisation had on your own organisation?

CONCLUSION

Both Europeanisation and globalisation are intensifying, and their impact on the UK's economy, society and organisations is increasing. This will affect all of us, as consumers, citizens, workers and professionals.

KEY LEARNING POINTS

- The European Union's key aims have always been to maintain peace in Europe (particularly between France and Germany) and to enhance prosperity.

- Although there is general agreement on these over-riding aims, there are considerable differences of opinion about the future direction of the EU, epitomised by the Single Market, Federalist and Integrationist perspectives.

- The Commission is the executive of the EU, initiating and implementing policy; the Council of Ministers is the political decision-making body, the Parliament is mainly consultative, while the European Court of Justice rules on the legal interpretation of the EU treaties and legislation.

- The EU expanded from 15 to 25 members in 2004, with the accession of mainly ex-communist countries from central Europe, and is likely to expand to 27 in 2007, with the accession of Bulgaria and Romania. This has necessitated the drafting of a new Constitution, published in 2004, which has caused considerable political controversy in many EU member states, particularly the UK and France.

- Since the mid-1940s, the world economic system has been regulated by three major international institutions: the IMF, the World Bank and GATT (now the World Trade Organisation). All have been criticised by the left as imposing capitalist norms on the developing world.

- Globalisation has been characterised as having three main elements: the expansion of markets, the transformation of politics and the emergence of new social and political movements.

- The theory of comparative advantage and international specialisation underpins the concept of globalisation. Globalisation has also become more feasible with modern developments in communications, particularly air transport and the Internet.

- Aisbett (2003) identified four main areas of concern over globalisation: an objection not to globalisation in principle, but to the way in which it is skewed in favour of developed countries; loss of sovereignty, to transnational corporations and to institutions like the IMF and the WTO; neo-liberal or 'Washington consensus' policies; and the rise of big corporations.

FURTHER READING

Micklethwait and Wooldridge's *A Future Perfect: The Challenge and Hidden Promise of Globalization*, 2000. This is an easily readable (but positive) introduction to globalisation. For a generally anti-globalisation perspective, check out websites like Oxfam (oxfam.org.uk) or Christian Aid (christianaid.org.uk).

For both the EU and globalisation, the way to keep up to date is read good-quality newspapers regularly. The same general advice applies as for Chapter 2: make sure you get a balance of left- and right-wing views.

Government Policy

INTRODUCTION

In this chapter we will analyse the evolution of government policy in social, economic and industrial fields, and the impact of government policy on organisations. As developments in the UK are heavily influenced by the actions of the EU, we will be concerned with both UK and EU policy. We start with formal legislative procedures in the UK and the EU, and then go on to consider informal influences on the evolution of policy. We then consider recent developments in policy in the UK.

THE LEGISLATIVE PROCESS IN THE UK AND THE EU
The UK

Most legislation originates in government departments and is directly sponsored by the Government. Some legislation, particularly on matters of conscience, starts as a Private Members' Bill. Most of these fail. Normally they only pass with substantial cross-party support, and support, or at worst neutrality, from the Government. Indeed, frequently the purpose of a Private Members' Bill is not actually to pass a new law, but to bring public attention to an issue which is important to an individual MP and those pressure groups which support him or her. In this section, we are only going to look at government Bills.

At least for Bills published relatively early in the life of a parliament, the general subject matter of the Bill will appear in the governing party's election manifesto – 'we intend to bring in legislation to put right the long-standing grievances concerning ...'

The next (optional) stage is a Green Paper. This is a consultative document setting out the case for the forthcoming legislation, and the pros and cons of various approaches to legislation. This does not commit the Government to anything, but forms a basis for discussion with interested parties and pressure groups. After consultation on the Green Paper, the Government may choose to:

- follow it up with a White Paper
- go straight to legislation
- drop the proposal.

A White Paper firms up on the proposal, but again does not commit the Government on detail. A lengthy period of consultation may then follow.

The parliamentary session normally starts in November, with the Queen's Speech, when the Queen sets out the programme of legislation for the coming year: 'My government intends to introduce legislation on ...'. The Government will then publish a Bill, drafted by specialist parliamentary lawyers. The Bill then goes through a number of formal stages, as follows.

- First Reading – a formal presentation of the Bill to the Commons
- Second Reading – a full debate on the principles of the Bill rather than the details
- Committee Stage – the Bill is then scrutinised in detail by a Standing Committee of the Commons, consisting of between 15 and 20 MPs, with a government majority. The Bill will be debated and voted on clause by clause, and some provisions may be amended
- Report Stage – the amended Bill goes back to the full Commons, where the Government has an opportunity to reverse any amendments forced on it at the Committee Stage
- Third Reading – this is formal, and not usually debated
- The Bill then goes to the House of Lords, and repeats the same stages as in the Commons. The Lords can amend the Bill or reject it. If they reject it, this delays the Bill for one parliamentary session. Having passed through the Lords, the Bill goes back to the Commons, which can reject any amendments made by the Lords
- Royal Assent – the Queen then agrees to the Bill, which becomes an Act. In theory the Queen could reject the Bill, but this has not been done for 300 years.

As a legal document, every word of an Act matters, and it is subject to interpretation by the courts.

The EU

This is very different from the process in the UK. Initial proposals for legislation are drawn up by the Commission, and must be based on one of the EU treaties (Rome, Maastricht, Amsterdam, Nice, etc.). Each treaty has to be unanimously ratified by the member states. By contrast, in the UK the Government has a free hand to legislate on anything that it chooses (including leaving the EU).

At this stage, the proposal is known as a draft directive (or after the implementation of the new EU Constitution of 2004, a draft framework law). The draft then goes out for consultation to the Council of Ministers, the European Parliament, and the Social Partners (the two employers' bodies Unice and CEEP and the trade union body ETUC). The Commission then revises its proposals, which are then formally presented to the Council of Ministers, which will take a decision on unanimity or qualified majority voting, depending on the nature of the legislation. The European Parliament has the right to debate and to comment on the proposed directive but, until the new Constitution is adopted, no right to amend or reject it. Under the new Constitution, the European Parliament will have the right to reject or amend the proposal, but only by a majority of more than half of all MEPs (not just those who vote).

The law will be adopted under the new constitution if:

- both the Parliament and the Council of Ministers approve it (by either unanimity or qualified majority, depending on the type of legislation)
- the Council of Ministers approves the parliament's amendments (if the Commission opposes an amendment, it must be approved by an unanimous vote of the Council of Ministers).

The directive then has to be implemented by member states – ie EU directives become law in the UK through a UK Act of Parliament. At the end of 2003, there were about 2,500 EU directives, and the compliance rate by member states ranged between 96 and 99 per cent (Mulvey 2003).

ACTIVITY 4.1

UK and EU legislation

What are the differences in passing legislation between the UK and the EU? Which system do you think is more democratic?

INFORMAL INFLUENCES ON POLICY

Political parties

Traditionally the electoral system in the UK has ensured a predominantly two-party electoral system (plus regional and/or nationalist parties representing Scotland, Wales and Northern Ireland) – a broadly 'right wing' party in favour of maintaining the status quo (the Tories in the early nineteenth century, the Conservatives from the late nineteenth century onwards), and a broadly 'left-wing' party in favour of change (the Whigs in the early nineteenth century, the Liberals in the late nineteenth century, Labour from the 1920s). The two wings broadly represented different class interests – the right wing the 'haves' who resisted change (the ruling class, and later the middle class), and the left wing the 'have-nots', those seeking change (the working class). Thus ideology and social class were seen as underpinning the UK party system. In Activity 4.2 you will explore how far this is still true.

The influence of members of political parties, even MPs, over government policy-making is small, and probably getting smaller. MPs are subject to party discipline, and although they can and do vote against their own government on occasions, every MP knows that if he votes to bring down his own government, his party career will be finished. Even massive revolts are unlikely to change government policy, as can be shown by the Labour revolt on university fees, and on the Iraq War, where even the resignation of a leading Cabinet member, Robin Cook, had no influence on policy.

Party conferences can pass resolutions critical of government policy, but governments have never had to take much notice of these. Policy is nowadays decided much more by focus groups and think-tanks. MPs do have the power to force an election for the post of party leader, and when the Conservatives ousted Margaret Thatcher and replaced her with John Major, the decision was taken solely by Conservative MPs. However, the Conservative Party, like the Labour Party, now elects its leader through a complicated electoral college system, where MPs, peers, MEPs, and party members all have a weighted vote.

ACTIVITY 4.2

Political parties

1 What arguments would you put forward if asked to support the argument that ideology and class no longer underpin the present party system?

2 David Farnham argues that there are two crucial differences between a political party and a pressure group (Farnham 1999, p137):

■ Parties try to win political control to use political power. Pressure groups seek to influence political decisions not to get in a position where they can make those decisions themselves.

■ The political programmes of parties are broad-based, while pressure groups tend to concentrate on a single issue.

Given the above, would you say that the UK Independence Party (UKIP), which won several seats in the EU elections in 2004, is a political party or a pressure group? What about the Ulster Unionist Party?

Pressure groups

A pressure group is 'any group in society which, through political action, seeks to achieve changes which it regards as desirable or to prevent changes which it regards as undesirable' (Forman and Baldwin 1999, p128). They can broadly be classified into two main types:

1 interest or sectional groups

2 attitude or cause groups.

Interest groups are those pressure groups which have a common interest, and they exist to promote the interests of that group. Classic examples are trade unions and employers' associations, but interest groups also include professional bodies, the Royal British Legion and the AA.

Attitude groups are those pressure groups whose members have attitudes or beliefs rather than material interests, and they seek to advance particular causes. Examples include the National Trust, Oxfam, Greenpeace, Liberty, and the RSPB. Some pressure groups appear to be hybrids. The Countryside Alliance, for example, would see itself as an attitude group, while its opponents would see it as an interest group.

Pressure groups have a number of important functions, as follows.

- Intermediaries between the Government and the public. The prime role of a pressure group is obviously to apply pressure on the Government (or sometimes on other political bodies like the EU, the IMF or a foreign government). They channel and express public opinion on key issues. Some pressure groups use professional lobbying organisations to put forward their point of view to decision-makers. American gaming interests are alleged to have spent £100m in 2004 in support of the Gambling Bill, which would introduce Las Vegas-style 'super-casinos' to the UK (Mathiason 2004). For a detailed analysis of the tactics used by the lobbyists in this case see Hencke (2004).

- Opponents and critics of government policy. Party discipline prevents governing party MPs from opposing government policy, while criticism from opposition parties tends to be ignored because everyone expects the Opposition to oppose. Pressure groups can provide detailed and (hopefully) constructive criticism of policy. Indeed, on some occasions pressure groups in effect write government policy for it.

- Agents of government. This is controversial. Increasingly, pressure groups which themselves provide services, particularly charities, receive government grants towards providing those services, which some feel may compromise their independence.

- Publicists to promote an interest or defend a standpoint.

ACTIVITY 4.3

A question of influence

Make a list of the ways in which pressure groups can influence the Government.

THE GOVERNMENT AND THE ECONOMY

Some key definitions

Before we can examine ways in which the Government can manage the economy, we need to define some key concepts.

Gross Domestic Product

The most common method of measuring the output of an economy is gross domestic product (GDP). This is the measure of the country's total annual output of goods and services. This is not the same as the sum of the outputs of all organisations in the economy, as this would involve double counting. For example, sales of cans of baked beans made by a supermarket are counted, but not sales of the tinplate for the cans made by a steelworks. When calculating GDP:

- indirect taxes and subsidies (like VAT) are normally ignored
- exports are included, because they form part of the output of the UK
- imports are excluded, because although they are consumed in the UK, they are part of the output of other countries.

An important distinction to make is between GDP and the standard of living or quality of life. Governments are concerned to achieve economic growth, defined as an increase in GDP over time. Individuals are much more concerned with their own standard of living.

ACTIVITY 4.4
Standard of living

How might an individual's standard of living increase without there being an increase in GDP?

Business cycles

The economy tends to move in a series of ups and downs in the short term, although the long-term trend is for the size of GDP to grow. These fluctuations, over a 5–10 year period, are known as the business cycle. Governments attempt to dampen the effects of these cycles, but have not succeeded in abolishing them entirely. The top of a cycle is known as a peak, the bottom as a trough. In the period between a peak and a trough, economic growth may merely slow down, as in the period 2001–03, following the terrorist attacks of September 11th 2001, or GDP may actually fall. If GDP falls for two consecutive quarters, this is technically known as a recession, as the UK experienced in 1973–75, 1979–81 and 1990–92. If a recession is both deep and long-lasting, it is known as a depression, as in the case of the Great Depression of 1929–33 following the Wall Street Crash.

Unemployment

Unemployment is a surprisingly complex concept which has significant social as well as economic consequences. It is not even simple to define unemployment. A person can only be unemployed if he or she is out of work and seeking work. But what about someone who is:

- working part-time but would rather work full-time?
- apparently seeking work, but has totally unrealistic expectations about the sort of job which he or she could obtain?

There are two main ways of measuring unemployment, as follows.

1 Counting those people who are claiming unemployment benefit (the claimant count). This means that those who do not have work, and are seeking work, but who do not qualify for benefit, are excluded. On the other hand, some people who are not genuinely seeking work may be included.

2 Carrying out a survey and ask people whether they are employed or unemployed. This is carried out through the Labour Force Survey, using internationally agreed definitions

provided by the International Labour Organisation (ILO). Here someone is classified as unemployed if they are

- out of work
- have been seeking work within the last 4 weeks
- available to start work within 2 weeks.

The ILO method is now the Government's preferred measure, but both are regularly published in the UK. The ILO figure comes out higher than the claimant count measure, mainly because it includes large numbers of women who are ineligible for unemployment benefit.

Inflation

Inflation is a general rise in the level of prices. In the UK it is measured in the following three ways:

1 RPI – the Retail Price Index. This is calculated by measuring monthly changes in the price of a basket of goods which is meant to represent the spending pattern of the average family. This is the measure used to assess yearly increases in pensions and other state benefits.

2 RPIX – the Retail Price Index excluding mortgage interest. Until November 2003 this was the Government's preferred target measure, as it represents the underlying rate of inflation in the economy (mortgage interest rates depend on the general level of interest rates, set by the Bank of England).

3 CPI – the Consumer Price Index. This is the agreed measure of inflation used throughout the European Union, and was adopted as the official inflation target in the UK in November 2003 (when it was known as the Harmonised Index of Consumer Prices – inevitably called hiccup!).

Balance of payments

The balance of payments is a measure of flows of money into and out of the UK economy. It is extremely complex as it has a number of different components. The most commonly used elements are as follows.

- The balance of trade. This measures imports and exports of goods.
- The balance of payments on current account. This measures imports and exports of goods and services.

Economic objectives

All governments, whatever their political complexion, are trying to achieve the following four main economic objectives.

1 Economic growth. Since the 1990s this has increased by around 2–2.5 per cent per annum, with some periods of falling GDP, and others when the growth rate in the short term has gone as high as 4 per cent.

2 Full employment. This does not mean that nobody is unemployed, but that there are, in theory, jobs available for those seeking them, at current wage rates. In practice, this means that full employment is achieved if the number out of work is matched by the number of unfilled vacancies.

3   Stable prices (or low inflation) – again there is some dispute about the optimum level of inflation, but most economists would agree that it is around the Labour Government's target of 2.5 per cent on the RPIX index in the late 1990s (re-stated as 2 per cent on the CPI index in November 2003).

4   Equilibrium in the balance of payments – ie that the value of goods and services exported should roughly equal the value imported. This has deteriorated in recent years, with the trade deficit expected to be around £60 billion in 2004, although this is offset to some extent by a strong surplus on the balance on services.

The New Labour Government since 1997 has been more successful than most governments, achieving full success on economic growth and inflation, and considerable success on full employment. The only blot on its record is a worsening balance of payments.

In addition, governments will have policies on other economic objectives. These might include the following.

■   Redistribution of income. This is seen as a social objective in its own right, but its prime economic function is a means to achieve economic growth.

■   Exchange rates. The exchange value of the pound is seen as a political virility symbol, but it is primarily important as a means of managing the balance of payments. UK entry to the euro is of course a long-running contentious political issue.

■   The level of taxation and the level of government spending – both in terms of their absolute level in the economy, and of the balance between them.

■   Interest rates. These are seen either as a means of controlling inflation or of managing growth.

■   Money supply. In the 1980s this was seen as an objective in its own right, but is now seen as a means of achieving other objectives.

■   Privatisation (or nationalisation). Linked with this is more general regulation or deregulation of the economy.

As you will see from the above list, economics is not value-free. Managing the economy inevitably has strong political and social, as well as economic elements.

The tools of government policy

A range of tools are available to the Government in its objective of managing the economy.

■   Fiscal policy
    This involves a manipulation of the level of taxation and/or government spending. The theory underpinning this was established by the economist John Maynard Keynes in the 1930s (Keynes 1936). If there is a persistent level of unemployment in the economy, he argued that this is fundamentally owing to a lack of demand. In order to increase demand in the economy, the Government can inject demand into it, either by increasing its own spending, which will directly lead to a higher demand for goods and services, or by cutting taxation, which will put more money into the hands of consumers, and so enable them to demand more goods and services. However, changes in taxation or public spending are subject to long time lags before

they take effect, and increasingly chancellors of the exchequer have not seen fiscal policy as an appropriate tool for short-term management of the economy. Instead, they have taken the view that the level of spending and taxation are much more issues of political rather than demand management policy. Gordon Brown has expressed this in his Golden Rule, which states that over an economic cycle, the Government should aim for a balanced budget, ie, the revenue raised through taxation should equal the amount spent on current goods and services. This policy does allow for some flexibility, ie for expenditure to exceed taxation during the trough phase of the cycle, so long as this is balanced by a surplus at the peak.

■ Monetary policy

Monetary policy was strongly in vogue during the 1980s, at the height of the power of Margaret Thatcher, and under the influence of the American economist Milton Friedman, who argued a direct causal link between the supply of money and the level of inflation (Friedman and Schwark 1963). Policies were therefore implemented directly to control the supply of money. However, as the leading monetarist economist Sir Alan Budd, who was chief economic adviser to the Treasury between 1991 and 1997, says, 'I hope I can say without offending anyone that the experiment in seeking to control inflation by setting quantitative monetary targets did not match the hopes of its most enthusiastic supporters, among whom I am willing to count myself' (Keegan 2004a). One of the main problems was not the existence of the link between money supply and inflation, but the difficulty in producing a watertight definition of money at a time of great technological change, including the explosive growth in the use of credit cards (which enable people to spend money they do not possess, and which does not exist until they spend it).

Monetary policy is now much simpler. It consists of control over interest rates, set by the independent Bank of England. The way in which this works will be explored in considerable detail below.

■ Competitiveness (supply-side) policy

Policy here is linked to the concept of NAIRU or Non-Accelerating Inflation Rate of Unemployment (the rate of unemployment which ensures a stable level of inflation). If the economy can be made more competitive, the rate of NAIRU should fall, and the economy will be able to operate at lower levels of inflation and unemployment. This involves deregulating the markets both for goods and services and for labour, through policies including privatisation and rigorous control of monopolies and cartels. It also involves a concerted drive to increase the rate of growth of productivity in the economy, by encouraging investment in research and development, and in the enhancement of worker skills. Again, this policy will be examined in depth below.

■ Exchange rate policy

It is possible to manipulate the exchange rate in order to achieve economic objectives. For example, if an exchange rate is set at a level below that justified by market forces, the currency will be under-valued. This will stimulate exports, which will be artificially lowered in price, and discourage imports, which will be artificially highly priced. An overvalued currency will have the opposite result. However, there are two major snags with this.

Manipulation of the exchange rate is only seriously possible if the exchange rate is fixed. However, since the 1970s, most currencies have floated, ie been subject to market forces.

Even in a fixed exchange rate system, it is very difficult in the long term to maintain an exchange rate markedly different from that implied by market forces

The other key issue in exchange rate policy is of course the euro. Should the UK join, or not? At the moment, the UK has an opt-out from Economic and Monetary Union, and thus from the Euro. However, the UK is qualified to join EMU if it chooses. In 1997, the Chancellor of the Exchequer postponed a decision on entry, saying that the UK would consider joining only if five economic tests were met. These were as follows.

1   Are business cycles and economic structures compatible such that the UK can live with euro interest rates?

2   Is there sufficient flexibility to deal with any problems which might arise?

3   Will joining EMU create better conditions for firms making long-term decisions to invest in the UK?

4   What impact will entry have on the competitive position of the City?

5   Will joining the Euro promote higher growth, stability, and a lasting increase in jobs?

If the Government decided that these tests were met, it would recommend entry to the Euro, but the final decision would be taken by a referendum. Public opinion in the UK appears to be heavily against euro entry, and entry is opposed by the Conservative Party and by significant elements in industry. In the last resort any decision on entry is likely to be political rather than economic. Labour may be in favour in principle, but will only hold a referendum if it is sure it will win. Most voters will probably make their decision on gut feeling, rather than the detail of the economic arguments. To no one's surprise, the Government decided in 2003 that the Five Tests had not been met, and, as a result, any decision in favour of entry has been postponed until the late 2000s.

CASE STUDY 4.1

Inflation and interest rates

The impact of inflation

We have already defined inflation as a general increase in the level of prices in the economy, measured in various ways – RPI, RPIX or CPI. In the last resort this is caused by excess demand in the economy, basically when the amount of goods and services which people want to buy is greater than the productive potential of the economy – 'too much money chasing too few goods'.

The generally accepted view is that inflation is harmful, and it follows from this that low inflation is beneficial, for the following reasons.

- Increased price competitiveness for UK goods. The important factor here is relative inflation – in order for UK goods to be competitive, UK inflation must be rising at a slower rate than that of our international competitors. Of course, if UK inflation is very rapid, it is likely that the value of the pound will fall, but this itself could generate further inflation, as import prices will rise.

- Distribution of income will be less distorted. High inflation benefits borrowers, particularly those with outstanding mortgages, which fall in value in real terms as the value of their houses tend to rise. In addition, the gap in money terms between wage settlements obtained by strong unions as compared with weak ones tends to be greater in times of rapid inflation.

- Reduced uncertainty. The more rapid the rate of inflation, and particularly the more variable it is, the more unpredictable the environment becomes for business and individuals. As a result, investment will be discouraged, as firms do not want to take risks, and the result could be falling output and rising unemployment.

- High inflation means high nominal interest rates. This puts pressure on the cash flows of borrowers if their main source of income is interrupted, for example by unemployment.

ACTIVITY 4.5
Deflation

If the effects of high inflation are adverse, would it be better to have falling prices (deflation?)

The link between unemployment and inflation

In the late 1950s, Professor Phillips found that over the previous 100 years there had been an inverse relationship between the rate of change of money wages and the level of unemployment (Phillips 1958). In the short term this intuitively makes sense. If unemployment is low, workers can demand higher wages, and vice versa. As wage inflation is a very important component of general inflation, it could thus be argued that there was an inverse relationship between unemployment and inflation – if unemployment rose, inflation would fall, and vice versa. This implied that governments could in principle choose the trade-off between inflation and unemployment which best suited their overall objectives.

Unfortunately, almost as soon as Phillips identified the relationship, it ceased to apply. Throughout the 1970s, both inflation and unemployment rose steeply at the same time, giving rise to a phenomenon known as stagflation. Gradually over the 1980s, inflation was squeezed out of the system through strict control of the money supply, but only at the cost of continuing high levels of unemployment. Since 1992, unemployment has fallen considerably, while inflation has stabilised at the 2–3 per cent level.

Clearly the simple concept of the Phillips curve no longer applies, but it has been replaced by the concept of NAIRU (non-accelerating inflation rate of unemployment). This is the level of unemployment at which inflation will be stable. NAIRU appears to have been about 7–8 per cent in the 1970s, but to have fallen to around 3–4 per cent (on the ILO measure) by the early 2000s. One prime objective of governments is to continue to improve the trade-off between inflation and unemployment by lowering the level of NAIRU. This can be done through making the labour market more competitive.

However, as the Bank of England says, 'The level of the NAIRU cannot be determined with any precision for the purposes of setting monetary policy … It is easier to construct plausible estimates after the event – ie once we have observed inflation – rather than in anticipation of it' (Bank of England 2004a). NAIRU appears to be much lower in the UK and USA, with largely deregulated labour markets, than in the eurozone, where labour markets are much more heavily regulated. Of course, there is a political and social, as well as an economic trade-off here: Which is preferable, a higher risk of unemployment in the eurozone, or the higher level of benefits which accompany unemployment there?

Interest rates

An interest rate is simply the price of money. However, unfortunately the real world is more complicated. As an individual, you are almost certainly paying and receiving several different rates of interest – on your bank current account, on your building society account, your Internet savings account, your mortgage, your credit card, your hire purchase agreement. Ultimately these come back to one rate, the official rate set by the Bank of England, and at which it will lend money to the banks and other financial institutions. This is set monthly by the Bank's Monetary Policy Committee.

If this official rate changes, the banks and building societies will change the rates for their own savers and borrowers. Equally importantly, an increase in interest rates affects expectations. If interest rates start to rise after a period when they have been static or falling, the expectation is that they will continue to rise in the near future. The Bank of England used this to great effect in 2004, when it made a series of quarter-point increases in interest rates, none of which was particularly serious on its own, but which had a big effect on expectations.

Interest rates and demand

When interest rates are changed, demand can be affected in a number of ways.

- Spending and saving
  An increase in interest rates makes saving more attractive and spending less attractive. Consumer spending is likely to fall. At the same time industrial investment will fall, as the margin between what an investment costs and the profit which it will produce becomes narrower.

- Cashflow
  Higher interest rates mean higher mortgage rates – normally paid monthly, and higher rates of interest on savings – normally paid annually. The short-term effect on the cashflow of individuals is likely to be negative, reducing demand.

- Asset prices
  A change in interest rates affects the price of stocks and shares. If interest rates go up, the price of stocks and shares tends to fall, as it becomes more attractive to hold cash. There will be a similar effect on house prices. An increase in interest rates thus marginally reduces individuals' wealth, again making them more reluctant to spend.

- Exchange rates
  At the same time, the exchange rate is likely to rise marginally, as it becomes more attractive to hold pounds rather than other currencies. This makes export prices higher, which again reduces demand. At the same time, import prices become cheaper, which immediately reduces inflation (Bank of England 2004b)

An increase in interest rates thus clearly reduces demand in the economy, which will lower the rate of inflation, However, as with everything in economics, this is subject to time lags. Some effects are almost immediate, such as the impact on the exchange rate, some take a matter of weeks, such as the impact on mortgage and savings rates, while others are long-term, like the wealth effect of falling share prices. The Bank of England calculates that it takes up to two years for the full impact to work through the economy. In making its interest rate decisions, the Bank of England thus has to make estimates of the level of inflation two years hence. This produces the apparently perverse result that the Bank can sometimes cut interest rates at a time when current inflation is above target, or vice versa.

Central banks and interest rates

The Bank of England

The Bank of England has been involved in setting interest rates for many years, and this system was formalised in the mid-1990s by the Ken and Eddie Show, when interest rates were set at a monthly meeting between the Chancellor, Kenneth Clarke, and the Governor of the Bank, Eddie George. However, in the last resort, the decision was the Chancellor's. This was changed in the first act of the incoming Labour Government in May 1997. To great surprise, Gordon Brown announced the granting of operational independence to the Bank. In future, interest rate decisions would be taken monthly by the Monetary Policy Committee, chaired by the Governor, which consists of both Bank and government nominees (a total of nine members).

Interest rate decisions were to be taken in line with the Government's inflation target, initially set as 2.5 per cent on RPIX, subject to a margin of plus or minus 1 per cent. The target was thus a symmetrical one, unlike the previous Conservative target, which was 2.5 per cent or less.

Under the Bank of England Act 1998, the Bank's remit was to:

- maintain price stability and
- subject to that, to support the economic policy of the Government, including its objectives for growth and employment.

In its remit for the Monetary Policy Committee, this was interpreted as 'The Government's central economic policy objective is to achieve high and stable levels of growth and employment. Price stability is a precondition for these high and stable levels of growth and employment, which will in turn help to create the conditions for price stability on a sustainable basis' (Bank of England 2003)

In December 2003, the target inflation rate was changed to 2 per cent on CPI, again plus or minus 1 per cent. This was a slightly looser target, as 2 per cent on CPI roughly equates to 3 per cent on RPIX.

If inflation moved away from target by more than one percentage point in either direction, the Governor was required to send an open letter to the Chancellor, setting out:

- the reasons why inflation has missed the target
- what the Bank is doing about it
- the time span for remedial action
- how the remedial action meets the Government's monetary policy objectives.

It is a measure of the success of the policy, that such a letter has never been required.

The European Central Bank

The ECB was set up in 1998, to manage Economic and Monetary Union, including setting interest rates for the eurozone. Interest rates are fixed on a monthly basis by the Governing Council, which consists of the Executive Board of the ECB, six members appointed by the eurozone countries, headed by the President of the ECB, the Dutchman Wim Duisenberg, plus the governors of the 12 central banks of the euro area.

The ECB is totally independent, and sets its own inflation target. The prime objective of the ECB is to maintain price stability, defined as 2 per cent or less on CPI. However, 'without prejudice to the objective of price stability', the eurosystem will also 'support the general economic policies in the Community', including 'a high level of employment' and 'sustainable and non-inflationary growth' (ECB 2004).

The Federal Reserve

The central bank of the USA is the Federal Reserve Board, headed by the octogenarian Alan Greenspan. It has no specific inflation target, but its remit is laid down by the Federal Reserve Act as to 'promote effectively the goals of maximum employment, stable prices and moderate long-term interest rates' (Federal Reserve 2004). Interest rates are set monthly by the Federal Open Market Committee.

ACTIVITY 4.6

Central Banks and 9/11

In 2001, the terrorist attacks of September 11th 2001 hit a world economy which was already sliding into recession. The three major central banks (the Bank of England, the ECB and the Federal Reserve) had already started cutting interest rates before the attacks, as follows.

	Previous peak	Rate at August 2001
Bank of England	6.25%	5.00%
ECB	5.75%	5.25%
Federal Reserve	6.50%	3.50%

After the attacks, all three central banks embarked on a medium-term programme of successive interest rate cuts, which troughed at 3.50 per cent (Bank of England), 3.00 per cent (ECB), and 1.00 per cent (Federal Reserve). In the case of the Bank of England and the Federal Reserve, most of the cuts were made in 2001, while the ECB made most of its cuts in 2002 and 2003.

By 2004, the UK and the US economies had made a robust recovery, while the eurozone still had low growth and high unemployment.

How far do you think that the relatively more effective recovery of the UK and USA from 9/11 was due to:

- the actions of the three central banks
- factors inherent in the terms of reference of the three banks?

CASE STUDY 4.2

Competitiveness

In the 1970s, the UK was widely seen as a failed economy. It was subject to wide fluctuations in economic performance, and suffered from high inflation and unemployment. Taxation was high, the economy was heavily regulated, and trade unions were widely seen as too powerful. Some of these shortcomings were tackled by the Thatcher Governments between 1979 and 1991, which lowered taxation, cut back on regulation and attacked the power of the trade unions. The result was an increase in the efficiency of the economy, although this was largely a function of the contraction of manufacturing. The manufacturers which survived were inevitably more efficient than those which had failed.

However, the impetus behind the reforms of the Thatcher Governments were as much political as economic. Policy changed with the advent of the Major Government in 1991. This was much less ideological. Policies were to be followed because they were effective, rather than because they were politically correct.

This approach was continued by New Labour in 1997, with an almost seamless transition from Ken Clarke to Gordon Brown as Chancellor of the Exchequer. Competitiveness became the watchword, and pragmatism the policy. The aim was to reform the British economy so that it could compete with the best in the world.

Productivity

Competitiveness has a large number of facets, from a tightening of anti-trust legislation to the promotion of a higher skills base in the UK, and stabilisation of macroeconomic policy. What ties them all together is the concept of productivity. This is a measure of how much the economy is producing per worker employed. This is dependent both on the efficiency of the worker and on the hours worked, so a better measure is probably output per worker hour.

In 2002, productivity measured by output per worker was 39 per cent below the USA, 15 per cent below France and 7 per cent below Germany. However, France and Germany work fewer hours than the UK, and the USA works more, so, on the better measure, output per worker hour, the UK is 26 per cent behind the USA, 24 per cent behind France and 11 per cent behind Germany. This is known as the productivity gap (Philpott 2002).

Since the 1950s, the underlying rate of growth of productivity in the UK has been around 2 per cent. Government policy is to try to increase this underlying rate, with a wide range of detailed polices put forward in two White Papers, *Building the Knowledge Driven Economy* in 1998 (www.dti.gov.uk/competitive), and *Opportunity for All in a World of Change* in 2001 (www.dti.gov.uk/opportunity for all). Success in doing so would increase the UK's long-term rate of economic growth, and would also lower NAIRU, allowing the UK economy to control inflation at a lower level of unemployment (Philpott 2002). A similar programme was launched by the EU at the Lisbon Summit in 2000 (EU 2004), which set the objective of becoming the most competitive, dynamic, knowledge-based economy in the world by 2010. Its detailed proposals included creating an environment which was conducive to business start-ups, a fully operational internal market, education and training suitable for a knowledge society, and a raising of the EU employment rate from 61 per cent in 2000 to 70 per cent in 2010, thereby creating 20 million new jobs. Of these, five million had been created by 2003 (Philpott 2003).

In 2004, a group appointed by the EU, under the chairmanship of the former Dutch Prime Minister, Wim Kok, reported on progress (Hutton 2004). They proposed:

■ EU members should spend 3 per cent of GDP on research and development (the UK at present spends 1.9 per cent)

■ there should be a European Research Council supporting centres of scientific excellence

■ degrees and qualifications should be mutually recognised, in order that researchers can develop career paths within the EU rather than joining the brain-drain to the USA

■ there should be an EU-wide patent law.

An increase in productivity depends on changes in a number of factors. These include the following.

■ *Capital investment.* The more modern the equipment with which people work, the more efficient they will be. Historically, investment in the UK has been low, and increases in productivity have come more through the shut-down of the most inefficient plant rather than the building of new plants. A telling comparison with the USA is that, while the UK produces the same volume of manufacturing output with half the capacity of the 1970s, the USA produces twice the output with the same capacity.

■ *Economic stability.* One key factor which deters investment is economic instability. Investors need to be convinced that there will be a consistent demand for what they produce, and that inflation will be stable. Here the UK has made great advances over the last decade. De Grauwe has argued that a comprehensive and reliable welfare state is also necessary, although this does not seem to be required in the USA (De Grauwe 2001).

■ *Research and development.* The UK is excellent at scientific research but much less good at the applied R&D needed to convert this into practical products and processes. It is significant that the UK's only world-class industry, pharmaceuticals, is the heaviest investor in R&D.

■ *IT and the Internet.* During the dot.com boom of the late 1990s, the Internet was seen as the Holy Grail of productivity, and some US economists put forward the concept of a New Economic Paradigm, where the business cycle was abolished, and growth would continue indefinitely. This rosy view was shaken by the dot.com crash in early 2000, and shattered by 9/11. Of the dot.com companies, virtually only Amazon, e-Bay and a few business to business (B2B) companies are profitable.

■ *Restrictive practices.* Restrictive practices by the trade unions were tackled by the Thatcher Governments, so the main concern is restrictive practices by industry. The UK has anti-trust laws (covered in more detail in Chapter 5), but they are much less tough than in the USA. One change here has been to make participation in price-fixing activities a criminal offence, subject to imprisonment – a measure in force in the USA since 1890 (Lennan 2001).

- *Management.* The quality of management in the UK is widely perceived as being poor, despite the spread of management qualifications such as the MBA. As with the whole of UK industry, there are some very good examples of management practice, but a very long tail of poor performers. The average standard needs to be raised to be nearer the best. Two main failings are a short-termist approach, which discourages long-term investment and development, and a failure to introduce modern management practices such as Just in Time and continuous improvement. Many sectors of industry still experience high levels of stress and alienation, and many managers refuse to consider a partnership approach with their workers.

- *Flexibility.* Industry must become more flexible in order to optimise its use of resources. This involves being

  Numerically flexible. Working time must adjust to meet customer demand – 'the 24/7 society'. This involves the use of techniques such as annual hours.

  Functionally flexible. Skills levels must be improved, and these skills fully utilised.

  Occupationally flexible. Workers must become multi-skilled.

  Wage flexible. Reward must be used as an incentive to higher productivity.

  Mindset flexible. Diversity must be encouraged in order to tap all available talent, and organisations must be family-friendly in order to encourage diversity (Briner 2001; Merrick 2001; Philpott 2002).

A key element is the need to develop workforce skills. A whole series of initiatives have been introduced, ranging from NVQs to TECs, ILAs to LSCs. The result has been an alphabet soup, without a great deal of impact on the skills base. As usual, the UK pattern is one of excellence at the top, with very effective degree-level provision, a gap in the middle, where technician-level skills are poorly developed, and a long tail of functional illiteracy and innumeracy.

However, it is becoming clear that workforce development is a dual responsibility, with the Government responsible for developing the basic skills of numeracy, literacy and IT (as stressed in the Tomlinson Report on the reform of age 14–19 education in October 2004), and industry being responsible for the development of workplace-specific skills.

The best that can be said at present about the effectiveness of competitiveness policy is that the UK is holding its own and not falling further behind its main competitors. Short-term gains are unlikely, and these policies should be seen as essentially long term.

In 2003, Michael Porter and Christian Ketels carried out a study for the DTI on the UK's competitiveness (Porter and Ketels 2003). Their conclusions were rather more optimistic. They said that successive governments have 'fundamentally changed the macroeconomic, and, more importantly, the microeconomic context for competition'. The challenge for the future was to manage the transition from an economy based on low cost to one based on unique value and innovation.

It is also important to remember that productivity per head is not the only driver of economic growth. As William Keegan pointed out in October 2004 (Keegan 2004b), superior economic growth in the USA is largely caused by factors such as:

■ a growing labour force, driven by high rates of immigration; this tends to lower the average age of the workforce, and also forces a high rate of investment to keep pace with the demand created by a growing population.

■ Long hours and short holidays.

■ Generally expansionary macroeconomic policies.

ACTIVITY 4.7

Investors in People

Investors in People (IIP) was introduced in October 1991. It is one of the key competitiveness-promoting initiatives which has been truly non-political, enthusiastically backed by both the Major and the Blair Governments. By 2001, 25,000 organisations had qualified for the standard, employing 24 per cent of the UK workforce.

Research carried out for IIP suggests that 73 per cent of organisations awarded the standard more than 12 months ago feel that it has increased their productivity. However, there is a counter-view, put forward by Scott Taylor of the Open University, that IIP frequently has little impact on performance (Brown 2001), and this is supported by research from the Institute of Directors, where only 15 per cent of 275 company directors felt that IIP had increased profitability, and a quarter thought it had increased productivity (Nelson 2001).

What arguments could be put forward to support Taylor's contention?

CASE STUDY 4.3

Economic development in India and China

Between 1985 and 1995, GNP growth in the developing world averaged 6 per cent a year, more than twice that of the developed world (World Bank 2000). This suggests that the developing world will soon catch up with the developed world. Unfortunately, this hopeful forecast ignores two key factors. One is the rapid rate of population growth in the developing world, When this is stripped out, and growth converted to GNP per head, the growth rate per head in the developing world falls to 3.8 per cent, while that of the developed world falls to 2.1 per cent.

Secondly, the developing country figures are distorted by the outstanding success of the two most populous countries, India and China, In the period 1985–95, India's GNP per head rose by 3.2 per cent a year, and China's by an impressive (although possibly unreliable) 8.3 per cent a year. Stripping out India and China from the figures, the rest of the developing world actually had a GNP per head which fell by nearly 1 per cent a year. Why have India and China done so well?

India and China have some distinct similarities in their economies. Both have huge populations, and a dominant agricultural sector, employing more than half the population. Both were among the world's most prosperous countries before they had contact with the West, and both subsequently declined. Both went through the same sequence of economic development, of emphasis on heavy industry and a planned economy, followed by agricultural reform, followed by export-led growth, with greater emphasis on the market (Goyal and Jha 2004).

The main difference comes in their political systems. China is a one-party state with power centralised in the Communist Party; India is a multi-party democracy. China is relatively homogeneous racially, with few religious or racial minorities, while India is a heterogeneous state both racially and religiously, with a very large Muslim minority population, and significant numbers of Sikhs, Buddhists and Christians.

As a democracy, India is relatively slow to take decisions, and to make major shifts in policy. On the other hand, decisions in India have democratic legitimacy. China can take quick decisions, and tends to be better at taking long-term decisions, as its government is not answerable to an electorate, while decisions in India are shorter term, and geared to the electoral cycle. As a result, China was better placed to make long-term investments in its education and health programmes. Despite its centralised political system, China has been very effective at decentralising economic decision-making. It has given a great deal of economic autonomy to the growth areas of Shanghai, Quangdong and Hong Kong.

China has also been more effective at opening its economy to the West and at encouraging foreign direct investment through a stable exchange rate and low real interest rates. India has gained through the widespread use of English in its higher education system, which has led to the outsourcing of large numbers of service jobs from the West. China has tended to gain from the outsourcing of manufacturing rather than service jobs. This has led to a big increase in Chinese exports, particularly to the USA and Japan.

Both countries clearly have economic systems which are highly effective at generating economic growth. As an authoritarian stare, China has been able to be more single-minded in its pursuit of growth, and as a result has achieved a higher rate of growth. However, there are costs in the Chinese system. As the development economist Amartya Sen has pointed out, no democratic country has experienced a devastating famine, whereas authoritarian states like China have (Steele 2001).

It appears that a combination of authoritarian political control and a decentralised market-run economic system seems to be highly effective at producing economic growth, but with accompanying costs like loss of freedom, economic inequality and social disruption.

However, it is possible to over-hype the success of China (Hilton 2004). It took until 1993 before China's exports were back at the level they reached in 1928, prior to the Japanese invasion, and despite its vast population, China's GDP in 2000 was only a quarter that of Japan. The dash for growth has also caused enormous environmental degradation. China has 16 of the world's 20 most polluted cites. It may be that in the long run the Indian tortoise will win the race with the Chinese hare.

SUMMARY AND CONCLUSIONS

This chapter has analysed the legislative process and influences on policy formation in the UK and the EU. The key components of the economy were analysed, as were the objectives of government policy and the tools which the Government can use to achieve them. Detailed case studies of inflation and interest rates, of competitiveness and productivity, and of Third World development were also analysed.

KEY LEARNING POINTS

- Legislation in the UK is normally initiated by the Government, whereas in the EU it is initiated by the Commission. The role of Parliament is much greater in the UK than in the EU.

- Political parties and their members have some influence on policy formation, but this influence is tending to decrease.

- Pressure groups are of two main types, interest or sectional groups and attitude or cause groups. They have considerable influence both on the evolution of government policy and on its implementation.

- There are crucial differences between gross domestic product and standard of living or quality of life.

- All governments, of whatever political colour, are striving to achieve economic growth, full employment, stable prices, and equilibrium on the balance of payments.

- Policy instruments available to governments include fiscal policy, monetary policy, competitiveness policy and exchange rate policy.

- Interest rates in the UK are set by the Bank of England, subject to an inflation target set by the Government.

- The inflation target in the UK is symmetrical, and therefore less restrictive than that of the European Central Bank.

- A drive to increase productivity and competitiveness is a key aim of both UK and EU economic policy, but does not lead to quick results.

- Despite their very different political systems, both India and China have been very effective at stimulating economic growth.

FURTHER READING

For the underlying economic theory, see Lipsey and Chrystal (recommended in Chapter 2). For the evolution and application of policy, the Bank of England (www.bankofengland.co.uk) and the Department of Trade and Industry (www.dti.gov.uk) websites are useful. John Philpott, the CIPD's chief economist, produces an occasional series for the CIPD entitled *Perspectives*, which is invaluable.

Regulation

CHAPTER 5

OBJECTIVES

By the end of this chapter, readers should be able to understand, explain and critically evaluate:

- the essential features of the UK legal system, including the sources and types of law and the courts system, including tribunals

- the significance of existing and new regulation for particular sectors and organisations and discuss the type and nature of responses to the regulation

- the nature of regulation in respect of contract, consumer and competition law and the implications for stakeholders to whom the law applies

- the effect regulation has on health and safety and employment law, advising on its current strengths and weaknesses.

INTRODUCTION

In March 1984, Arthur Scargill led the miners' union into a national strike to try to improve working conditions in the mines and to prevent a massive programme of pit closures. He dismissed the legislation passed two years earlier requiring a ballot before a strike action could be taken, taking the view that 'bad laws should be ignored', just as the Trades Union Movement had successfully done in 1972 against earlier Tory trade union legislation. In a defining moment of the Thatcher administration, the Government brought the full force of the establishment – police, army, public opinion – to restore the 'rule of law', supporting the concept that laws passed in a proper democratic process must be obeyed by individuals and organisations. The view was widely promulgated that 'societies where the rule of law can be flouted with impunity cannot survive' and it was the almost unanimous support of this view across the UK that ultimately sealed the miners' fate.

The legal system, then, is at the heart of a democratic society. It sets out the rules within which people and organisations live and do business with each other; it reflects the current views on morality held by the majority of its citizens; it defines the punishments for breaking these rules; it establishes the nature of the contracts between the individual, the organisation and the state whereby the state is paid (through taxation) to protect the interests of all parties in a fair and impartial way. It allows everybody to plan their lives with the fair certainty of foreseeing what actions and behaviour are allowed and what is forbidden.

This chapter provides a general introduction to the structure of UK law, details some of the specific legislation that sets out a level playing field for business and the consumer, indicates the main protection for employees in the workplace, examines how law regulates particular sectors and labour markets and suggests ways that employers can respond to new legislation. Law is a complex subject and organisations and individuals regularly call on experts to advise them, so the outline provided in this chapter is primarily to raise awareness of the legal contours.

LEGAL CONTOURS

Legal concepts

There is a clear *division of authority* between the judiciary and the executive, a factor that distinguishes true democracy from a dictatorship. Judges are independent and, once appointed, cannot be dismissed, except in extreme cases such as where they are convicted of corruption or another serious offence. If they take decisions that the Government does not like (and this is increasingly happening with the increased use of judicial review), the Government simply has to accept their decisions.

Precedent requires courts to follow decisions laid down in earlier cases where the facts are broadly similar. To give an example, in decisions made on unfair dismissal claims soon after the Act was passed in 1972, higher courts confirmed the circumstances under which an employee could claim constructive dismissal, including the need for the individual to immediately resign and leave the employment once the incident had occurred. If a claim reaches a tribunal today and the claimant delayed by a few weeks in leaving the employment after the incident occurred, then the tribunal would be required to follow the precedent and throw out the claim.

When lawyers are advising on a case, then, they need to be well read not just in the law itself, but in the way it has been interpreted by the courts as shown in the precedents involved. They need to read the *obiter dictum*, which are the judge's recorded comments justifying their decisions. Faced by precedents which indicate that a case would be unsuccessful, a lawyer would either advise their client to withdrawal or the lawyer would try their best to argue that the facts of the case were significantly different so that the precedent did not apply.

That is not to say that precedents cannot be changed. One of the duties of the Court of Appeal is to examine precedents argued before them and judge whether such precedents are out of date for changing social times or preserve a system which is clearly unfair. In such cases, it may decide they need to be altered at the margins or completely reversed. A well-known example of reversal was the Walker v Northumberland County Council case (see Example 5.1).

In serious criminal cases (and surprisingly, civil cases for libel or slander), the final decision is made by a jury – one is *judged by one's peers*. In jury trials, even the judge's advice can be overturned under the belief that it is a matter of whose word can be trusted and a jury of 12 people is the best way to test this.

EXAMPLE 5.1

Changing a precedent

John Walker was a social work manager who returned to work having had a mental breakdown brought on through an excessive work load. He requested a reduction in his duties and additional resources to allow him to cope with his responsibilities and serve the community. His employer did very little to help him and he subsequently suffered a further extended breakdown which ended his career. Prior to this case, the precedent had been that the employer had a clear duty of care in respect of preventing foreseeable physical illness but not mental illness brought on by stress. The Court of Appeal confirmed that this duty of care should be extended to foreseeable mental illness because there was no logical reason why it should be excluded from the scope of the Health and safety at Work Act. Walker was awarded £175,000 in damages and this decision established a change in precedent. Consequently, employers have had to give much more careful consideration to issue of foreseeable stress and subsequent mental illness among their staff.

Source: Walker v Northumberland County Council 1995 IRLR 35/95

Types of law

The law is divided into two main divisions, as follows.

Civil law

The ground rules dealing with relationships between individuals and between an individual and an organisation are laid down under civil law. Where one side believes that the law has been broken, they will take the case up in the civil courts and aim to have the wrong righted and/or obtain compensation. The main areas under which civil cases are brought are *breach of contract* (where it is claimed that one party has broken the terms of a legally enforceable contract) and *torts,* which are civil wrongs independent of contract, such as negligence, nuisance or defamation (see example).

EXAMPLE 5.2

A tort

Your next-door-neighbour has allowed a tree to grow so large that parts are overhanging your small garden and takes away most of your light. You have asked him civilly to take some action but nothing happens. You therefore bring a case claiming *nuisance*. Before the case comes to court, a gale brings down a large branch which smashes your fence and greenhouse. You therefore add a further claim for *negligence* to the case.

The remedies you can obtain are:

- compensation (damages) – but only to the extent of your proven loses, plus costs you have expended
- Specific Performance – where the court instructs the plaintiff to carry out an action (see example)

■ injunction – where the court instructs the defendant to NOT carry out an action, such as demolishing a listed building.

EXAMPLE 5.3

Specific performance

You have successfully bid for a painting at an auction but you learn subsequently that the owner decided to withdraw the painting for sale. You believe you have a valid contract and ask the court to instruct the owner to complete the contract and deliver the painting to you. You have set your heart on obtaining that unique painting and no alternative or compensation would satisfy you.

Criminal law

Here offences (crimes) are defined which society believe need punishing. The court case is a result of a police investigation and a case brought by the Crown Prosecution Service. Very occasionally, a private prosecution takes place, such as by the parents of the murdered teenager Stephen Lawrence in the 1990s. In general, however, these have a very low success rate and can be stopped by the Attorney General if they are not regarded as being in the public interest.

Cases are divided into *indictable offences*, generally serious crimes – murder, rape, serious fraud – where conviction can result in imprisonment, and *summary offences* –parking, petty theft – which are less serious and where conviction normally brings a fine.

ACTIVITY 5.1

In 1994, a small outdoor pursuits company in Dorset was convicted of manslaughter after the death of four teenagers on a canoe trip. Its owner, who was identified as being ultimately responsible for decisions relating to the trip which resulted in the deaths, was subsequently sent to prison. Under what other circumstances can an organisation commit a criminal offence?

From where does the law originate?

We are so used, these days, to a flood of new legislation (*statute law*), emerging from parliament each year that it is a common fallacy to believe that this process, explained in Chapter 3, is the only source of law. However, there are two other main sources, as follows.

Common law

Up until the nineteenth century, most law was 'common', which meant that it had come into effect through judges recognising custom and practice (and common sense) and this was spread around the country by judges on their circuits. These decisions made up the precedents. In most areas today, common law decisions have been incorporated into statute, but there are a number of fundamental common law concepts that remain, such as those relating to the law of contract and employee rights (see later in the chapter). There also remain some more isolated specific rights under common law, such as those grazing rights held by New Forest Commoners.

Codes of practice

Although not technically law, formal codes have a strong influence on decisions taken by the courts. For example, an organisation facing a tribunal claim for unfair dismissal who has not followed closely the ACAS Code on Disciplinary and Grievance Procedures is less likely to make a successful defence. Similarly, an employer facing an equal pay claim should ensure that the Commission for Racial Equality's Code on Equal Pay has been incorporated into their procedures.

It should also be noted that much of the statute law originates from the *European Union* whose legislative processes are set out in Chapter 3.

Courts system

In Figure 5.1, the courts system for England and Wales is set out. (Scotland has had its own somewhat different system for more than 500 years.) Courts are distinguished through their regulation of civil or criminal law and whether they are courts of first instance or whether they hear appeals or both.

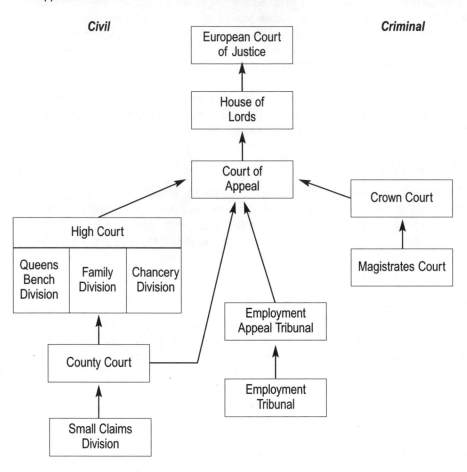

Note: the Tribunal route indicates the process for employment law only

Figure 5.1 *Court System in England and Wales*

Civil cases

Claims start in the *County Court* or, if the amount at issue is less than £3,000, the Small Claims Division. Speed, accessibility and informality are the keynotes here with representation frowned upon, with costs normally limited to the value of the summons. The judge acts alone as the arbitrator. It provides an opportunity for businesses and individuals to claim small debts and for torts to be examined and resolved. One day an overhanging tree dispute may be being resolved, the next, a claim from an ex-employee for unpaid overtime. There are around 300 crown courts situated in cities and market towns with judges still going on 'circuits' to try to ensure a degree of consistency, although small claims courts are generally overseen by a registrar.

In the County Courts, actions for less than £25,000 are heard together with some others up to £50,000 by agreement with the parties, depending on their complexity. Additional subject areas at the County Courts, apart from contract and tort cases include probate disputes, bankruptcy, undefended divorce, consumer credit issues and some land questions. Around 2.5 million summonses a year are taken out at County Courts but only around 5 to 10 per cent arrive in court and an even smaller percentage are actually defended.

Summonses valued at over £50,000 go directly to the High Court. This has three divisions which deal with cases of first instance and appeals from lesser courts. The *Queens Bench Division* is the busiest with jurisdiction over high value contract and tort cases, and a special commercial court dealing with banking, insurance and other financial services cases. It also has an Admiralty Court to hear cases involving ships and aircraft while it also hears some appeals from the County Court and a comparatively small number of criminal appeals from Crown Courts. The *Family Division* handles matrimonial cases, including wardship, adoption and custody claims. Finally, the *Chancery Division*, the oldest court of all, has jurisdiction over high value tax cases, trusts, partnership disputes, patent and copyright actions and land disputes.

Criminal cases

The *Magistrates Court* manages most of the criminal cases, determining around 98 per cent of all crime. Around half of its two million or so caseload consists of motoring offences. It handles all forms of petty crime with the maximum penalty it can apply six months' prison sentence, although few prison sentences are awarded. It has special arrangements to handle juvenile cases and it acts as a preliminary hearing in serious crime cases, deciding on 'committing' to a Crown Court and agreeing bail/custody arrangements. There are 550 Magistrates Courts, with 27,000 magistrates on the bench. They are a mixture of stipendiary (paid) officials and unpaid appointees. Stipendiary magistrates can sit alone. It is possible for those accused at a Magistrates Court to decide to be heard in front of a jury at a Crown Court, usually in the hope that juries convict less often than hardened magistrates. This right may be removed under pending legislation. Appeals (there are few) go generally to the Crown Court.

There are close to 100 *Crown Courts*, the most famous being the Central Criminal Court (Old Bailey). Cases are heard by juries, although the judge has a strong influence through control of the proceedings, interventions to clarify issues and the summing up.

Higher courts

The *Court of Appeal* hears both criminal and civil court appeals with three to five judges in attendance and a majority decision prevailing with each judge's reasons published. Their judgments are extremely influential, much used to clarify the law and to set the ultimate precedent. Cases are sometimes referred to this court when new evidence has come to light that casts doubt on the validity of criminal convictions, cases that may have been held as long as 20 years or more ago. The appeal to the *House of Lords* can only be on a legal issue and the decision is final, except where the case comes under European law, where much of employment law resides. If so, the case is heard by *the European Court of Justice,* which gives a ruling and then refers the case back to the UK court for implementation.

Tribunals

The most well-known tribunals are those in employment areas, such as Unfair Dismissal and Sex, Race and Disability Discrimination. However, there are numerous tribunals set up by statute in other areas. There are Rent Tribunals, set up to help protect tenants from unscrupulous landlords, Social Security Appeal tribunals, to provide an opportunity for citizens to questions decisions made about their right to benefits, such as unemployment and sickness, and various tribunals related to appeals over taxation. They all have the same intention, which is to provide a formal yet accessible process for the aggrieved citizen to have their case heard fairly, impartially and thoroughly by persons not involved in the original decision. The accessibility comes about through, first, some discouragement of legal representation, as with the Small Claims Court, by generally not awarding costs and secondly, by ensuring that help in the initial stages is provided by the tribunals themselves and by volunteer bodies such as the Citizens' Advice Bureau.

In the employment area, the tribunals are bound by rules of evidence and precedent but the three member tribunals are allowed to operate a much more informal and inquisitive approach than the higher courts. Appeals to the Employment Appeal Tribunal and subsequent appeals to higher courts can only be on the basis of law.

Ombudsmen

A final grouping of quasi-legal intent are the sets of ombudsmen, set up by legislation to investigate complaints of maladministration, mostly in the public arena. There are a number of commissioners (Ombudsmen) in areas such as local government, the National Health Service and parliament whose reports have no precise legal standing but put pressure on the bodies concerned to rectify mistakes and improve their services. More recently, a commission has been set up for the pensions industry.

LAW OF CONTRACT

Introduction

Contracts are at the heart of all business and employment activity and the Common Law governing their operation goes back further in time than most other law. For centuries, the judges interpreted the law in a way that reflected the 'laissez-faire' approach to all business, with the state interfering very little and people in business and employment were left alone to run their affairs. This was partly to preserve the inequality of the 'master and servant' relationship and partly because most business contracts were on a relatively equal basis. To buy a pair of shoes, a customer went to the local cobbler and negotiated a price on a fairly equal basis. However, this was to change by the mid-nineteenth century as the industrial revolution and the development of capitalism had created large enterprises in commerce and industry, which produced many unequal bargaining situations. In the next section, we shall see how the state has intervened over the last 100 years by introducing legislation to provide a more balanced situation.

The essence of a contract is to provide a legally binding format for a set of mutual promises. In general, the contract involves one party providing goods or a service and the other paying for them, and a typical organisation will have scores of contracts with suppliers, customers, service providers, intermediaries, staff and contractors. These contracts do not have to be in writing to be legally binding (apart from those related to land), although for clarity and certainty, most of them are confirmed in this way. However, any informal changes that both parties agree to, even if not confirmed in writing, will supersede those written into the contract, so long as one side can produce compelling evidence that such an informal arrangement took place.

Interestingly, there are some very important contracts where the parties have agreed that they are not legally binding. These are agreements between employers and trade unions where, by tradition, both sides reserve the right to go back on the deals they make should they choose to do so. This is an interesting reflection on the trust between the parties under British employment relations.

There are six main elements in any contract, as shown below.

Offer and unconditional acceptance – for each contract, the offer must state all the terms, be communicated effectively and must be clear and unambiguous. It is different from what is known as an *invitation to treat*. When shops first started putting prices in their shop windows, the courts were asked to intervene to distinguish between what appeared to be a legal 'offer' and what was merely an invitation to people to come into the shop and start negotiating. They decided that the prices marked on goods in the shop window or in advertisements are not 'offers' (or even 'special offers') and a potential customer cannot go into the shop and demand the legal right to buy the goods at the prices shown. It needs the shopkeeper's acceptance to make this a contract.

Acceptance must be unconditional and within the stipulated (or reasonable) time. An offer can be withdrawn at any time prior to acceptance. If the acceptance stipulates conditions, then this becomes a counter-offer. If both parties act as if they are working under an agreement, then a contract is deemed to have been agreed.

An area that still provides some difficulties with the courts is that of standard terms and conditions. One business will ask for tenders for providing goods (an invitation to treat). Another company will respond, making an offer on documentation which has its standard terms and conditions of trading printed on the back. The first company then accepts the offer on documentation with its own standard terms and conditions on the back. If the terms differ, it could be held to be a counter-offer, of course. If there is a dispute over some small detail which differs between the companies, the courts have tended to decide that the last set of documentation applies but will be influenced by the actions of the parties and any evidence that can be offered to support the view that a particular term applied. It still does lead to problems, however, which are regularly resolved by an arbitration service.

There must be *genuine agreement.* Each party must have the same understanding of what makes up the contract and there must be no misrepresentation. For example, if the car seller knowingly indicates a mileage that is not genuine, then the contract will be void and the buyer can claim damages. What often needs to be clarified under this heading is what were 'representations' (I think this is a most reliable motor) and what were actual terms of the contract (the tyres are 3 months old). A buyer acting on representations has no redress. Contracts must not be entered into under duress or undue influence, including drink or drugs. If this is the case, the contracts can be voided.

The parties must have the *capacity to contract.* So minors are excluded, except for necessities, (such as sweets and bus journeys!) but not for larger items. The same applies to those of an unsound mind. An interesting area is that it can be assumed that employees of an organisation who appear to have the authority to contract do in fact have this authority. This is to avoid the situation where an organisation can go back on a contract they subsequently decide is not in their favour.

There must be an *intention to create legal relations.* In general, legal relations between close relatives are rarely upheld by the courts, unless there is clear evidence to the contrary. The opposite applies to all business relationships where the presumption is that there is an intention present.

The contract must be for *legal purposes.* A contract is void if, for example, payment is made as 'cash in hand' where national insurance should be paid or any contracts set up which are purely to evade taxation.

There must be *consideration.* This is normally money, although it can be any right or benefit which can be held to be of monetary value either currently or in the future and contracts of barter are legal (ie international contracts of grain in exchange for oil). Without consideration, as in an agreement to paint the house of a friend for nothing, there can be no enforceable contract. In the voluntary world, this still provides some problems of course. The payment must refer to the future and not to some past payments or obligations. Finally, the payment does not have to be adequate, fair or reasonable – that is up to the parties concerned.

A *contract of employment* arises directly out of contract law. A job must be offered and unconditionally accepted. There must be genuine agreement with no misunderstanding of the essential terms and conditions, such as the need to work night shift or the type of company car; the contract must be legal, with no illegal activities such as ' cash in hand'; there must be consideration, a wage or salary, as voluntary work is not enforceable and only those aged over 13 can have an employment contract with strict regulations relating to the employment of those under 18. Interestingly, the courts recognise the employment of wives and husbands so long as there is clear evidence of a contract existing.

There are more details on employment law on p. 92.

REGULATING BUSINESS AND PROTECTING THE CONSUMER

On a hot summer's day in 1930, a bottle of ginger beer was bought at the end of a walk by a young man for his lady friend. She gratefully drank up but, in finishing the opaque bottle, the remains of a decomposed snail appeared and, not surprisingly, she became very ill. On recovering, she wanted recompense for her unhappy experience but she could not sue the shopkeeper because she had no contract with him, nor could she sue her boyfriend because there was no consideration – the bottle was a gift – nor did she have a contract with the manufacturer. However, a lengthy legal case was commenced which, 2 years later, appeared at the House of Lords (Donaghue v Stevenson), where the landmark decision was reached that manufacturers can be guilty of the tort of negligence.

Prior to the case, 'caveat emptor' (let the buyer beware) applied in all consumer purchases but Donaghue v Stevenson established that manufacturers have a duty of care to their customers not to be negligent and to avoid any acts or omissions which can be reasonably foreseen to kill, injure the consumer or member of the public or to damage property. Subsequent cases have clarified guidelines: for example, drugs manufacturers have a greater duty of care than newspaper publishers because the consequences of faulty goods are far more serious.

The above-mentioned case was an important one and the outcome was a distinct improvement in the degree of protection for consumers. By the late 1960s, however, governments started to take a more supportive view for the consumer. There were a number of reasons for this, as follows.

- The growth of huge multinational corporations made it much more difficult for the view to be held that a contract was made between equal partners.
- Mergers and acquisitions were growing to the stage that some companies had control of substantial sectors of the market-place and could dictate terms.
- There was a growth in the practice of large organisations inserting 'small print' into contracts where special conditions were inserted and liabilities excluded to the detriment even of the observant consumer.
- Pressure had developed from consumer organisations, such as *Which* magazine, which helped develop consumer awareness of shady practices, and politicians appreciated they needed to take notice of this pressure.
- Britain decided to join the European Union in the early 1970s and some legislation was required to bring the UK in line with European law.
- Trading practices were changing in line with technological and monetary developments and there were gaps in the law in these areas.

The legislation can be divided into the *macro* area, to control and enhance competition generally and in the *micro* area, where specific unfair business practices are made illegal.

Controlling and enhancing competition

Fair Trading Act 1973
It was considered essential that a watchdog with wide powers of investigation should exist to champion the consumer interest and provide independent advice for the Government. The Office of Fair Trading (OFT) took this role and its powers have been increased with subsequent legislation, including the **Competition Act 1998** and the **Enterprise Act 2002**. The Director-General of Free Trading has responsibility to investigate commercial activities which may appear to be against the interests of consumers and advise the Government if it is

believed that action is necessary. The scope of activities investigated is wide, covering all sectors, businesses large and small and dealing with contract terms, selling methods, packaging and promotion. Although its powers have limits, the fact that an investigation can take place and that orders can be sought from the Government to stop certain activities are, in practice, strong deterrents and have often changed the way business is carried out. In its early days, it investigated pyramid selling and ensured its abolition.

Restrictive Trade Practices Act 1976/ Competition Act 1998

This legislation was passed to prevent the use of monopoly power either by individual companies or groups of companies colluding. A restrictive practice is defined as collusion on prices, terms of supply, manufacturing processes and any activity that is likely to have the effect of restricting, distorting or preventing competition. The OFT has the right to enter premises and demand documents and to enforce restrictions on movement or destruction of evidence. If an organisation refuses to co-operate, then it can be penalised to the extent of 10 per cent of turnover.

When a practice is found to exist, it can only be successfully justified by the argument that it

- protects the public from injury
- is a counterweight to another monopoly (such as in negotiations with the Royal Mail)
- provides extensive benefits to exports.

Examples of investigations in recent years include extended warranties (see Case 5.1), operation of small pharmacies and the major chains, private dentistry, consumer IT services and estate agencies. The OFT has also investigated some business methods, including doorstop selling and public sector procurement. A number of investigations were carried out in the 1980s and 1990s regarding price-fixing by cement companies which eventually resulted in the cartel being broken up and cement prices substantially reduced.

CASE 5.1

OFT report on extended warranties

In 2002, the OFT carried out an investigation into the £500 million market in extended warranties, chiefly for electrical goods and referred the matter to the Competition Commission to decide on action. They found that the bulk of warranties were purchased at the point of sale of the goods, and could add 50 per cent to the price of the product and were generally poor value. Bad practice reported included the following.

- Sales staff emphasised the risk of product failure.
- Customers were told that independent repairs were difficult to obtain and were expensive.
- The consumer was not encouraged to shop around.

It was also reported that self-regulation had not worked and that the large electrical retailers were exploiting their monopoly situation to the detriment of consumers.

Source: OFT website 2002

The OFT reports to the Government, who can decide to refer the matter to the **Competition Commission** either for a decision or, in the case of an impending merger where the organisation will have 25 per cent or more of the market, a fuller inquiry to decide if the merger is in the public interest and under what terms the merger would be allowed to progress. Full-scale investigations by the Commission in recent years have included one into the position of Nestle (where it found it did not have excessive monopolistic power on coffee prices), video games (where it recommended the abolition of licence controls) and UK car prices (where it found that the exclusive dealership system operated against the public interest).

Investigations of potential wrong-doing, or the threat of referral to the OFT or the Competition Commission, have a huge impact on organisations or their future planning of possible mergers. A raid by the OFT on premises can cause a company's share price to drop 10 per cent and many mergers have been decided by the policy of the Competition Commission. In the case of Safeway Supermarkets, at one stage there were five companies making a bid, but the policy decisions of the Competition Commission ensured that one company, Morrisons, would be successful, owing to fears of monopoly power should another company, such as Tesco, be successful.

ACTIVITY 5.2

The OFT carried out a survey of doorstep selling in response to complaints from the Citizens Advice Bureau. Their report in 2004 recommended that legislation needs to be updated to combat the psychological tactics employed by many salespeople.

The study into the practice of selling goods and services on the doorstep and in the home, worth at least £2.4 billion a year, found that a range of sales tactics and influencing techniques can lead consumers to make inappropriate purchases which they later regret. This highlights a gap in consumer protection. The current legislation gives consumers who are cold-called a 7-day period in which to cancel a contract. This protection does not apply to consumers who asked for the visit.

Buying in the home provides a unique setting for a business transaction – salespeople effectively have a captive audience. Nearly 40 per cent of consumers have bought goods or services in the home. While 70 per cent of those were satisfied, a significant minority of 30 per cent experienced problems: at least 15,000 complaints a year are made to trading standards departments regarding doorstep sales. Most respondents to the OFT's consumer survey said they felt buying in the home was more pressurised than other settings.

The OFT recommends that Government should extend the legislation to give cancellation rights to solicited visits as well as unsolicited. The OFT will also run a consumer education campaign in conjunction with interested groups to raise awareness of consumers' rights and alert them to the psychological techniques used and how to combat them.

Look up the Office of Fair Trading's website and examine two more of its recent investigations, including the remit to the OFT, the decisions it has made and the justification for those decisions.

Consumer protection

Economic theory would argue that rational behaviour by consumers makes their protection unnecessary. Poorly performing products would not survive and consumers would simply walk away from poor service. To a large extent that it is true but the consumer is not always in a position to behave rationally. They may not have sufficient information about the product (hence the need for product description on the label), they may not have a choice of products if an uncontrolled monopoly exists and they may not be able to challenge a large and unscrupulous supplier. So a whole raft of legislation has been passed in recent years covering all business–consumer relationships and attempting to tighten up on legal loopholes. Much of the legislation encoded the Common Law in place and then extended it. Here is a brief summary of the key features:

Trade Descriptions Act 1968 / Consumer Protection Act 1987

These two acts protect against traders who deliberately give false descriptions in the price, quality and nature of service. These are criminal offences and can result in fines and even imprisonment for repeated offences. The act is policed by local government Trading Standard officials, who, incidentally, also assist the Office of Fair Trading in gathering information. Examples of cases include:

- advertisements showing massive price reductions when the prices had only been increased the day before (regulations now state that goods must have been at the pre-reduction price for 28 continuous days during the previous six months).
- cars being advertised with 'one owner' which was a leasing company that had leased the car out for long periods to five different drivers.
- prices being advertised but with no indication that VAT is to be added.

LAW IN PRACTICE 5.1

MFI was fined £18,000 in 1993 by magistrates in Enfield, North London, for giving out false information on nine counts. It advertised 'massive reductions on' and '30 per cent off' furniture suites when, in fact, the prices had been the same for the previous 6 months, with a number of suites actually having gone up in price at the time of advertising.

The Consumer Protection Act also places strict (but not absolute) liability on suppliers for damage and death/injury caused by defects in their products. There is no need to prove negligence or a contractual relationship but there is a defence that the state of scientific and technical knowledge at the time the product was supplied was not sufficiently advanced for the defect to be recognised (the 'state of the act' defence).

Unfair Contract Terms Act 1977

Introduced to prevent 'small print' removing consumers' rights, generally without their knowledge, the act has two parts. First, the seller cannot remove the liability for death or injury through negligence under any circumstances. Secondly, a trader cannot enforce a contract term that the courts hold to be unfair. For example, a coach company advertised a tour by luxury coach with videos, toilet, etc. but added in their small print that they reserved the right to substitute a coach of inferior quality. The courts held this to be unfair as it gave too much leeway to the coach company and most customers would not have picked up this particular item within the small print. The claimant was awarded compensation.

A number of well-publicised cases and the constant vigilance of consumer societies have resulted in much greater honesty in communicating the real (and generally reasonable) contract terms by suppliers since this act was passed.

Sale of Goods Act 1979/ Supply of Goods and Services Act 1982
This Act enables dissatisfied customers to take civil action against the supplier. The Act requires that:

- Goods and services must match the description.
- They must be of merchantable quality – in appearance, finish and durability.
- They must be fit for the purpose.
- Services provided must be carried out with reasonable skill and within a reasonable time.

As the Acts have been interpreted, the issue of reasonableness is key. A very cheap pair of canvas shoes is fit for the purpose if they last 6 months while a pair of expensive, hand-made leathers would not be fit if they wore out after 4 years' light wear. In essence, it has been for the court to decide what the bounds of reasonableness are and we shall see this again in the field of employment law.

If the product fails to meet the tests under the Act, the consumer has the remedy of the right to their money back, or receive a credit note, or for the goods to be replaced free of charge or the consumer can take the goods at a reduced price.

Consumer Credit Act 1974
This Act was introduced following the boom in hire purchase and credit agreements in the 1960s and 1970s which led to high pressure selling, especially in people's homes, and high rates of interest. The Act took two main directions. First, it aimed to clean up the industry by enforcing licensing of lenders for all credit activities, including credit cards. The licensing involves an inspection regime and a requirement for effective staff training and proper funding of the business.

The second direction was to ensure that contracts were not oppressive. All credit contracts and all contracts signed outside of business premises have a 7-day 'cooling-off' period where the consumer can cancel without loss to either party. The terms of the credit can be altered by the courts if they regard the rate of interest as excessive. The consumer has the right to full details of the agreement before signing, including the annual rate of charge (calculated by means of the OFT current formula), the full cost of the loan, the debtor's right to pay the loan off early and the terms under which they would do so. The Act does not apply to loans over an upper limit, currently £25,000 and only applies to consumer credit, not corporate credit.

On p. 106 we will look in more detail at the effect these laws and additional regulations have in specific sectors and industries.

EMPLOYMENT LAW

The regulation of employment relationships has changed out of all recognition over the last 40 years. Originating from the individual 'master–servant' contract, the fundamental inequality of the parties to the relationship became clear by the mid-nineteenth century and a political party (the Labour Party) was set up essentially with the aim of rectifying these inequalities through legislation by establishing employee rights and removing legal restraints on collective bargaining. It was clear that there was a major difference between a conflict on the one hand over an employment contract which can lead to unemployment and suffering abject poverty, and on the other hand a difference between two parties over buying a pair of shoes. Moreover, the evidence of unscrupulous use of dominant employer power was widespread.

Although much progress was made in these areas in the early twentieth century, especially in the collective bargaining field, the stimulus to enacting more radical and extensive employee protection has come from the European Union. At the same time, the political consensus in recent times has been that the rights granted to trade unions in the collective bargaining field went too far and they were reined-in by Conservative governments in the period between 1980 and 1992.

Sources of the employment contract

The terms of an employment contract come from a surprising number of sources. It is not just the **express terms**, which are those specifically included in the contract (usually set out in the offer letter) such as salary, notice and holiday entitlement. Other sources are of equal importance:

- There are a number of **implied terms**, originating from Common Law. These include the duty of the employee to co-operate with the employer in such areas as reasonable changes to the job, exercise due care in looking after the employer's goods and property, and show loyalty demonstrated by not disclosing confidential information. The employer also has duties, such as to exercise due care over the employee's health, safety and well-being (see p. 98), to provide work, indemnify the employee if he or she incurs loss, expense or liability in carrying out the employer's instruction and to pay wages on time and correctly.

- Many contracts incorporate **collective terms**, negotiated between the employer(s) and union(s) either at a local or national level. These may deal with issues such as overtime payment, holidays and disciplinary procedures.

- Contract terms are also incorporated through the **employee handbook**, which sets out rules and policies set out by the employer which the employee must sign up to.

- Many more unwritten contract terms reflect **employment laws** covering employee rights and benefits (see p. 96).

An additional complication is that the *contract terms do not need to be written down*. Rules relating to, say, employees swapping shifts, which have operated informally for some years (ie through custom and practice) with the full knowledge of management, become part of the contract. In claims for unfair dismissal, the tribunal is very keen to establish whether terms written into contracts are those that actually operate in practice. For example, if an employee is dismissed for fighting (as clearly laid out in the employee handbook) but it comes to light that on the last two occasions when a similar incident occurred, the employees were merely warned, the tribunal can take the view that custom and practice is that dismissal is not the normal punishment under the contract.

That is not to say contractual terms cannot be changed by either party. An individual employee can request changes to his or her holiday arrangements which are different to the standard contractual terms. Or changes can be negotiated on a collective basis usually through unions but sometimes through a works council. An employer can change shift arrangements and introduce different work practices and systems. In doing so, it should consult with the workforce, be able to justify the changes for business reasons and ensure they are published widely. It does not need to obtain every individual's signed agreement to the changes. An employee who continues to work under the changes has deemed to have accepted the changed contract.

A further complication is differentiating between the normal employee contract, called a *contract of service* and the contract for the self-employed, who work under a *contract for services*. The legal implications are great in that a different tax regime applies (hence the considerable interest shown by the Inland Revenue in this area) and the self-employed have none of the rights and benefits detailed below. Legal tussles have occurred in areas such as commission-only sales people and those providing occasional but regular services, such as consultants. Although a complex area, the courts examine the degree of control and the nature of exclusivity of contract which can sometimes overcome the apparent clarity of the payment and tax arrangements.

Under the Employment Rights Act 1996, employers are required to give to each new employee within two months a long statement of certain contract terms under 16 headings, which includes details such as the date that continuous employment started, hours of work and holiday entitlement. This is called the 'principal statement' but, to repeat, it is not the actual contract of employment.

Employee rights

The bulk of employment law since the 1970s has been enacted to improve the minimum level of benefits for employees and to protect them from potential employer abuse. There was some earlier legislation in this area, such as the prohibition of child labour and the 9-hour working day in the coal mines applied in the nineteenth century, but recent legislation has taken the process much further and allowed employees to benefit extensively from the changes.

Employee protection has been enhanced in a number of areas, as discussed below.

Protection from discrimination
Since the 1970s, groups seen as vulnerable in the employment field because of well-evidenced discrimination, harassment and bullying, have been given legal protection. The various acts make it unlawful to discriminate on the grounds of sex, ethnic origin, disability, age or religion. Discrimination has taken three forms:

Direct discrimination
An instance here would be to advertise for a 'Girl Friday' or to use different criteria for selection for promotion. In the case of race discrimination, it may relate to an employer

indicating to a recruitment agency that it does not want black casual workers; or an employer may turn down a deaf or partially sighted applicant specifically because of this disability. In each case, an individual or group is treated less favourably than another on the grounds of sex, race or disability. The employer has no defence even if it genuinely believes what it is doing is right. The motives are irrelevant.

Indirect discrimination

This occurs where the employer treats all applicants or employees the same but a practice, condition or policy adversely affects one sex or race more than another, or if it affects the disabled more than the able-bodied or the elderly more than the young. The way it normally adversely affects that group is because the proportion of people from a particular group able to meet the condition or policy is considerably smaller. Moreover, the employer cannot objectively justify the practice, policy or condition. If the employer cannot convince the tribunal that the defence is genuine and substantial, the employer will lose the case. Tribunal cases have included:

- the requirement to restrict applicants geographically by residence to a specific area which discriminated against ethnic minorities, whose representation in that area was slight
- recruiting only through word of mouth in an employment site dominated by white males
- promoting internally when the workforce is unbalanced.

The Equal Pay Act (1970) prohibits discrimination in pay and benefits between men and women, where work is 'like' or rated as similar under a job evaluation scheme. In addition, an employee can claim that their work is of 'equal value' as that of another employee of the opposite sex.

Harassment and bullying

Described as 'unwanted behaviour which a person finds intimidating, upsetting, embarrassing, humiliating or offensive', the courts have increasingly punished harassment and bullying, using both the concept of an employer's duty of care and discrimination legislation, supported by the EU Equal Treatment Directive (amended in 2000). This reflects the changing social attitudes in society where a predominantly male, white culture in workplaces, where power may be exercised over staff in a vulnerable position, is no longer acceptable in a modern state. It has been accepted by the courts that the judgment as to whether behaviour is acceptable or not comes from the subject(s) of the harassment. There can be additional compensation awarded for 'loss of feelings'.

No service requirement is necessary in any area of discrimination. Protection applies from day one of employment.

Protection from unfair dismissal

Since 1972, employees with one year's service have been protected from arbitrary and unfair dismissal. To successfully defend a claim, the employer has to show that it has a justifiable reason for dismissal (usually based on poor performance, conduct or redundancy) and that it has carried out the dismissal using the correct procedures. If it fails, the tribunal awards compensation up to a maximum of £54,000 (2004), and, occasionally, can order the employer to reinstate the employee.

ACAS has provided codes of practices in dealing with dismissal and redundancies which organisations need to observe to defend against claims successfully. For example, where the offences are deemed to be misdemeanours (timekeeping, attendance, poor performance), warnings are required whereas with gross misconduct (theft, violence), instant dismissal is permitted. Employees' rights, including a fair hearing, a colleague to help support their case and a fair appeals procedure, must be observed.

The same protection is also afforded against dismissal due to pregnancy or for being a union activist.

Protection from working excessive hours
Arising from an EU directive and essentially a health and safety measure, the Working Time Regulations 1998 have had a controversial history. They have established that employees cannot be forced to work in excess of 48 hours a week, averaged over 17 weeks. Employees should have 11 consecutive hours of rest in any 24-hour period and a 24-hour rest in every 7-day period, plus a 20-minute break if the shift exceeds 6 hours. The regulations also insist on the provision of four weeks' holiday.

The controversial aspect is that employers and employees can agree to 'opt out' of the regulations, so they often apply as a voluntary measure. How 'voluntary' they are and whether the opt-out should remain is discussed later.

Protection when being transferred
The Transfer of Undertakings (Protection of Employment) Regulations 1981 (known as TUPE) were introduced as a result of the EU Acquired Rights Directive. The philosophy here is that employees need to be protected when their organisation is sold to or merged with another organisation, or when they are outsourced with their work. Prior to these regulations, employees' terms could be fundamentally and unilaterally altered with the employees having the choice to accept or leave.

Under the Regulations, all employment terms and conditions are protected (except pensions) and prior service is recognised. This does not stop the new employer changing terms at a later date. Full consultation must take place with the employees being transferred.

Protection of deductions from pay
Under the Employment Rights Act 1996, employees have the right of an itemised pay statement and deductions can only be made with prior authorisation from the employee in writing.

ACTIVITY 5.3

In the 2005 budget, Gordon Brown gave another commitment to reduce 'red tape' for businesses, which included reducing the number of agencies monitoring and inspecting businesses from 35 to 9. Read reports on these budget actions (such as in the *Sunday Times*, 20 March 2005) and set up a debate over the issue of whether the protection of employees has now gone too far. Has employers' ability to act competitively been restricted by UK and EU legislation and is there too much bureaucracy involved in employing people?

Benefits

A summary of the minimum benefits introduced through legislation are set out in Table 5.1.

Table 5.1 *Employee benefits introduced through legislation*

Minimum benefit	Legislation	Summary of key details
Minimum wage	National Minimum Wage Act 1998	Provides low minimum (£4.85 (Jan. 2005) for employees age 22 and over); Lower rates for employees under 22. Aims to eradicate exploitative pay in vulnerable sectors, such as home workers and hospitality
Maternity pay	Employment Rights Act 1996, amended by Employment Act 2002	Payable by employers for 26 weeks. Six months qualifying period paid at 90 per cent of average earnings for six weeks then £106 per week (Jan. 2005) for remaining 20 weeks
Ante-natal care	As above	Right to paid time off during working hours for all ante-natal care and treatment
Maternity leave	As above	On top of paid maternity leave, an additional 26 weeks' unpaid maternity leave can be taken, with the right to the same job back upon return
Paternity leave and pay	Employment Act 2002	Six months' qualifying period. Applicable to father of child, mother's husband or partner, who are expected to have some responsibility for upbringing of child. Paid for two weeks at £106 per week (Jan. 2005)
Adoption leave	Employment Act 2002	One of the parents can take up to 26 weeks' unpaid leave when an adoption takes place. Six months' qualifying service
Parental leave	Maternity and Parental Leave Regulations 1999	Parents with children under five (or disabled children under 18) can take up to 13 weeks' unpaid leave with the right to return to the same job. One years' qualifying service
Time off for dependents	Employment Rights Act 1996	Reasonable unpaid time can be taken off to provide assistance when a dependent dies, falls ill, gives birth or is injured/assaulted; or for any school problems or resulting from disruption to existing care arrangements. It is not applicable simply to provide normal care on a regular basis and only applies to an immediate crisis. In Qua v John Ford Morrison Solicitors, EAT confirmed a fair dismissal when Qua took 17 different days to look after her child who had medical problems
Flexible working	Employment Act 2002/ Employment Rights Act 1996	Provides the right of a parent of a child under six (18 if disabled) to apply for change in working arrangements, including to work flexibly in order to care for the child. Employer can refuse on the basis of burden of additional costs, detrimental effect on ability to meet customer demand or quality of service, disruption of staff/ department. Six months' qualifying period
Time off for public duties	Employment Rights Act 1996	Reasonable unpaid time can be taken off relating to work as a member of a local authority, health authority or similar
Time off for trade union duties	TULRCA 1992	Officials of independent trade unions have right to time off with pay during working hours to carry out reasonable and relevant trade union duties and to undertake training, as specified by ACAS Code of Practice
Statutory sick pay (SSP)	Social Security Contributions and Benefits Act 1992/Statutory Sick Pay Act 1994	Employers are responsible for payment of SSP for up to 28 weeks of sickness/injury in any single period of entitlement
Redundancy consultation, time off and pay	TULRCA 1992	Consultation with employees/representatives must take place 90 days before redundancies take effect if 100 or more employees are redundant (30 days if between 20 and 99 employees) and adequate information must be provided by employer. Redundancy pay entitlement at one week's pay (1.5 weeks at age 41 and over, 0.5 from 18 to 21) for each year of service, up to 20 years. The maximum week's pay is £280 at Feb. 2005. Reasonable time off with pay must be given to look for alternative work

Notes: 1. These benefits are correct at the time of writing but are subject to amendment both in terms of the pay arrangements and in other details.; 2. These are minimum benefits and employers can (and do) improve them by granting pay where there is no entitlement under the legislation, increasing the rates or enhancing the terms and conditions.

Regulation of contracts through collective bargaining

In the nineteenth century, government legislation was put in place to stamp out the infant trade unions, which were attempting to interfere with the employment contract. Over the last 200 years, the pendulum has swung, first to provide a legal framework for union immunity so union activities are protected in tort, and then back the other way under Thatcherite reforms, where tight restrictions on this immunity were introduced to protect employers from arbitrary union power.

Under a variety of Acts passed during the period 1980–95, legal immunity is only available for unions in leading their members to break their contracts through strikes or other industrial actions when they:

- have a secret ballot before action is taken (with strict requirements as to notifying the employer, how the ballot should be carried out and who is entitled to vote)
- only take action against their own employer (so-called secondary action against suppliers or customers is not protected)
- carry out picketing only at their own place of work and in very small numbers (to prevent the dangerous and oppressive mass picketing which took place during the 1984 miners' strike)
- do not insist on a 'closed shop' – employees can join or not join a union as they wish
- ensure they elect their full-time officials on a regular basis under strict governance and follow their own rules on disciplining and expelling members.

Since the 1997 election of a Labour Government, the pendulum has somewhat swung back towards improving the regulation of relationships with the workforce, chiefly through organised labour. First, the Statutory Recognition procedures in the 1999 Employment Relations Act has served to support union members who wish to formally negotiate in the workplace. Secondly, the European-initiated Information and Consultation Regulations (in force from April 2005) give rights to employees to be informed and consulted about the business for whom they work.

ACTIVITY 5.4

An application was made to the Central Arbitration Committee in 2004 by the Amicus union for the right to carry out a recognition ballot for manual staff at Japan Airlines. The employer had provided a number of reasons why this should not take place, concerned mostly with the nature of the bargaining unit requested. The union claimed that 110 out of the 210 manual employees were already union members. CAC carried out an investigation and, although they found only 96 to be members out of 229 total staff, they approved the bargaining unit in 2005 and the right for the union to carry out a recognition ballot.

Look up the website for the Central Arbitration Committee and examine a further two of the decisions that they have taken recently, including the parties involved, the background to the dispute over recognition and the justification for the decision.

REGULATING HEALTH AND SAFETY

Introduction

Regulation of health and safety in the UK is very extensive with over 100 current pieces of legislation. Although there has been a steady decline in the number of deaths and serious accidents over the last few decades, over 300 people are killed in accidents at work each year, including 100 members of the public. Not only is this a huge waste of human resources but it is very costly for the economy. The main aim of the regulations, therefore, is to reduce the number of accidents and resultant ill-health and to ensure that a safety-conscious culture becomes widespread so that business can operate more efficiently.

This section begins with an introduction to main legislation, examines how it is enforced and considers the important role of human resources in ensuring that initiatives are taken and that the law is followed so that all employees work in a safe environment.

Health and Safety at Work Act 1974 (HASAWA)

This influential legislation, born out of a consensus between the political parties, is essentially an 'enabling' Act, with wide-ranging, if imprecise, provisions which require interpretation by the courts or putting into effect through Regulations sanctioned by Parliament.

The main aim of the legislation was to provide comprehensive cover for all employees and to protect all personnel on-site and impose criminal liability to ensure compliance. At the same time it was important to encourage self-regulation through developing codes of conduct and emphasising personal responsibility from everybody involved – managers, employees, sub-contractors and designers.

Duties on employers

The Act lays down a fundamental 'duty of care' towards the health, safety and welfare of all employees, which is the starting point of all considerations, as illustrated by Case 5.2.

CASE 5.2

Hickson and Welsh

In 1992, five workers were killed at the chemical company, Hickson and Welsh, in Castleford, West Yorkshire. The accident followed the first cleaning in 30 years of the sludge from a tank of volatile mononitrotoluene (MNT). The job had not been properly assessed for risk and was left to a junior team leader who had only recently returned to the MNT section. Incorrect cleaning tools were used, a monitoring thermometer was inadequate, the sludge content had not been analysed and the whole approach had been 'casual'. During the cleaning operation, a fireball suddenly burst from the tank, torching a frail control cabin next door and leaving the factory's main office block with shattered windows and burnt-out rooms.

The company was fined £250,000 with £150,000 costs in the High Court for breaches of their safety duties and for not providing a safe system of work. The managing director of the plant, the operations director and manager all left the company shortly after the accident.

Source: Wainwright (1994

Section 2 sets out the general duties on employers, which cover:

- the provision of systems of work, equipment and a workplace that are all safe
- arrangements for the use, handling, storage and transport of articles and substances that are all safe
- adequate and necessary information, supervision, training and instruction to ensure effective employee safety
- ensuring that there are safe means of getting into and out of premises
- adequate welfare provision.

The duties also extend to sub-contractors working on the premises and to members of the public. Throughout this section of the Act, the words *as far as is reasonably practicable* are mentioned for each clause. This limits the absolute responsibility to employers and allows them to achieve a balance between the assessed risk of an unsafe practice and the cost of avoiding that risk. Employers each day need to consider issues such as replacement of older, potentially dangerous machines, reducing noise levels and improving ventilation, and balancing the cost and practicality against the safety requirements. These may be finely judged decisions and, ultimately, should an accident or incident arise before the employer has acted, it would then be up to the courts to decide if the action was 'reasonably practical' or not. If the court decided that the employer should have taken action as part of their 'duty of care' then the employer could be punished for its failure to carry out its statutory duty.

There is a requirement to use 'best practical means' to solve safety problems. This is an ever-tightening noose trying to prevent employers from carrying out botched jobs or taking short cuts. In industries where safety is absolutely paramount, such as nuclear power or defence, then 'state of the art' safety systems are the expectation.

The duty of care extends, to a degree, of monitoring sickness, absence and health in the organisation. Each establishment has its own specific areas of danger and certain places are prone to a higher level of sickness if nothing is done.

Duties on employees
The Act recognised that responsibility for safety was not just one-way. Confirming the Common Law implied term of the employment contract that the employee is obliged to follow the safety instructions, sections 7 and 8 go further by stating that the employee must co-operate with safety initiatives and the training that accompanies them, take reasonable care of their own health and safety and not recklessly interfere with machines, plant or processes so as to make them unsafe. The clear implications are that employees have to wear the required safety gear and follow all authorised safety rules. They also risk dismissal if they refuse to follow other important health and safety instructions, including restrictions on smoking in the workplace.

Duties on designers, manufacturers, suppliers and installers
Duties here under Section 6 include incorporating safety features at the design stage, testing for risks to health and providing full safety instruction and hazard details. Again, this aspect clarified the rather unspecific Common Law obligations and has made a large difference in the way products are designed and marketed. Since the act, for example, all commercial

guillotines require the operator to have both hands on separate buttons for it to operate. Furthermore, one manufacturer of numerically controlled tools was successfully prosecuted because the design allowed the override of a guard while the machine was still working.

The Health and Safety Commission and Health and Safety Executive

Both the Health and Safety Commission and the Health and Safety Executive were set up under HASAWA. The Commission has between six and nine lay members drawn from bodies representing employers, trade unions and local authorities. It is primarily an advisory body and its main responsibility is for carrying out the policy of the Act and providing advice for local authorities and others to enable them to discharge the responsibilities imposed upon them by the Act. The Commission arranges for research to be carried out, submits proposals for new regulations, produces codes of practice and generally works to reassure the public that risks are being properly controlled through information and responsiveness to public concerns. The Health and Safety Executive are responsible for the policing and enforcement of the Act and other acts involving safety.

Control of Substances Hazardous to Health Regulations (COSHH) 1988

These regulations and associated codes of practice are designed to protect employees who work with any substances which could be hazardous to their health unless they are handled and utilised in a properly controlled way. They apply to all workplaces, large and small, and include all substances except for those where regulations were already in force, such as lead and asbestos.

The principal requirements in these regulations are five-fold.

1 A *risk assessment* must be made to identify all potentially hazardous substances and to set out the precautions required. Employers are required to carry out the risk assessment every five years.

2 A system must be put in place to prevent or control these risks. Consideration must be given to replace hazardous substances or to provide better controlled working arrangements where they are used.

3 The employer must make sure these controls are effectively put to use and keep records of the monitoring process.

4 Employers must regularly conduct health surveillance of staff engaged in work associated with these substances where there is a known identifiable risk.

5 Employees must be informed of the hazards and trained in the control processes, including the precautions that they need to take.

Regulations arising from European Union Directives

It has been an objective from the early days of the European movement that laws relating to Health and Safety should be applied consistently across Europe. This ensures that the free market between states can operate efficiently without manufacturers and traders having to deal with different regulations in each country. The *Framework Directive*, implemented by member states in 1992, contained general safety principles and objectives, such as the prevention of occupational risks and providing balanced participation between the parties affected. Regulations arising from this directive include the **Manual Handling Operations regulations 1992,** covering requirements on systems and training for lifting and the **Health**

and Safety (Display Screen Equipment) Regulations 1992, covering the requirements on regular eye testing, design of work stations and the need for regular breaks.

Regulations have also come into effect relating to the provision and use of protective equipment, the control of asbestos at work, measures to set minimum standards for the safe use of machines and equipment and the protection of young people and pregnant women in the workplace.

Reporting of Diseases and Dangerous Occurrences Regulations (RIDDOR) 1995

All statistics on safety arise from a system of reporting by employers and this revised system was introduced to produce more accurate information and extend it to dangerous situations where nobody was hurt. All deaths and serious injuries must be immediately reported and a written report sent within 10 days. Lesser accidents which cause an employee to be off work for more than 3 days must lead to a completed accident form being sent to the enforcing authorities, this also applying to some work-related diseases such as skin cancer or dermatitis.

ENFORCING THE LAW

External authorities

Local authority enforcement officers mostly deal with the service industries such as hotels, restaurants, offices and warehouses while inspectors, working for the Health and Safety Executive, deal with factories, mines, railways, schools and hospitals. Their enforcement authority consists of rights to:

- enter premises, with or without notice, at any reasonable time (accompanied by the police, if obstructed)
- take samples, measurements and photographs or recordings
- carry out tests
- direct that work be left undisturbed
- examine books and documents
- take statements from any employee concerned.

Their main enforcement activities, if persuasion has not achieved the desired results, is to issue improvement notices and prohibition notices. *Improvement notices* are issued where the inspector is satisfied there has been a contravention of a statutory provision. The improvement notice will give the employer a certain time within which that contravention must be remedied. Work can continue in the meantime. A *prohibition notice*, which means the work must immediately cease, is issued when the inspector considers that the activity involves a risk of serious personal safety or a severe safety hazard to the employees or the public. Around 15,000 notices are issued each year and the records of such notices are on public view for up to three years, providing a deterrent to safety transgressors.

Internal authorities

The main authorities within an organisation are *safety officers* and *safety representatives*. There is no specific requirement for an organisation to have a safety officer but most industrial sites with over 200 employees usually have a full-time appointment. Smaller organisations may have a part-time employee or make use of consultants. The role of the safety officer is to ensure that the safety requirements imposed by legislation are met by the organisation. They will set up safe systems of work, carry out risk assessments, investigate accidents and dangerous occurrences and generally try to ensure that a 'safety culture' operates in the workplace.

Safety representatives are appointed or elected by the employees, either directly or through their trade union. Their rights are set down in the **Health and Safety (Consultation with Employees) Regulations 1996.** They must be recognised by employers, involved in the consultation process through a safety committee and given reasonable paid time off to carry out their duties together with basic facilities such as the use of a telephone and a filing cabinet. Their duties are, to a large extent, carried out in tandem with those of the safety officer with whom they will work closely in practice, in that they investigate accidents, make regular safety inspections, assess risks and bring forward employee complaints and suggestions regarding safety. If two or more safety representatives request the formation of a *safety committee,* the employer must set one up.

RISK ASSESSMENT

Risk assessment does not only apply to materials and substances under the COSHH regulations, although these regulations stimulated interest and experience in this process. Under the 1992 Code of Practice for the Management of Health and Safety at Work, it became a legal duty for employers to assess and record health and safety risks and requires the appointment of 'competent persons' to assist in this and other safety tasks.

There are three main stages in the process of assessing and controlling risks:

1 identifying hazards (the potential causes of harm)
2 assessing risks (the likelihood of harm occurring and its severity) and prioritising action
3 designing, implementing and monitoring measures to eliminate or minimise risk.

Risk assessment continues to be a matter of balance. The test of 'reasonably practical' is still used in the context of cost and difficulty balanced against likely danger. It is important, therefore, that organisations have set out policies and procedures which help them to achieve a fair balance and which will highlight actions that they have to take speedily.

ACTIVITY 5.5

Suggest how a system can be set up which identifies and assesses the seriousness of risks and the action that should be taken that can apply to any working situation.

Occupational stress

Stress has become one of the most serious health issues of recent years. A survey by the HSE (2002) estimates that stress costs nearly £4 billion per year in the UK, over 1 per cent of gross domestic product, or £150 per employee per year. The number of work-related stress cases reaching the courts has increased from 516 in 2002 to 6,428 in 2003 (Palmer and Quinn 2004). 150,000 employees take at least one month off for ailments caused by stress at work. Employees aged between 34 and 44 suffer the most, while the problems worsen the longer they stay in the same job.

The causes of occupational stress are numerous. They are associated with perceptions of job insecurity, increase in work intensity, aggressive management styles, lack of effective workplace communication, overt or insidious bullying and harassment, faulty selection for promotion or transfer and lack of guidance and training (Cartwright and Cooper 1997). Employees may be exposed to situations which they find uncomfortable, such as continually dealing with customers, excessive computer work, repetitive or fragmented work or having to make regular public presentations. Probably the most common cause, however, is the constant fear of organisational change through restructuring, takeovers, mergers or business process re-engineering. A lack of control over their work, their environment or their career progression can also be stressful (Rick et al 1997).

When a work environment containing these cultural aspects is added to personal problems, such as divorce or separation, ill or dying relatives, difficult housing conditions and financial problems, then it is not surprising that the employer will be faced with a good proportion of employees with stress-related problems.

Stress is manifested not only in high absence levels; fatigue, increases in infections, backache and digestive illnesses are commonly found. Irritation, hostility, anxiety and a state of panic can arise in the workplace with knock-on effects on working practices and relationships between employees. The end result may be that the employee is 'burnt-out', and unable to cope with pressures that previously had been regarded as challenging and stimulating. Employees may also turn to palliatives, such as alcohol or drugs.

The employer who neglects the problem of occupational stress may face legal action. The first legal breakthrough for an employee was John Walker, a social work manager with Northumberland County Council who, having had a mental breakdown arising from his occupation, returned to his job but received no positive assistance from his employer to help him to cope successfully. The details of this case have been set out at the start of this chapter in Example 1 (Walker v Northumberland County Council 1995, IRLR 35/95).

Later cases have included a primary school head who won £100,000 after suffering two nervous breakdowns allegedly caused by stress brought on from bullying and harassment, and an out-of-court settlement reached in 1998 between an NHS trust and the bereaved spouse of an employee who committed suicide. In a later case, Birmingham City Council admitted liability for personal injury caused by stress when they moved a 39-year-old senior draughtsman to the post of a neighbourhood housing officer without sufficient training. The nature of the work was so different and the inter-personal demands so great that she had long periods of ill-health leading to early retirement on medical grounds. She was awarded £67,000 (Miller 1999).

Greater clarification as to the employer's responsibility in the case of psychiatric injury based on exposure to unacceptable levels of stress was given by the Court of Appeal in 2002 (Sutherland v Hatton). The court held that an employer was entitled to assume that an employee was able to withstand the normal pressures of the job and to take what the employee said about her own health at face value. It was only if there were indications which would lead a reasonable employer to realise that there was a problem that a duty to take action would arise. In terms of whether the injury to health was foreseeable, factors that should be taken into account include whether:

- the workload was abnormally heavy
- the work was particularly intellectually or emotionally demanding
- the demands were greater compared to similar employees.

If the only way of making the employee safe was to dismiss him or her, then there would be no breach of duty by letting the employee continue if he or she was willing to do so (IRS 2002).

All of these cases show that employers need to carefully consider the way in which work demands affect their employees and ensure that they investigate each case, taking appropriate action to ameliorate potentially health damaging situations (Earnshaw and Cooper 1996). A further consideration is the level of employees' expectations on welfare provision. A sure sign of a sympathetic and caring employer is one which will make special provision for the personal and individual needs of employees. Finally, a CIPD study (Tehrani 2002) has shown that employers who have some form of 'wellness' programmes incurred reduced annual employment costs of between £1,335 and £2,910 less per employee than employers who do not.

ACTIVITY 5.6

You have been brought in as a consultant to carry out a review of the level of stress in an organisation. Having investigated safety and welfare statistics, and carried out an employee attitude survey, you report on the following indicators of stress:

- The absenteeism levels had risen from 6 per cent to 9 per cent over the last three years, of which 3 per cent was reported as being caused by stress-related illnesses.
- The number of staff on long-term sickness had increased from 8 to 14, with six incidents of stress or other mental problems.
- The level of reported accidents had doubled from 12 to 24 over the same period.
- There had been three incidence of violence inside the site, two alcohol induced. Five employees had been dismissed arising from these incidents. Two of these dismissals had resulted in claims to employment tribunals.
- The staff attitude survey showed that over 70 per cent considered that they worked excessive hours, which caused stress 'occasionally' or 'regularly'.
- 20 per cent of staff found that their relationships with their managers were 'poor' or 'very poor'.
- 30 per cent of staff believed that urgent improvements in their physical environment was required.

What advice would you give to the employer to alleviate the causes of stress in this organisation?

ROLE OF HUMAN RESOURCES

In the majority of organisations in which separate human resources departments exist, such departments have responsibility for health, safety or welfare issues or play a major part therein. The main activities consist of the following:

Formulating policies and procedures
This activity is more than a formality required by law. It is essential that new employees understand how safety works within a new organisation and the policies and procedures will set out how the safety responsibilities are structured and the requirements from each employee. Specific references to certain areas (such as responsibility for checking lifting gear, or guards) should be clearly spelt out. The document should give a statement of management intent as to how safety issues will be treated in the workplace. Detailed procedures should be set out for dealing with emergencies, safety training, information arising from the investigations under COSHH, and procedures should be set out for all departments wherein hazards have been identified. Human Resources should ensure that such documents are logical, readable and have been circulated correctly.

Monitoring policies and procedures
At regular intervals, all procedures need examining to see if they need updating to take account of new processes, materials and layouts. By attending management and safety meetings, Human Resources can ensure such necessary revisions can be identified and put into place.

Advising management and employees on safety legislation
New regulations continue to emerge, especially from Europe, with different levels of importance and different implementation dates.

Designing, providing and recording health and safety training
Systematic training is essential if procedures are to operate properly. It should start with induction training to ensure that employees who are involved in any hazardous operation have instruction in key areas before they set foot on the work-site. Safety instruction should be incorporated into any new processes or where new materials are introduced onto site. New safety representatives have the right for time-off for training and this should be encouraged by the organisation so they can operate efficiently.

Liaising with the safety inspectorate
Building a relationship with the enforcing authorities is essential. Making use of their advice and extensive knowledge can be valuable, especially where new processes or production lines are being planned. A list of necessary actions arising from a late visit by the factory inspector could result in an expensive delay to a new production facility.

Helping create a healthy working environment
All the research indicates that a healthy workforce will be a successful one and a higher performing one so being proactive in introducing and encouraging initiatives to support health programmes can make a substantial difference to organisational performance, as shown in Case 5.3.

> ## CASE 5.3
>
> ### Improving employee health at Kimberley-Clarke
>
> Kimberley-Clarke, which makes products such as Kleenex and Huggies nappies, has made cost savings of £500,000 per annum and reduced long-term staff absence from 6.8 per cent to 0.5 per cent after launching schemes in 2002 aimed at improving the health of its 174 UK staff. Under the programme, the company introduced work-life balance coaching sessions, massages for desk workers and sleep management workshops to improve employees' sleep quality. It also provided free fruit twice a week to promote healthy eating. Evidence that the scheme was getting immediate results was that, after six months, only 19 per cent admitted they suffered sleep problems, which was down from 68 per cent before the scheme started.
>
> *Source: Watkins (2003)*
>
> Originally published in *People Management* 18 December 2003, and reproduced with permission

A test of overall success is whether a safety-conscious culture pervades the organisation. This is shown through the management operating systems and procedures not just because of the legal requirements but because they see that it makes good business sense, both in terms of reducing costs arising from accidents and from establishing a caring relationship with the labour force.

IMPLICATIONS OF REGULATION

On pp. 86–91, the roles of the Office of Fair Trading and Competition Commission in disseminating, regulating and enforcing commercial and consumer legislation were set out. Additional industry-specific regulation has been put in place over the last 20 years and this section will examine the operation of a selection of these regulators and the implications in the fields of privatised utilities, financial services, communications and areas of the public sector.

Industry regulators – privatised utilities

During the period 1980 to 1995, public utilities in the UK were privatised in what is now seen as a momentous and generally successful business revolution. The Labour Party ideology of nationalisation of key industries, which led to coal, steel, gas, electricity, railways and many other industries coming under state control in the post-war period until 1976, was replaced by the free trade and competition philosophy, promulgated by Milton Friedman (1970). It had become clear that the philosophy of veering towards a centrally controlled interventionist state operation, which had operated for the previous 20 years in the Western economies, had failed to produce the economic success that had been promised. Managers in state-controlled industries complained of constant ministerial interference, starvation of investment and regular changes in strategic direction. At its peak, almost 10 per cent of GDP came under government control in the UK. By 2002, after privatisation, this had been reduced to only 1 per cent.

Detailed studies (Martin and Parker 1997; Electricity Association 1998) have shown that labour productivity has risen at an average of 15 per cent per annum, service provision has improved substantially and prices have generally fallen, especially in telecommunications and electricity.

The model for privatisation was essentially one of attempting to break up state monopolies, introducing a variety of methods to stimulate competition and keeping a measure of control through regulation in the interests of the consumer. Unbundling has involved separating out the potentially competitive areas (eg electricity generation, telecommunication value-added services) from the monopoly part (eg transmission and distribution grids, telephone lines to homes). This picture has been repeated across Europe with only a handful of mostly Scandinavian governments owning the state telecommunications company, reinforced by EU Directives requiring member states to establish independent regulatory agencies to provide a 'level playing field' for potential competitors (Curwen 1997; Pollack 1997).

In each sector privatised, a *regulator* has been appointed to oversee the operation of the business for the benefit of the consumer (business and private) and to try to ensure that the form of privatisation actually worked in practice. The main responsibilities of the regulator are:

- to set out the pricing model (with or without agreement from the participants)
- to establish and monitor service standards
- to encourage the working of a competitive market
- for products such as gas and electricity, to ensure stable sources of supply
- to prevent the exercise of any remnant of monopolistic power
- to ensure the industry meets social and environmental responsibilities.

The regulator is appointed by the Government but is independent of government control. Each industry has been faced by a specific business context and the model of regulation has constantly been changed as the nature of the competitive challenges within each sector has altered. For example, one of the major issues in the telecommunications industry has been the role of the dominant provider, BT, which originally controlled landlines into most UK homes. The challenge for the regulator was to encourage competition with respect to this control, achieved mainly through encouraging the development of cable and mobile phone systems and through complex agreements allowing other companies access to the landlines to provide alternative services and through acting as a mediator in resolving disputes between the parties, such as the dispute in 2004 over NTS discounts. In telecommunication, for example, the industry moved from one monopoly provider in 1984 (BT) to over 70 providers in 2004. As another example, companies in the water industry were allowed by the regulator, Ofwat, to make a substantial increase in prices in the early 1990s to fund the substantial investment required to transform sewage treatment and reduce effluent discharge and, thereby, improve water quality around the UK coastline.

An example of the nature of the regulation occurred in 2004 when Ofgem fined Powergen £700,000 after the company stopped more than 20,000 domestic customers from switching to new gas/electricity contracts.

The ability to set pricing models (unsuccessfully challenged in the courts in the mid-1990s by the gas industry) and to discipline players in the industry has given the regulator substantial power over operating companies. However, the need for establishing a fair pricing model has been reduced in recent years as more sophisticated markets have been introduced into gas and electricity, allowing more providers to enter the market and create more competition, while natural competition has developed in the telecommunications industry.

Industry regulation – Financial services (FSA) and Communications (Ofcom)

A second strand of regulation covers two industries that the state regards as needing special forms of regulation, namely financial services and communications. These are industries which, generally, have not been government owned (apart from the BBC and BT), but where there is a strong public interest. This interest is not just to preserve or encourage competition but to inspire confidence in the financial or communication systems, to regulate ethical behaviour and to act as a watchdog over technical developments.

Ofcom, set up in 2003, covers activities previous controlled by, among others, the Broadcasting Standards Commission, Radio Authority, Oftel and the Independent Television Authority. It has a duty to 'balance the promotion of choice and competition with the duty to foster plurality, informed citizenship, protect viewers, listeners and customers and promote cultural diversity'. Its activities include:

Competition policy

- reform of public service broadcasting, assessing the effects of digital television on the BBC's channel provision and the regular licence review
- developing and implementing policy on awarding of radio and ITV licences
- developing and implementing policy on television advertising under a single terrestrial commercial provider (ITV)
- advising the Government on foreign takeover of major communications players, such as national newspapers.

Protecting small players – producing codes on the ability of independent programme producers to retain their programming rights

Technology reviews – advising on digital switchover, scheduled for 2010

Protecting public morals – advising on television programme content in terms of sex and violence.

Regulating financial markets has, in recent years, been a key part of government economic activity. Understanding that confidence is at the heart of a country's financial system and fearful of the 'melt-down' that could occur should this confidence suddenly evaporate, governments have established systems of financial supervision to try to avoid rogue activities. Much of this authority has been delegated to the Bank of England but a good part of the detailed supervision, investigation and enforcement has gradually been taken up by the **Financial Services Authority (FSA)**, whose main aims are set out in Table 5.2 below.

The FSA certainly has teeth. Examples of disciplinary action over a short period in 2004 included:

- fining Bank of Scotland PLC £1,250,000 for failing to keep proper records of customer identification under Money Laundering rules
- banning six directors of Chiyoda Fire and Marine Insurance Company (Europe) for their role in distorting their financial results, and clearly failing to act with honesty and integrity

Table 5.2 *Aims of the FSA*

Securing the right degree of protection for consumers	Vetting firms and individuals trading in specific areas, such as financial advisers and credit providers, for honesty, competence and financial soundness
Monitoring how these standards are met in practice	When problems arise, investigation takes place and, if appropriate, disciplinary action or prosecution results
Promoting public understanding of the financial system	Communications and publicity to try to ensure that the consumer is more knowledgeable and can manage their financial affairs more effectively
Maintaining confidence in the UK financial system	Supervising exchanges, settlement houses and market infrastructure providers (IT, etc.), conducting market surveillance and monitoring transactions
Helping to reduce financial crime	Investigating cases that may involve money laundering, fraud and dishonesty and criminal market misconduct such as insider trading

- fining Interdependence Ltd £125,000 for serious failings in its supervision of representatives who were advising customers to withdraw cash early from their pension schemes
- fining Peter Bracken, former Head of Whitehead Mann Group, £15,000 for misusing unpublished confidential information for his personal gain (a profit, in fact, of £2,430 in share dealing).

Regulation and the public sector

The Audit Commission carries out a different form of regulation in the public sector. It is a true 'watchdog', carrying out investigations into the operations of local authorities, health services and government departments. It principally examines issues of efficiency and ethical behaviour, endeavouring to establish realisable targets and examples of best practice and to shame poor performers into change by publicising their faults. Although it has no executive power to change an organisation's policies or practices, the Government take note of its findings when it takes decisions over funding, especially with regard to local authorities. It has had a degree of success in leading public organisations to carefully examine their methods of operation and benchmark their performance against that of similar bodies.

Regulation and other sectors

Although most sectors operate without a specific regulator, they are touched by regulation in a number of ways, as follows.

- Their practices may be investigated by the OFT and Competition Commission, such as the doorstep selling example explained on pp. 86–91.

- A planned merger or takeover can be referred to the Competition Commission to decide if it breaches the monopolies guidelines, such as was threatened in the 2003 battle over Safeway Plc. Here, the OFT decided that the purchase of Safeway by Morrisons would be allowed without a full Commission investigation because the combined sales did not reach 25 per cent and the geographical coverage was different. Tesco's bid, however, would not be allowed because competition in some areas would have been substantially reduced and the combined sales would have breached 25 per cent.

- Their detailed operations can be constrained by UK or European law in areas such as labelling and packaging, information to consumers or environmental regulations.

- Planning laws have become increasingly intrusive, such as the government policy in 2000 to reject any further out-of-town shopping developments, including supermarkets, because of their effect on traffic growth and decline of the local high street.

Codes of practice

Each of the regulators is authorised to produce codes of practices. Ofgen, for example, have produced a code of practice for the action that should be taken when a provider proposes to cut off a consumer's gas or electricity supply and Ofcom has a Code of Advertising Practice. These codes do not in themselves have a force of law but they have strong influence on business behaviour. They help to raise standards throughout the industry, stopping organisations from indulging in dubious practices which, although not illegal, give the industry a bad name. Many organisations are happy to accept and influence the production of a code rather than having legal restrictions imposed on them.

ACTIVITY 5.7

What are the benefits of a regulatory system as opposed to a state-controlled system?

KEY LEARNING POINTS

- UK Law can be divided into criminal and civil law and originates chiefly from legislation emanating from the European Union, the UK parliament and Common Law. Courts are bound by precedent.

- The last 30 years have seen a substantial increase in the volume and intensity of legislation to protect employees and consumers with increased regulation of business activity.

- The burden of this legislation has been borne by businesses, which need to adapt their operations to ensure compliance.

- A larger emphasis has been put on organisations carrying out safety audits and risk assessment to ensure accident prevention and a healthier workplace.

- Few sectors now manage to avoid a form of regulation with a substantial presence in the privatised utilities and the financial and communications sectors where regulators have considerable legal powers.

- Consumers are also protected through the regulation of markets to prevent the use of monopolistic powers by large organisations.

Demography

INTRODUCTION

Demography looks at populations – their sizes, characteristics and the way they change. It sounds like a dry and academic subject but that is far from the truth. Population changes throughout the ages have been one of the major determining factors in economic development, political activity and social change. A growth in population can have a number of consequences. It can lead to wars, such as when the Roman Empire constantly fought with the barbarians in the search to extend its boundaries to secure more extensive food supplies for its growing population, or to the hordes sweeping out of Mongolia and the Far East a few centuries later. It can also lead to extensive economic growth. It was only possible for the industrial revolution to get under way in the UK factories in the late eighteenth century with the growing supply of surplus labour from the countryside, following the enclosure movement and technological agricultural developments. Nor would the vast choice of international food and restaurants we enjoy today have happened without the post-war migratory patterns, first from the new commonwealth countries, followed by young entrepreneurs from all around the world.

OBJECTIVES

By the end of this chapter, readers should be able to understand, explain and critically evaluate:

- **the key demographic statistics in a local, national, European and international setting**

- **the important effects produced by changes in demographic influences**

- **how demography has major influences on businesses and government, who need to respond in a positive way**

- **the appropriateness of responses by business and government to take advantage of major demographic changes.**

POPULATION GROWTH

In the year 1000, world population is estimated to have been at around 300 million. It grew slowly over the next 750 years to 728 million in 1750. Over the next 250 years, there was a spectacular growth, with a doubling of population to 1,500 million by 1900 and a further doubling to 3 billion by 1960. It has taken only 40 years for the population to double again to 6 billion.

The breakdown by continent of the growth from 1800 to 2000 is shown in Table 6.1.

Table 6.1 *World population 1800 to 2000 (millions)*

Year	1800	1850	1900	1950	2000
Asia	635	809	947	1,402	3,683
Africa	107	111	133	224	784
Europe	203	276	408	547	729
Latin America and Caribbean	24	38	74	166	519
North America	7	26	82	172	310
Oceania	2	2	6	13	30
World total	978	1,262	1,650	2,524	6,055

It can be seen that the growth in population has not been consistent across the world. Up until 1900, population increased rapidly in the developing world, but stayed relatively subdued in the poorer developing world. Since 1900, the bulk of the world population growth has been in the developing world with an astonishing tripling of population in Africa and Latin America since 1950. This has been accompanied by a rapid slowing in growth in the developed world, especially in Europe, with some countries, such as Germany, showing an absolute decline in recent years.

In the UK, as shown in Table 6.2, the spurt in population took place in the nineteenth century and has slowed considerably since 1900 with growth in Scotland almost negligible. The effects of the potato famine and lack of industrial development in Ireland can be seen with an actual decline in population from 1851 to 1901 when vast numbers of young people left Ireland to go to the English mainland, America and the colonies. In fact, Ireland has also reversed the UK trend with a considerable growth in population since 1951, reflecting a more buoyant agricultural and industrial economy arising principally from joining Europe in 1973; greater economic opportunities have also halted mass migration abroad.

Table 6.2 *UK population (thousands)*

Year	1801	1851	1901	1951	2001
England	8,305	16,764	30,515	41,159	50,035
Wales	587	1,163	2,013	2,599	2,988
Scotland	1,608	2,889	4,472	5,096	5,258
Northern Ireland		1,443	1,237	1,371	1,701
Total	10,500	22,259	38,237	50,225	59,982

Drivers of population change

Taking the world as a whole, the only two factors controlling population change are the level of the *birth rate* and the level of the *death rate.* Within any particular country or region, another factor is important, namely the *migration into and out of* that country or region.

Birth rate

The *birth rate* is usually expressed in terms of the number of live births per 1,000 population. The fertility rate is the average number of births for each woman of child-bearing age. A rate of 2.1 is required to maintain the population over an extended period of time, excluding migration.

Table 6.3 *Birth statistics – UK*

	Actual births – average for decade (thousands)	Fertility rate
1900	1,091	3.5
1931	824	1.8
1951	839	2.2
1961	962	2.6
1971	736	2.0
1981	757	1.8
1991	744	1.7
2001	639 (estimate)	1.8

Source. Office of population censuses/ Office for national statistics

The birth rate is determined by:

- the number of women in the population who are of child-bearing age and
- the proportion of this group of women who actually have children.

It is clear from Table 6.3 that there has been a steady drop in the birth rate since 1900, with the exception of a baby boom in the 1960s (plus a similar shorter boom in the period 1946-49). The birth rate has mirrored the fertility rate, although the latter has had greater variations. It is currently well below 2.1 and this has been the main cause of the slowing down in the rate of population growth. However, in the early part of the twenty-first century, there are indications that the fertility rate is starting to gently rise again.

Table 6.4 provides a comparison of the UK with other countries in terms of fertility rate, showing that it is generally higher than for the rest of Europe, but lower than for most developing countries.

Table 6.4 *World fertility rates in 2003 – selected countries*

Russia	1.2	Bangladesh	3.3	USA	2.0	**Averages**	
Spain	1.1	Greece	1.1	Germany	1.3	Developing countries	3.9
China	1.8	Sweden	1.6	Switzerland	1.5	Developed countries	1.4
Canada	1.6	Australia	1.8	UK	1.6		

Source: United Nations (2005)

The suggested causes of the reduced fertility rate are as follows.

- Women are taking charge of their fertility. The widespread use of the contraceptive pill and other modern devices from the 1970s onwards allowed decisions to be taken on family planning unheard of previously. Many women (and couples) have decided not to have families or to have just one child, often so that two careers can be pursued. This is connected with postponing starting a family until later. Having children usually brings a savage reduction in household income as one member, usually the mother, may stop working or go part-time.

- It is no longer necessary to have a large family as an insurance against obtaining care in older age. The extended family has generally declined in importance as the state has stepped in to provide or support services that have traditionally been carried out by family members.

- The cost of bringing up families has risen, especially if university costs are expected, so the average expenditure on children has not fallen with the birth rate – it is simply a case of each child representing a larger financial investment, despite government financial incentives.

- In the wider world, children are no longer as useful as they once were. Fewer people live on farms where children can help out and child labour, although still as area of international concern, is far less prevalent and strong attempts have been made to eradicate this practice in recent years.

Death rate

As measured by deaths per 1,000 population, the UK rate has fallen from 23 in 1851 to 11 in 2000. The advances of medicine, reduced infant mortality and generally improved health, clean water supply and sanitation facilities have allowed life expectancy to increase, as shown in Table 6.5.

Table 6.5 *Life expectancy in the UK*

UK life expectancy	Male	Female
1901	48	52
1950	66	72
1990	72	78
2002	76	80

The UK life expectancy is around the European average but some developed countries such as Japan and Singapore exceed our rates. So, as people live longer, the death rate falls. The actual number of deaths, however, has not fallen by the same proportion because the population has substantially increased over this period. In 1900, the number of UK deaths was 624,000 and the figure for 2004 was 514,000.

The picture is not rosy throughout the world. 28 per cent of all countries have a life expectancy of less than 60. There are still Sub-Sahara African countries where societies live with the appalling situation of life expectancy being less than 50 with the worst example – Sierra Leone – currently only 39 for women and as low as 36 for men. On top of poor health, there are numerous outbreaks of war, disease (especially HIV/AIDS) while poor living conditions are very common.

In developed countries, the main feature of a dropping death rate is the rapid ageing of the population with a rapid growth in the numbers over retirement age.

Migration

The third factor determining population levels is the number of people migrating into or out of a country. Clearly, if more people enter a country than leave it, then the population will rise. International migration has always been substantial. Man's original ancestors migrated out of Africa to populate the world and most of North and South America, Oceania and parts of Southern Africa have been colonised by migrants who have replaced the small indigenous populations.

It has been estimated that about 125 million people live outside their country of birth or citizenship (Martin and Widgren 1996). Political, social, economic and environmental upheavals have been the spur to large-scale movements. Religious dissention encouraged puritan migration to America in the seventeenth and eighteenth centuries and persecution has forced Jewish populations to leave their homelands, be it Russia in the nineteenth century or Germany under the Nazis. Owing to very poor economic and social prospects, the Irish migrated all over the world for 150 years, Chinese labour was used to build the American railroads and much of Dubai's current building boom uses Nepalese and Indian skilled craftsmen. Britain eagerly recruited in the West Indies and the Indian sub-continent in the early post-war years to staff the health service and public transport when local labour was in short supply. At the same time, there was a substantial outflow of skilled labour to take up new lives in Australia, Canada, New Zealand and South Africa, often under 'assisted passages' incentives.

On a world scale, certain migration paths are especially important as Dicken explains:

> " ... there are massive movements across the Mexico–United States border and from parts of Asia to the United States. Australia has become an important focus of migration from South East Asia ... and from countries around the Mediterranean to Germany."
>
> Dicken (2003), p521

In general terms, the twentieth century has seen far more restrictions placed upon migrants by governments fearful of the economic and social consequences of mass immigration. Although immigration was never easy (both America and Australia veered towards operating a 'whites only' policy for decades) the latter half of the twentieth century has seen severe restrictions imposed by countries all over the world.

In the case of the UK, the Commonwealth Immigration Act in the mid-1950s imposed limitations on free entry for mostly ethnic would-be migrants and subsequent legislation tightened the regulations further. Commonwealth immigration dropped sharply from 150,000 per annum to a third of this within a few years and has continued at around this rate since that time. However, since the mid-1990s, the net inflow of migrants has escalated substantially as shown in Table 6.6.

Table 6.6 *Average annual migration into and out of the UK 1989 to 2002 (thousands)*

	1989–1993			1994–1998			1999–2000		
	Inflow	Out	Net	Inflow	Out	Net	Inflow	Out	Net
New Commonwealth	50	26	24	49	23	26	71	23	48
Old Commonwealth	53	58	–5	57	51	6	84	68	16
European Union	66	61	5	84	62	22	83	80	3
USA	25	35	–10	30	25	5	23	27	–4
Middle East	9	11	–2	11	9	2	12	11	1
Rest of Europe	12	9	3	13	12	1	17	10	7
South America	2	3	–1	3	3	0	5	3	2
Africa & Others	24	19	5	29	19	11	86	56	30
All countries	241	222	19	276	204	73	381	278	103

Where the figure is negative, a net outflow of population is indicated. These figures show the substantial rise in migration in recent years. From a net balance of only 19,000 per annum in the four years up to 1993, this has risen to 103,000 by 2000, which continued to rise sharply to 160,000 in 2002. The increases have been from all areas of the world including, surprisingly, the Old Commonwealth countries, such as Australia.

There has been a significant rise recently in asylum seekers to the UK which totalled 76,000 in 2000 rising to 103,000 in 2002. Government action to speed up the system of dealing with applications has caused some reduction in applications but not eliminated the total. Only around 20 per cent of asylum seekers have their application accepted but many are able to stay in the UK while their appeal is heard, which can take many months.

The reasons for the increasing numbers of migrants include the following.

- Britain's economic performance in since the mid-1990s has been very positive, better than for most of Europe.
- There is a strong culture of entrepreneurship, with open opportunities for small businesses to flourish, perhaps more so than other parts of Europe, although not so strong as in America.
- There are established ethnic communities from all parts of the world, allowing greater ease of transition and community support.

- The number of low-paid unskilled jobs available is very high, especially in the hospitality, caring and building industry. Some are in the black economy, encouraging asylum seekers and illegal immigrants.

- In the education field, there has been a huge growth in undergraduate and post-graduate courses taken up by international students, who are able to help their financing through part-time work.

Europe has been faced with a similar situation. While the UK's number of asylum seekers represents 1.7 per cent of the population, Sweden's 33,000 represents nearly 4 per cent, while Austria has a figure of 5 per cent. Asylum seekers to France and Germany are currently running at around half the UK rate.

Ethnicity of population

An inevitable development of the increase in migration has been a growth in the ethnic variation in most developed countries. In the UK, around 7 per cent of the population, around 4.0 million, are from ethnic minorities, double the figure in the 1970s. The largest group are from the Indian subcontinent – around 55 per cent of the total, while West Indians make up a further 15 per cent (actually a declining proportion as many retire back to their countries of origin), with the remainder from Africa, Asia and the Middle East.

Those from ethnic minorities have generally settled over the years in urban localities, with large congregations in inner East London boroughs and towns in the Midlands and the North. As a whole, they have a lower age profile with a much smaller percentage aged over 65, chiefly because migrants tend to be in lower age categories. Also, many migrants retire to their countries of origin. The effects of the increase in ethnic minority sectors is discussed in Chapter 7.

Ethnicity of population is far greater in the United States, as shown in Case Study 6.1.

CASE STUDY 6.1

'Latinos' are a major force in the US economy

People of Hispanic origin ('latinos', as many prefer to be called) make up 12 per cent of the US workforce today but this will become at least 25 per cent in 50 years' time, owing to their much larger families and current age profile. They originate from across Latin America but predominantly Mexico, and their growth rate is 3 per cent per annum, compared to 0.8 per cent for the rest of America. As a group, they are a key catalyst for economic growth. In some of the larger cities, such as Los Angeles, they make up the majority of the under-18 age set. Their disposable income jumped 29 per cent from 2001 to 2004, double the rate for the rest of the population and they have a growing influence on all consumer patterns, especially food, clothes and entertainment.

The latino boom brings a welcome charge to the economy at a time when others countries' population growth has slowed to a crawl. Without a steady supply of new workers and consumers, a greying USA might see a long-term slowdown along the lines of ageing Japan.

Yet this demographic change produces potential problems. One of the major issues relates to language. With a huge Spanish-speaking minority, there could be pressures for recognition of an official second language, much as French is in Canada today. This could harm assimilation and encourage a form of separatism in states such as California, just like it has been a major cause of conflict in Quebec.

Another issue is the perception that large numbers of poorly educated, non-English speakers undermine the US economy. Although the steady influx of low-skilled workers helps keep America's gardens tended and floors cleaned, those workers also exert downward pressure on wages, causing friction with other groups of workers in this sector.

Source: Business Week (2004)

Migration is a very emotive subject, bringing to the mix a number of political, economic, social and psychological issues. Broadly speaking, there are a set of reasons for encouraging migration and another set for discouraging it, as follows.

Encouraging migration

- We live in a global economy and we need to make the best use of all talents from whatever the source.
- Migrants have energy and enthusiasm and a willingness to succeed. They have made a substantial effort to move from their home country and practice indicates that they are motivated to work hard.
- Most migrants are in the age group 18-40 and, in an ageing population, it is important to have a good source of younger labour.
- Migrants can fill the low-skill jobs that are currently difficult to fill – they prevent wage rates rising too high.
- It is not unusual for migrant entrepreneurs to offer ethnic goods and services, which expands the market-place to be benefit of the consumer. Thai food and ethnic textiles are obvious examples.
- It is arguable that it is more beneficial for the UK economy for migrants to carry out work in the UK rather than that work to be outsourced to a migrant's home country.
- Why should migrants be prevented from benefiting from the UK's successful economy? – after all, for 200 years, the UK benefited from running the economies of its colonies so it is time for those benefits to be shared.

Discouraging migration

- The UK is very densely populated and an inflow of immigrants leads to pressure on housing and jobs.

■ Where there is a large source of low-skilled labour, it discourages employers from becoming more productive by automating production or innovating the services provided.

■ Too much migration encourages the black economy, which reduces tax revenue and is associated with crime.

■ The process of policing and administrating prospective migrants is very expensive and difficult to carry out efficiently and fairly.

■ Migrants can be socially marginalised, staying in their own communities, retaining their own cultures and religions and not integrating effectively. This can create social problems and difficulties with the next generation.

OTHER DEMOGRAPHIC CHANGES

Working population

The state of the mid-2004 UK labour market is shown in Table 6.7.

Table 6.7 *UK labour market 2004 (thousands)*

	Male	Female	Total
Employed	12,600	12,100	24,700
Self-employed	2,600	1,000	3,600
Total labour market	15,200	13,100	28,300
Part-time	1,600	5,700	7,300
Temporary	700	800	1,500
Unemployed			1,400
Economically active			29,700 (79%)
Economically inactive			7,800 (21%)

Compared to the early 1990s, there has been a growth of around 4 million in the total working population, made up of a natural growth in the population, a reduction in unemployment and an increase in the participation level. The rate of employment for women has risen much more steeply that for men, with the women's total rising by more than 2 million over the last 10 years. The steady fall in unemployment, which has halved in the same period, has also led to a more confident labour market, so the number of temporary employees has declined. The number of people self-employed has stayed steady in risen years, having increased substantially in the 1980s under the Thatcher period, when entrepreneurial activity was strongly encouraged.

The decline in the birth rate leading to an ageing population has already affected the size and nature of the potential working population, those within the age range 16 to 60 or 65. Table 6.8 shows this starkly.

Table 6.8 *UK population – age distribution 1901 to 2026 (%)*

	Under 16	16–24	25–44	45–64	Over 65
Males					
1901	34	20	28	15	4
1931	26	18	29	21	7
1961	25	14	27	25	9
1991	21	14	30	22	13
2001	21	11	31	23	13
2011*	19	12	27	27	15
2026*	18	10	26	26	19
Females					
1901	31	20	28	15	6
1931	23	17	30	21	8
1961	22	13	25	26	14
1991	19	12	28	21	18
2001	20	10	29	23	18
2011*	18	11	26	26	18
2026*	17	10	25	26	22

* forecast

Source: Office for National Statistics

In Table 6.8 it is shown that the younger male working population, age 16–44, has fallen from 48 per cent of the population in 1901 to 39 per cent in 2001 and is expected to decline further to 36 per cent by 2026 with the same picture for women. The percentage in the age group 16–24 has actually halved. On the other hand, there has been a considerable growth in the older employees groups. In fact, the number of employees aged 50 to 59 (women) and 64 (men), has increased by 1.3 million (about 26 per cent) in the 10 years up to 2004. Not all pensioners are an immediate drain on the economy as many choose to work after retirement age. There are around a million in this category, a figure that has risen by 34 per cent over the last 10 years.

Given that far more young people go on to further and higher education, with the government target of 50 per cent attending some form of higher education, this reduces the younger working population even further.

ACTIVITY 6.1

A development in the working population in recent years has been the growth of what is known as 'atypical employment', which is not full-time 9 to 5 employment. It covers part-time, shift-work, teleworking and a host of variable working arrangements. What are the driving forces for this growth?

Participation rates

People used to work until they reached pensionable age (many, of course, did not last that long, worn out by heavy industrial work or poor diets). As late as 1975, 84 per cent of men aged 60–64 were 'economically active' in the UK but this fell to 50 per cent by 1994. This was chiefly the result of the recession in the early 1990s when many older men lost their jobs and found it difficult to obtain alternative employment. Many were disabled and obtained disability benefits, which are higher than unemployment benefits. Organisations also encouraged older employees to take early retirement, sometimes providing generous redundancy payments or enhanced pensions.

By the early 2000s, this position was changing. For example, in the 12 months to December 2004, the number of people age 50 and over in employment rose by 190,000, including a 73,000 increase in those over retirement age. Participation rates for men age 50 to 64 rose from 65 to 72 per cent from 1995 to 2003 and for those over retirement age it has risen from 7.5 to 9.2 per cent (Economist 2004). This is partly to do with the prosperous economy wherein many part-time jobs are available, especially in the service sector, and partly to do with the decline in pension prospects arising from the stock market crash of 2000, the value of personal pensions having declined by as much as 50 per cent as a result.

For women, there has been a substantial increase in the participation rate, rising from 63 per cent in 1979 to 74 per cent in 2004. Women have developed their careers, continued at work while raising a family or returned to work much sooner than in previous decades. They have also taken up new careers and skills through obtaining qualifications, many via some form of government initiative. Other support has come through the strengthening equal opportunity legislation, where the barriers to women's employment and development have been steadily removed.

The growth in European participation rates mirrors the UK situation, although the average rate was still lower at 78 per cent for men and 60 per cent for women in 2000. In France, for example, the male rate was 75 per cent and female 62 per cent while the Italian rate for women was as low as 46 per cent in the same year.

ACTIVITY 6.2

Two organisations, described below, have just set up in an area of high unemployment and low participation, with the support of various government grants and loans.

Jones Supermarkets have set up a regional distribution centre to employ 450 staff in warehousing and logistics positions on 24/7 operations.

Williams Toys and Games have established a manufacturing and distributing centre to employ 200 staff. There is a seasonal element to the work so a number of staff will be working flexibly, including evening shifts and weekends for the busy autumn period. Most of the toys and games are imported finished or semi-finished so the work is essentially unskilled and semi-skilled and involves a high element of packing and distribution.

Given that setting up in the area will help reduce the unemployment rate, are there ways in which the organisations can help further improve the participation rate?

Sectoral employment

The number of people working in *manufacturing* has been declining since the 1950s where it stood at over 6 million. The 1990s, however, saw a particularly steep drop both in real terms and as a percentage of total employment as shown in Table 6.9.

Table 6.9 *Sectoral employment 1993 to 2004 (thousands)*

	1993	**2004**	**Change**
Manufacturing	3,952	3,360	−592
Construction	966	1,260	+296
Service sector	17,419	20,994	+3,575
Sections of the service sector			
Warehousing/retailing	3,906	4,572	+666
Hotels, catering	1,360	1,785	+425
Post, telecommunications	437	551	+114
Real estate	256	367	+117
IT, renting, research, etc.	2,546	3,587	+1,041
Public administrations	1,467	1,500	+33
Education	1,892	2,293	+401
Health	2,511	2,942	+431
Other community/ personal needs	1,069	1,375	+92
Financial services (banks, etc.)	1,014	1,094	+80

Every part of the service sector has increased with the sharpest increases (more than 25 per cent) in hotels and catering, telecommunications, real estate, IT associated business activities and community/personal needs. This, of course, is a reflection of the changing pattern of consumer demand: we spend much more money on leisure activities – staying away from home, eating out, talking on the phone and visiting the hairdressers. In fact the highest rate of growth of any individual work activity from 1990 to 2002 was seen in hairdressing. We are also obsessed with our houses, hence the increased numbers employed in estate agencies and associated activities.

But the biggest increase of all is the category involving computer-related jobs (although this category is a rather vague one and does include some non-computer activities), which has shown a rise of 40 per cent. This will reinforce what you will read in Chapter 8 on Technology where IT developments (automation, communications) have replaced the need for skilled and unskilled labour in manufacturing. The major improvements in productivity have all taken place in this sector so output has risen, prices have come down and overall industrial employment has diminished. Also, much of the manufacturing has migrated to parts of the world where labour is cheaper and the products are then imported into the UK.

ACTIVITY 6.3

Consider the scenario wherein the main manufacturing employer in a country town, employing 1500 staff, announces it is closing down. What are the implications for the local economy? What are the overall implications for the UK of the decline in manufacturing employment?

Changes in family structure

The move to smaller families and a higher participation rate for women has led to changes in the structure of families and the role of family members. Working women (especially those in full-time work) spend less time in domestic routines, which has led to a considerable growth in industries devoted to convenience foods, eating out and hired-in domestic help. Information from the Family Expenditure Survey shows that the proportion of income spent on eating out has increased by 50 per cent over the period 1980 to 2000. The changes in the labour market have led to changes in the nature of society, as shown in Research Focus 6.1.

RESEARCH FOCUS 6.1

Changing society in South Wales

Doreen Massey carried out a survey of the implications of the massive closures of the steel and coal-mining industries in the early 1980s and identified the difference between the former labour market, which was heavily male-dominated with a high proportion of manual and semi-skilled labour, and the new labour market that has grown up with economic re-structuring. The latter was typified by new jobs in the electronics industries and a high level of female employment. The previous labour market had created a patriarchal society that had remained relatively stable over many generations. The new market offered less stability and less security and led to changes in social patterns and family organisation.

Source: Massey (1984)

ACTIVITY 6.4

What actions can the Government take to mitigate the negative consequences of areas of declining manufacturing?

Other changes have involved the caring responsibilities for children becoming more shared between spouses, while there are many examples of active grandparents taking a substantial responsibility for day-to-day care of younger children.

On the other hand, there is the challenge of looking after older relatives, with around half living into their 80s and many into their 90s and beyond. In the past, many have lived-in, creating an extended family setup, but, in Europe, this practice is declining (although it is still the norm in Japan). The need for a degree of personal privacy, the day-to-day medical and psychological challenges of coping with an elderly relative and the widespread growth in sheltered accommodation have been reasons for this trend.

Another trend has been the decline in marriage, as shown by Figure 6.1.

1970	415,000
1980	370,000
1990	331,000
2001	286,000

Figure 6.1 *Marriages in the UK*

This is not just a UK phenomenon. In Scandinavia, over 50 per cent of children are now born out of wedlock (Kurtz 2004). The issue of declining marriages and rising divorces (157,000 in 2001) will be discussed further in Chapter 7 but the rising number of single-parent families and the dependence of many such families on the benefits system, which is especially strong in the UK, presents a further financial challenge to governments as well as implications for housing provision and, in certain areas, an effect on crime (Haskey 1993).

Changes in geographical population location

A final aspect of demography is the internal movement of population within countries. For over 200 years, there has been a steady movement away from the land and into the cities around the world as agriculture has become mechanised and farms have undergone consolidation. In the last 100 years or so, this movement has extended in certain countries to widespread geographical patterns. In Italy, there has been a mass movement from the poor, rural South to the more prosperous urban North. In the UK, the movement is in the opposite direction with a general move from the industrial areas, especially in the North, to the more balanced economies of the South and East (Stilwell, Rees and Boden 1992). The population of the north-eastern counties of England actually dropped in the 1990s and population increases in Yorkshire and Lancashire were quite small. On the other hand, counties in the south-east, such as Cambridgeshire, increased by 10 per cent or more in population as an estimated 250,000 citizens moved from north to south (Brindle 1999).

AND THE FUTURE?

If the world's population were to continue to increase at its current rate, all estimates show such a growth to be completely unsustainable. Food and energy would run out, leading to the Malthusian nightmares of war, pestilence and disease, causing a decline in population to sustainable levels. Economists have been divided as to the scenario in 2050 with some estimates of population at 10 billion and still growing and other economists indicating a more conservative outcome. Happily, those with an optimistic viewpoint are becoming more plentiful. At a 2002 United Nations conference, the director of the population division, Joseph Chamie, confidently predicted a peak of 8 billion at 2040 followed by a falling world population at 2050 for the first time since the Black Death.

The conference was called to discuss the implications of unexpectedly fast declines in fertility in dozens of countries, including some very large ones. Mexico, India and Brazil have all forecast a decline in their birth rate below replacement level within 20 years. The assumption that, as nations developed their economies, women settle down to 2.4 children, now appears erroneous. Women in developing countries appear to be to striving for the freedoms achieved in the developed countries where the decisions open include deciding not to have a family at all or just one child. Bangladeshi women today have 3.3 children while the Vietnamese have halved their fertility rate in 10 years to 2.3, just above the replacement level (Pearce 2002). A continuation of the trend for fewer births will automatically result in eliminating population growth.

There is also a question mark over increasing life expectancy. It is still likely that we can all expect to live a little longer every decade but AIDS has had a serious effect in sub-Saharan Africa and is spreading its tentacles into other areas with a rapid growth in HIV in Eastern Europe, South America and the Far East. So the increase in life expectancy, although having in itself important consequences, will only marginally influence the long-term decline in population.

In the UK, the apparent slow but steady decline in the fertility rate will inevitably bring to an end the natural population growth, probably around 2035 or 2040 when it will peak at around 66 million, according to latest predictions. However, the Government Actuary's Department has reported that life expectancy is growing faster than previous predictions and should rise to 81 for men and 85 for women by 2030 (Doward 2003). If this occurs, then the population will continue to grow for a little longer, although the average age of the population will rise.

However, there is no doubt that *the population will become older*. In 2030, 15 million people will be over current pensionable age, compared to 11 million now. As early as 2007, there will be more pensioners than children. The average age is set to rise from 38.8 in 2000 to 42.6 in 2025.

The factor that is unknown is the net migration effect, which depends on government policy and the way the policy works out in practice. One government estimate is that net migration will be as high as 135,000 per year for the next 25 years (Baird 2001), adding over 3 million to the population over this period.

To summarise, over the next 20 years the world population will continue to grow rapidly but this growth will then start to taper off and will probably reverse by the mid-century point. Populations in developed countries will become distinctly older and internationally diverse. Populations in developing countries will also age but from a very low base figure and will become internationally mobile.

IMPLICATIONS OF DEMOGRAPHIC PREDICTIONS

As indicated at the start of this chapter, demographic trends will have substantial implications across the world at local, national and international levels. We will examine these implications in outline for the following groups:

- organisations, especially in the UK private sector
- governments, especially the UK Government
- international society.

IMPLICATIONS FOR ORGANISATIONS

A slow-down in population growth and an ageing population has effects both on the nature of the market-place and on sources of labour. Adaptations to their current business practices could take the following forms.

Sources of labour: With far fewer school leavers and younger people generally, organisations will have to look elsewhere for labour, particularly if the economy continues to grow steadily under the full employment conditions we have seen in the late 1990s and early 2000s. Alternative sources may involve moving away from the traditional full-time 9- to-5 job design and moving to a more flexible model where much greater use is made of part-time jobs, job shares, flexible hours and working from home. These flexible modes can meet the working needs of those with caring responsibilities, principally (but not exclusively) women, and older people generally who are retired or semi-retired. Some retailers, such as B & Q and Tesco, have specifically targeted older potential staff, which has led not just to an easing of recruitment difficulties but to considerable customer satisfaction arising from the knowledge such staff bring to the job. As a spokesperson for Nationwide Building Society explained:

> **" Many customers prefer dealing with more maturity and experience and older workers tend to be more loyal and committed. "**
>
> *The Economist* **2004**

An example of a local authority following the same path is shown in Case Study 6.2 involving Bridgend Borough Council.

CASE STUDY 6.2

Age positive success at Bridgend Borough Council

In the late 1990s, Bridgend Council began to appreciate the growing demographic effects as their employees' average age had risen to 41 and the reduced number of school leavers were being snapped up by major competitors in the area, such as by Sony and Ford. Action was needed to ensure the continued maintenance of a skilled workforce and to ensure that suitable employment was available, irrespective of age.

Recent initiatives have included:

- the abolition of age limits in advertisements
- eliminating the date of birth on the application form
- employees who work beyond their normal retirement ages able to continue to contribute towards their pension scheme up the maximum of 40 years' service
- introducing a mentoring scheme that will involve those who intend to retire coaching younger employees to ensure valuable skills are not lost
- ignoring an employee's age when considering training and development opportunities.

What has been more important is the changing culture where being 'Age Positive' is built into the way the Council is run, where it is seen as open-minded, flexible and committed to people's development. For example, employees are encouraged to continue working so long as everybody is comfortable. This has worked well in areas such as social care where maturity can be a positive benefit and with specialist positions, such as continuing to employ a fitness instructor (well into his 70s) on a part-time basis.

Success in this area has been recognised by a national award from Age Positive – the government body campaigning to tackle workplace ageism.

Source: Persaud (2004)

 Originally published in *People Management* 29 July 2004, and reproduced with permission

It is also unlikely that the offers of early retirement with enhanced pensions will be so generous in the future. The UK Government has already moved away from funding such arrangements centrally, requiring each department or agency to bear the costs involved. This has already led to a substantial reduction in such offers and employees choosing early retirements now mostly have to fund this out of their own pension schemes.

Change in markets: As the patterns of population change, their consumer needs alter accordingly. With an ageing population, there will be a *decline* in demand for products for the young, such as baby foods and prams and, eventually, for products for teenagers and the age group 18–25. The brewing industry has seen a substantial decline in the demand for beer as the largest consumers have traditionally been those aged 18–25, a declining age group, although their drinking habits have also changed. Similarly, sales of teenage fashion goods – clothes, compact disks, jewellery – have become sluggish in recent years. Although the per capita spending has increased as the general level of prosperity has risen, it does not make up for the reduced population in these age brackets.

On the other side of the equation, there are some sectors of industries which *gain* from an ageing population. The most dramatic change is seen in the travel and tourism industry as older people spend a higher proportion of their income on holidays than most other groups. For a number of cyclical reasons, they also have become a much more wealthy segment of the community. Saga, floated on the stock market for close to £1 billion in 2004, is the clearest winner, providing a vast range of holidays – active and inactive – for a growing market, broadening their product range to insurance and other financial services. Stannah lifts has become another household name while magazines devoted to older readers (such as *Yours*) have substantially increased their circulations.

ACTIVITY 6.5

Summarise the effects of an ageing population on the tourism, retailing and banking industries.

Housing presents an interesting reflection of demographic changes. Although the population is now growing only slowly, the price of houses has risen substantially owing, mostly, to a somewhat unexpected higher demand. This has come about because, as the fertility rate drops and the population ages, there is no corresponding drop in the number of households. Whereas young children live with their parents, older people live mostly in their own housing unit. Many stay in their own homes looking after themselves to the end, or nearly the end, of their lives, assisted by a benefits system that encourages such behaviour. Add to this the increase in divorce which often creates additional demand for housing and the rise in students living away from home, and perhaps the rise in house prices is not so unexpected. Winners here have been the construction companies that provide retirement homes, such as McCarthy and Stone and property companies that invest in buy-to-rent.

Other clear winners in the demographic stakes are those who market *products specifically for the elderly*. Anything from mobility products to products aimed at improving healthcare, from pharmaceutical products to private hospitals. The same reasoning can be applied to the next age group down – call it 'middle age' – where their demands for financial services (savings products, pensions) and some luxury products (Mercedes cars, boats and homes in the sun) have grown very strongly in recent years.

IMPLICATIONS FOR GOVERNMENTS, ESPECIALLY THE UK GOVERNMENT

For governments, the biggest potential difficulty arising from the ageing population is the increase in the *dependency ratio* (see definition).

DEFINITION

Dependency ratio

The dependency ratio is the ratio of working-age population to the dependent population.

The dependent population is children under 16 and older people over retirement age.

As the proportion of the population over retirement age increases, it puts a much greater strain on the working population who need to fund the services for older people. As detailed above, there has been a much greater reliance on the state for looking after older people. There is no doubt a far greater strain will be with us soon, as Figure 6.2 indicates.

1901	12.5
1931	10.0
1961	5.5
1991	4.3
2001	4.3
2011	4.1
2026	3.2

Figure 6.2 *UK dependency ratio – ratio of 16–64-year-olds to over-65s*

Figure 6.2 (which does not take into account numbers of dependent children under 16) shows the startling change in dependency that has occurred already and will get worse in the future.

Currently just over four employees provide earned income to support one pensioner. This will decline to just over three by 2026. The position is worse for other countries. For Germany and Japan, the ratio will be less than three by the same year and it is estimated that the rate for Germany will be around two by 2040.

The problem for governments is how to raise the increased revenue required from what could be a dwindling resource of working-age population. It has been estimated that each pensioner costs the government around £10,000 per year, net of any tax receipts, through the old-age pension, a variety of benefits (housing, disability, etc.) and the vast range of medical care available (primary care, free prescriptions, hospital stays). Older people are much more prone to illness and therefore impose much greater costs on the health services. It could be argued that some of the additional money required can be raised by savings on services to young people with reduced expenditure on maternity units and compulsory schooling, although any closure or reduction in services is met by solid resistance from the community. One research estimate is that the additional required funding for health is about £1 billion a year, which can be saved by reducing school expenditure, but state pension provision will cost an additional £4 billion a year under existing arrangements (National Institute of Economic and Social Research, quoted in McCrone 1999). Because employees in their 40s and 50s earn more than employees in their 20s, it is expected that increased tax revenue will go some way towards filling this gap.

The *pension implications* are tough for the UK and America, but at least there is reasonable private pension provision that is located in properly funded systems. This, however, is the exception compared with the rest of the world. For most of Europe and other developed countries, the proportion of pensions paid by the state is very much higher and this is funded as transfer payments under a Pay As You Go (PAYG) basis, ie directly out of taxation income, rather than from an actual fund of money that has been invested.

Table 6.10 shows the implications for selected countries in terms of the huge government expenditure necessary to fund pensions as a proportion of GDP (gross domestic product).

Table 6.10 *Public pension expenditure as a percentage of GDP*

Year	1995	2020	2040
UK	4.5	5.2	7.1
USA	4.1	5.2	7.2
Netherlands	6.0	8.4	12.1
France	10.6	11.6	14.3
Sweden	11.8	13.9	14.9
Spain	10.0	11.3	16.8
Germany	11.1	12.3	18.4
Italy	13.3	15.3	21.4

Source: Eurostat

There are already substantial problems in France, Germany and Italy over the substantial public sector borrowing. The European Union attempted during 2002–04 to fine these countries as part of the stability pact arrangements made at the time of the establishment of the Euro to prevent governments incurring excessive expenditure in buying their way out of financial difficulties. Many commercial organisations are moving production out of these countries to the UK, Eastern Europe and the developing world to avoid existing high taxation rates. So how such pension liabilities can be met is sorely testing the economic advisers and central banks in these countries.

ACTIVITY 6.6

Not all writers regard the pension liabilities problem as insurmountable or see the necessity of huge increases in taxation or reductions in benefits to solve the pensions problem. What do you consider to be the basis for their optimism?

A further problem arises from *irregular internal migration*. Those parts of the country that attract population are faced by considerable pressures on housing, transport and infrastructure services. For example, the housing shortages in London and the South-East have produced continuous shortages in workers in the essential public services sector, especially teachers and nurses, who cannot find affordable housing, particularly early on in their careers. (Similar problems occur in the Milan and Turin areas of Northern Italy.) The UK Government is therefore faced with planning dilemmas. If it allows housing on green-belt land around London, massive opposition is stirred up. If new roads are built to alleviate traffic congestion, traffic merely increases within a short space of time and again clogs up the system (Champion 1993).

Finally, there are problems associated with the *skills base*. As Jackson (1998) explains:

> **One reason why the market has been unable to absorb the ... unemployed has been the increasing demand for employees with appropriate skills and capabilities. Gaining entry to the labour market has become more difficult as manual occupations have declined and as employers have become more selective about recruits to jobs in the service and quaternary sectors. Britain needs a better trained workforce if it is to meet the challenge from its competitors in Europe and overseas and the current skills gap means that many find themselves excluded from the opportunities of employment.**
>
> **Jackson (1998) p125**

Options for governments

Governments will need to either raise taxes or reduce benefits. Some countries have already taken bold steps, such as New Zealand abolishing the universal right to an old-age pension, and the UK Government is raising the age at which women can claim the pension to 65 by 2010. However, this can be very damaging politically and is not taken lightly. Certainly people can be encouraged to increase their savings for the future by making a larger contribution to their pension schemes, which is done by most governments. In Japan, this has been very successful and the Japanese are the highest savers in the world. (Incidentally, this high saving and reduced consumption has contributed to a prolonged recession in Japan through most of the 1990s and early 2000s.)

It is also likely that when the full effects of the higher dependency ratio reach the population as a whole, society will be much more affluent and willing to pay the additional costs as part of the understanding that a measure of the decency of a society is how it looks after vulnerable groups, such as the elderly.

An alternative approach is to attempt to reverse the demographic trends and to encourage bigger families. This can be done by providing greater financial incentives (tax reliefs and maternity/child benefits) and by encouraging organisations to be more family friendly so that women are able to combine motherhood and a job more easily. The problem is that such actions by governments, such as shown by Japan in Case Study 6.3, appear to have only a marginal effect on the indigenous population. Despite actions in similar forms by many governments in developed countries, it has done little to reverse the flagging fertility rate.

One form of drastic action could be to open the doors wider to migrants from developing countries. This makes a great deal of long-term economic sense but has a number of political obstacles to overcome in terms of the perceptions of migrants 'taking jobs' and the additional pressures on housing and transport.

CASE STUDY 6.3

Bribing mothers – the Japanese response

In 2002, the Japanese Government announced that every Japanese woman who gives birth is to receive the equivalent of £1,700 plus up to £15,000 worth of help with child care. The fact that this initiative is likely to cost around £5 billion indicates the degree of anxiety over the continuing decline in Japan's birth rate: it has been estimated that if it continues at its present rate, the population of Japan will halve by the year 2100. A rapidly ageing population, supported by fewer and fewer working people could keep Japan in a state of semi-permanent recession. It is estimated that if current trends continue, young people in 2025 will have to pay around 25 per cent of their salary as a tax to simply keep pensions at their current level.

The main difficulty is a cultural one. A rigid, male-orientated working structure, coupled with the traditional view that a woman's place is in the home, has come up against the career aspirations of women and has led them to indulge in a 'baby strike'. The perceived high financial, social and emotional costs of motherhood in Japan has not helped the situation. In Tokyo, the fertility rate has dropped to 1.0 while nationally it hovers around 1.33, well below the stable population figure.

It remains to be seen whether the financial inducements, the availability of 'baby shops' to help women with childcare and 'grandmother networks' to support young families will make any difference or whether women will continue to wait until their aspirations in the workplace have been better satisfied.

Source: Norton (2002)

One response to the overcrowding in some parts of a country has been to attempt to disperse government departments (as long ago as the early 1970s, the Department of National Savings was moved to Durham, for example) and to provide additional tax and benefit incentives to businesses to move to poorer regions, which is a major pillar of the European Union's economic policy.

Not everybody, however, insists that an ageing population is so great a problem. Mullan (2002) argues that demographic ageing has no determinate relationship to national economic activity and that modest levels of economic growth will be more than sufficient to create the wealth required to sustain the costs brought on by greater numbers of elderly dependents.

IMPLICATIONS FOR INTERNATIONAL SOCIETY

The global economy

The most worrying aspect of the current demographic changes is that a mature and ageing population appears to lead directly to reduced economic growth. Europe and Japan have seen the fastest decline in fertility rates and has also seen the slowest economic growth in the early twenty-first century. America, on the other hand, has had a milder strain to endure and has managed to maintain a faster growth rate over the period. In the 'Tiger' economies – China, Korea, Taiwan, and on the Indian sub-continent, where fertility rates, although falling, still remain at or above replacement level, there is a much higher rate of economic growth.

The United Nations has projected that America, with its higher fertility rate and greater levels of migration, will equal Europe's population by 2040 (currently it is 100 million less) and exceed it by 40 million by 2050. The economic implications are far-reaching. The working population of Europe will start to decline in 2010 but, for America, the current steady growth in its workforce will even start to *accelerate* in 2025. This will result in the US economy growing twice as fast as that of Europe for the next 50 years. In 2000, America accounted for 23 per cent of global gross domestic product (GDP) compared to Europe's 18 per cent. By 2050, the United Nations estimate America's share will be 26 per cent while Europe's will have shrunk to only 10 per cent. By 2050, the American economy will be 2.5 times as big as Europe's with all the additional political clout that this implies (Smallwood 2003).

In reality, the only way this situation could be reversed would be by radically changing Europe's tight immigration controls, which is a very unlikely event, or if America's fertility rate dropped sharply, as it becomes a mature economy.

International migration of work

In the early 2000s, Barclays Bank and other financial institutions announced that they would be cutting their workforces and transferring chunks of their customer service and 'back-office' administration work to other countries, particularly India. The costs of carrying out this work in developing countries is just a fraction of UK costs and the workforces are young, educated, English-speaking and flexible in their approach to working hours and the nature of the work. These decisions were made because the demographic changes, and the responses made by governments (India has invested heavily in English-language education) have made such countries good substitutes for UK-based labour.

CASE STUDY 6.4

Examples of German jobs exodus 2002–2004

Lufthansa: European ticket sales based in Cracow, Poland. Aircraft engines serviced in Hungary, China and the Philippines.

Motorola: 600 engineering jobs moved to China. Repair work moved to Eastern Europe.

Deutsche Bank: Deutsche Software subsidiary moved to India with 4,000 jobs.

SAP, business software and systems: Created 1,500 jobs in Bangalore, India and new 120 strong R&D centre in Shanghai.

Continental Tyres: Three German factories closed – work transferred to three new factories in Romania, Czech Republic and Slovakia.

Source: Woodhead (2004)

This situation has been replicated around the globe. In America, work migration is an important issue dividing the political parties, while German unions have had to respond to threats to move industrial work from factories such as Volkswagen to Eastern Europe by agreeing to reduce hourly wages (see Case Study 6.4).

ACTIVITY 6.7

In 2003, the South African Government placed a prohibition on UK companies recruiting qualified nurses to work in the NHS, viewing the exodus of skilled workers such as nurses as a matter of long-term disaster for the country. Do you agree with this viewpoint? Discuss the issue from both viewpoints.

WORLD'S RESOURCES

In the twentieth century, the inventiveness, organisational powers and application of technology from farmers, merchants, entrepreneurs and companies of all sizes, allowed the tripling world population to be adequately provided for in terms of food, water and power. Not completely of course, with intermittent famines and a growing imbalance between rich and poor countries. However, it had been considered unlikely that such expansion of resources could continue at this breakneck pace for another 100 years.

The forecasts of a levelling out of the population by mid-century must be regarded, therefore, as good news for everybody. The strains on space and exploitation of a limited land mass, especially where global warming appears to be reducing capacity, may now be much lessened, although these pressures are brought about not just by numbers of population but by their overall demands. A richer, more consuming population still has the capacity to wreak enormous damage on our planet's infrastructure.

KEY LEARNING POINTS

■ The major demographic trends across the world are a major decline in the birth rate, population ageing and increasing migration, both of people and jobs. These trends are strongest in the developed world, especially Europe.

■ These trends are likely to continue to produce a reversal of world population expansion around 2050. Developed countries are likely to be faced by declining populations before that time unless they change policies and allow higher rates of migration.

■ These demographic changes provide opportunities for organisation to move into new product and service areas. The reduction in the availability of younger labour means that organisations will need to re-organise work patterns to encourage greater participation from women, older people and other groups.

■ Governments will increasingly be faced by the need for higher expenditure on pensions, benefits and health services as a result of demographic changes. At the same time, the higher dependency ratio is likely to necessitate higher levels of taxation to finance this expenditure. Initiatives to combat these difficulties can include encouraging larger families through incentives, reducing benefits and stimulating personal savings for pensions and health.

■ It is likely that an ageing population will be less production-oriented, providing challenges for the world economy and wealth creation. There has been a rapid transferral of jobs and services around the world as an outcome of globalisation.

Social Trends

OBJECTIVES

By the end of this chapter, readers should be able to understand, explain and critically evaluate:

- major theories of social stratification

- the main socio-economic classifications used in the UK

- the nature and extent of social mobility in the UK

- reasons for the slowing rate of social mobility in the UK and its effects

- the extent and nature of inequality and poverty in the UK

- changes in the industrial and employment structure in the UK, and the growth of flexible forms of organisation

- the nature and importance of the psychological contract

- work-life balance

- similarities and differences between equal opportunities and diversity

- the changing nature and role of trade unions, particularly New Unionism.

INTRODUCTION

This chapter will analyse recent trends in society and social structure in the UK. We start with an analysis of social stratification, including a discussion of social class. We then analyse social mobility and inequality, and the continuing existence of poverty in the UK. We then look behind the class structure and analyse the factors which have led to social change, including changes in the industrial structure, the nature of work and attitudes to work. We conclude with an analysis of the current role and position of trade unions.

CLASS

Karl Marx

The concept of class as a social concept goes back to the writings of Karl Marx in the mid-nineteenth century. To Marx, class was related to ownership of the means of production. He divided society into two classes, the bourgeoisie, or capitalists, who owned the means of production, and the proletariat, wage workers, who owned only their own labour. The relationship between the two classes was one of exploitation. The capitalists, through their ownership of the means of production – factories, machines, etc., controlled the production process, and used this power to exploit the workers. In particular, the capitalists pocketed the difference between what they paid the workers and the value of the goods produced – what Marx called 'surplus value'.

One thing which will strike you immediately about Marx's analysis is that he recognises only two classes – capitalists and workers. There is no mention of the class which is generally seen as numerically dominant today, the middle class. This is inevitable given Marx's approach. You were either a 'have' (a capitalist) or a 'have-not' (a worker). He recognised that there were managers who ran the factories on behalf of the capitalists, and who would not see themselves as workers. These managers later became a key segment of the middle class, but Marx dismissed any aspirations which they had to separate themselves from the working class as 'false class consciousness'. In the last resort, he saw them as being as much pawns of the capitalists as the proletariat was.

Max Weber

The German sociologist Max Weber, writing at the end of the nineteenth century, argued that Marx's class system was over-simplistic. Class, based on the ownership of property, was important, but it was only one element of social stratification. Unlike Marx, he recognised a significant middle class, including the self-employed, civil servants, clerks and professionals. Weber argued that status and power were also important. Status is a measure of social standing, and refers to the way that society regards individuals and groups. For example, in many societies, doctors or teachers have a high social standing, based on their education and skills. Power is the ability to influence decisions, This is mainly to do with access to political power, which could be used to gain wealth and prestige, as in Italy in the 1980s, or much of Africa in the 1990s.

His concept of class was different from Marx's. Whereas Marx emphasised the ownership of property, Weber saw class as being much more a function of market capacity – the skills and attributes which individuals bring to the labour market, and which determine their success or failure.

Runciman has combined the Marxist and Weberian approaches by stressing the concept of economic power (Runciman 1990). He sees this as having three dimensions, as follows:

1 ownership – legal title to the means of production (nowadays more often through shared ownership rather than direct ownership

2 control – a contractual right to direct or manage the means of production (ie managers)

3 marketability – skills or capacity with a value in the labour market.

An individual's position in the social hierarchy can derive from any of these dimensions.

Putting the Marxist and Weberian models together, and incorporating Runciman's approach, we can produce a stratification system as follows (Table 7.1):

Table 7.1 *Stratification system based on Marxist and Weberian models*

Upper class:	Owners of the means of production Very advantageous life chances
Middle class:	Non-owners of direct productive wealth, but owners of personal wealth and some indirect productive wealth (houses, pension funds, unit trusts, etc.) Advantageous life chances due to market capacity from non-manual skills
Manual workers:	Non-owners of productive wealth, very little personal wealth Disadvantageous life chances due to falling demand for manual skills
Underclass:	Non-owners of any sort of wealth Grossly disadvantageous life chances due to marginal position in the labour market

Source: adapted from Bilton *et al* 1996

SOCIO-ECONOMIC CLASSIFICATIONS

There are several different ways in which social stratification is measured in the UK. One of these is the National Statistics Socio-economic Classifications Scale, (NS-NEC) used by the Government for the first time for the 2001 census. This divides the population into the following eight categories:

1 higher managerial and professional occupations; this is subdivided into:

1.1 employers and managers in larger organisations (company directors, senior civil servants, senior police and armed forces officers)

1.2 higher professionals (doctors, lawyers, clergy)

2 lower managerial and professional occupations (nurses, journalists, actors, prison officers)

3 intermediate occupations (clerks, secretaries, driving instructors)

4 small employers and on account workers (publicans, farmers, taxi drivers, window cleaners)

5 lower supervisory, craft and related occupations (printers, television engineers, train drivers)

6 semi-routine occupations (shop assistants, hairdressers, bus drivers)

7 Routine occupations (labourers, waiters, dustmen)

8 those who have never had paid work and the long-term unemployed.

The theoretical underpinning for this classification is to differentiate social position in relation to type of employment relationship. The key criterion is thus how much freedom someone has over their work, rather than the amount of money they earn. The higher the degree to which someone controls the terms and conditions of their working life, the higher their classification (ISER 2002).

A similar classification is the JICNARS market research classification:

■ upper middle class: higher managerial, administrative or professional (bank manager, bishop, coroner, professor)

- middle class: middle to senior management and professionals (police chief inspector, priest, probation officer, senior buyer)
- lower middle class: junior management, supervisory, secretarial and clerical (accounts clerk, bank cashier, staff nurse, receptionist)
- skilled working class: manual trades (bus driver, bricklayer, carpenter, train driver)
- working class: semi- and unskilled workers (dustman, bus conductor, ratcatcher)
- pensioners, widows and those on the breadline.

ACTIVITY 7.1

Social stratification

1 How useful do you think the NS-NEC and JICNARS classifications are in explaining social class in the UK?

2 If you were a marketing manager, what further classifications would you find useful for your job?

SOCIAL MOBILITY

Social mobility is the movement of people up or down the social hierarchy, either within one generation (intragenerational mobility) or between generations (intergenerational mobility). Intergenerational mobility is easiest to measure, by taking the occupation of fathers and comparing this with the occupation of their offspring. Another distinction is between absolute social mobility (the number of proportion of people who move from one social class to another) and relative social mobility (the probability of a member of a social class moving to another class.) Opportunities for social mobility represent one dimension of an individual's life chances, the chance to better their quality of life. Other dimensions are the absence of poverty, and access to decent standards of health and education. Quality of life varies with social class, ethnic group, gender and locality (Aldridge 2004).

Until the Second World War, there was considerable absolute social mobility in Britain, but downward mobility was nearly as common as upward. Since the Second World War, upward absolute social mobility has considerably outweighed downward, with the trend increasing – it is much higher for men born in 1950–59 (the latest available figures) than for men born in 1920–29 (the first group to have reached maturity after the Second World War). The main reason for this upward mobility is that there is 'more room at the top'. In 1900, the middle class made up 18 per cent of the population, while the working class made up 62 per cent. By 2000, the middle class was 42 per cent of the population and the working class 38 per cent.

While the picture on absolute social mobility looks positive, the picture is very different when one looks at relative mobility. Because the middle class is bigger, this means that children of middle class parents have less risk of falling down into the working class, ie downward social mobility has fallen. The result has been that the chances of a working class child making it to the middle class have changed little – it is estimated that a working class child is 15 times less likely to make it into the middle class than a middle class child is to stay in the middle class.

Most worryingly, there is some evidence that social mobility, however it is measured, is slowing down. This is best shown by figures on income. Studies have been made of the correlation between fathers' earnings and earnings of offspring. A correlation of zero would imply complete income mobility between generations, ie that a father's income has no influence on his offspring's income, while a correlation of one would imply total immobility, ie that an offspring's place on the income scale is exactly the same as his or her father's. For the UK, correlations have been found of between 0.4 and 0.6 for earnings of sons, and between 0.45 and 0.7 for those of daughters. The higher the correlation the less income mobility, and, by implication, the lower the level of social mobility.

Closer examination of the correlations shows two disturbing trends:

1 Correlations are much higher in the UK than in countries such as Canada, Sweden or Finland.

2 A comparison of those born in 1958 with those born in 1970 shows the correlations increasing – ie social mobility in the UK is falling.

ACTIVITY 7.2

Social mobility, education and the meritocracy

■ After the Education Act of 1944 it was thought that the 11-plus examination, which determined whether children would go to a grammar school (and receive an education leading to middle class occupations) or to a secondary modern school (leading to working class occupations) would increase social mobility, by selecting on the basis of intelligence rather than fathers' social class. By the 1970s, the theory behind this was discredited, and a switch was made to comprehensive education, whereby all children, whatever their intelligence or social background, would go to the same school. This does not seem to have been effective in increasing social mobility. Why do you think that changes in the education system seem to have failed to increase social mobility?

■ In 1958 the sociologist Michael Young published *The Rise of the Meritocracy*. In this book he examined the likely consequences of a society in which success was based solely on merit (ie on ability) rather than on social background, and in which there was total social mobility – in other words something very like the aspirations of the 1944 Education Act. However, Young saw considerable downsides to this. What do you think these downsides could have been?

■ The slowdown in social mobility is of increasing concern to Labour politicians. Typical is a speech made by Alan Milburn to the Institute of Public Policy Research in November 2004 (Milburn 2004). Why do you think that New Labour would be concerned about a fall in social mobility?

INEQUALITY

Inequality in society can be measured in a number of ways, but the easiest is distribution of wealth or income. Wealth is extremely unevenly distributed in the UK, although rather less unevenly than in the 1950s (Table 7.2).

Table 7.2 *Distribution of wealth UK (%)*

	1954	1975	1981	1994
Top 1%	43.0	23.2	18.0	19.0
Top 10%	79.0	62.4	50.0	51.0
Top 50%		92.0	93.0	93.0

Source: adapted from George and Wilding (1999)

Several points can be drawn from these figures, as follows.

■ Inequality in wealth fell over the period 1954–1981. The main reason for this seems to have been the spread of home ownership, from perhaps 20 per cent just after the War to around 75 per cent by 1994. For the first time this gave most of the middle class, and some sections of the working class, access to wealth.

■ Wealth inequality has widened since 1981 (in reality from the election of the Thatcher Government in 1979. Drastic cuts in the higher rates of tax, privatisation and the long-term rise in the stock market have all contributed to this trend, which has not been reversed under New Labour.

■ The bottom half of the population has never owned significant wealth, and this has not changed in recent years.

A slightly less pessimistic picture comes if we include the right to a state old-age pension as part of wealth. If we do this, the share of the top 50 per cent for 1994 falls from 93 to 83 per cent.

The same pattern emerges if one examines distribution of income, as shown in the following table (Table 7.3).

Table 7.3 *Distribution of income (UK) (before housing costs)*

	1961	1979	1994	1997
Top 10%	22.0	21.0	26.0	26.0
Top 20%	37.0	35.0	41.0	41.0
Top 50%	70.6	68.0	72.0	72.0
Bottom 10%	4.0	4.2	3.1	3.1

Source: adapted from George and Wilding (1999)

Key points from this table are the following.

■ Income inequality narrowed marginally between 1961 and 1979, but has widened again since 1979.

■ Income distribution in 1997 was more uneven than it had been in 1961.

■ Margaret Thatcher's 'trickle-down' theory, that increasing the wealth and income of the rich would produce a trickle down of greater income and wealth lower down the scale, appears to be a myth.

■ Even when inequality was lessening, this did not benefit the bottom 10 per cent.

Since 1997, the share of the bottom 10 per cent has improved slightly, largely as a result of Gordon Brown's use of tax credits targeted at the poorest, but inequality generally seems to have continued to increase. An increased emphasis on indirect rather than direct taxes, which started well before 1997, has tended to hit the bottom end of the distribution harder than the top. Since 1979, the proportion of income paid in tax by the lowest 20 per cent of taxpayers has risen from 31 to 42 per cent, while the proportion paid by the highest fifth has fallen from 37 to 34 per cent (Clark 2004). Yes, the poor pay a higher proportion of income in tax than the rich!

A method used by statisticians to measure inequality is the Gini coefficient. This expresses income distribution on a scale of 0 to 100, with 0 representing total equality. The higher the figure the more uneven the distribution. The Gini coefficient figures (Table 7.4) have changed as follows:

Table 7.4 *Gini coefficient (before housing costs)*

1961	1970	1979	1991	1997	2002
26	26	25	34	33	36

Source: George and Wilding (1999) and Clark (2004)

On the Gini figures, inequality was constant over the period 1961–79, widened under the Thatcher Governments, narrowed slightly under the Major Government, and has widened significantly under New Labour since 1997.

POVERTY

Absolute poverty in the Ethiopian sense does not exist in the UK. A more useful definition is relative poverty, and this is inescapable in a society in which income is distributed unevenly. However, relative poverty can be defined In many different ways – assistance level, assistance level plus x per cent, half median earnings, 60 per cent of median earnings, before or after housing costs. The definition standardised throughout the EU is household income below 60 per cent of median income (after housing costs) – approximately £12,000 a year in 2004. On this definition, poverty rose steadily throughout the Thatcher and Major years, reaching a peak of 13.9 million people (nearly a quarter of the population) in 1997, falling since to 12.4 million in 2004 (Clark 2004). Of 16 industrialised countries measured for poverty in 1995, the UK was twelfth, with twice the level of poverty of Sweden or Finland, and slightly less than Ireland, Greece, Italy and the USA (Aldridge 2004).

Poverty is particularly influenced by the following three factors:

1 *Children:* the percentage of households with incomes below 60 per cent of the median was around 20 per cent of the whole population in 2001, but around 30 per cent for households with children. The proportion for single-parent households was even higher.

2 *Gender:* despite 30 years of equal pay legislation, average female hourly earnings are still only around 75 per cent of male earnings, and women on average work fewer hours than men. This particularly hits single-parent households headed by women (the vast majority).

3 *Ethnicity:* ethnic minority groups are likely to have lower incomes than whites – average weekly male pay in 2000 was £297 for whites, £264 for Chinese, £254 for Afro-

Caribbeans, £222 for Pakistanis, and £142 for Bangladeshis. Only Indians, at £307, have a higher income than whites. However, after we take account of the fact that Indians on average have higher educational qualifications than whites, their 'like-for-like' earnings are lower. In 1995, more than a third of the ethnic minority population was in the poorest fifth of the population (George and Wilding 1999). In 1991, unemployment rates for all ethnic minority groups were twice those of the white population, and unemployment rates for Bangladeshis were three times as high for men and five times as high for women.

Poverty matters because it affects future life chances. Infant mortality rates are twice as high for unskilled manual groups than they are for professionals. Life expectancy for male professionals in 1997–99 was 79, and for female professionals 83, while for unskilled manual groups the corresponding figures were 75 and 77. The lower your income, the more likely you are to be a victim of burglary.

The percentage of children aged between 5 and 15 experiencing mental disorders is between two and three times higher for those living in households with an income of less than £100 a week than they are for those in households earning over £700 a week. Most poor children fail. Their depressed parents are unable to give them aspirations (Toynbee 2004).

ACTIVITY 7.3
Poverty and inequality

- In 2001, the average chief executive officer in the UK earned £509,000, while the average manufacturing worker earned £20,475, a differential of around 25:1. German CEOs averaged £298,000, 11 times a German manufacturing worker's income. The ratio in the USA was 32:1. Executive pay in the UK had soared by 29 per cent between 1999 and 2001, and has risen relative to average wages since 2001 (Duncan 2001). What do you think the impact of these differentials is likely to be on the motivation of manufacturing workers in the UK?

- Why should social inequality matter to employers? What can they do about it?

- What can the Government do to increase social mobility and equality of opportunity, and to reduce poverty?

TRENDS IN EMPLOYMENT
Changes in the industrial structure

In 1951, manufacturing accounted for a third of GDP and nearly 40 per cent of employment. By 2001 employment in manufacturing had fallen to 14 per cent of the workforce, although as the size of the workforce has increased considerably, the number working in manufacturing has only fallen from 8.7 to 3.7 million. Part of the reason for this fall is the shift of manufacturing jobs to Eastern Europe and the Far East, a consequence of globalisation. Another reason is peculiar to the UK – the chronic over-valuation of the pound since the late 1970s, which made UK manufacturing uncompetitive, and which triggered recessions in the early 1980s and early 1990s. The trend continues – the pound is still high, and there is much talk of a two-speed economy – booming services and recessionary manufacturing. Where manufacturing has survived, the nature of work within it has changed, from skilled and semi-skilled manual work to much more knowledge-based and less manual work.

The fall in mining and quarrying has been even more marked, from 880,000 workers in 1951 to 76,000 in 2001 (Philpott 2002). The share of public services in GDP has fallen markedly since the early 1950s, although employment has remained more or less constant at around 5 million. Falls in privatised public corporations and the armed forces have been matched by growths in education and the NHS. Services of all kinds have boomed, and have grown from about half of employment in 1966 to around three-quarters in 2001 (Gallie 2000).

There have also been changes in the occupational level of the workforce. The share of manual workers in the workforce fell from 64 per cent in 1952 to 38 per cent in 1991, with the biggest proportionate fall among unskilled manual workers, whose percentage has fallen by nearly two thirds. Skilled manual workers have fallen from 25 per cent of the workforce in 1951 to 12 per cent in 2001, while the managerial professional and technical workforce has risen from 12 per cent in 1951 to nearly 40 per cent in 2001, and relatively poorly paid service sector jobs have also increased.

The above trends are typical of most of Western Europe, although the proportion of workers in manufacturing is higher in Germany and Italy, and the proportion working in services higher in the Netherlands (Gallie *op cit*).

The feminisation of the workforce

Male participation rates (the proportion of the population of working age who are in employment) have fallen steadily since 1951 (and indeed since 1911). They were 88 per cent in 1951 and had fallen to 71 per cent in 1998 (Gallie *op cit*). The fall is explained by early retirement, and greater levels of sickness incapacity. Female rates over the same period have risen from 33 to 54 per cent. As a result the share of women in the labour force has risen from 30 to 44 per cent. All of the gain in female employment has come about as a result of an increased participation in the labour force of married women. The single participation rate has fallen from 73 per cent in 1951 to 64 per cent in 1991, while the married women participation rate has risen from 22 to 53 per cent. It is difficult to remember that in the early 1950s women in occupations like the civil service were routinely expected to resign when they married!

Women are under-represented in the higher professions, as managers and administrators, and in manual work, while they are over-represented in the lower professional grouping and as technicians (primarily education and the NHS), clerical workers, and salespeople. Women are expected to account for two thirds of all expected job increases over the period to 2010 (Green 2003).

ACTIVITY 7.4

Social class

'There is no such thing as society' (Margaret Thatcher); 'the classless society' (John Major); 'we are all middle class now' (anon).

Explain each of these statements. Do you agree with any of them?

ACTIVITY 7.5

The Harlow economy

Harlow is a New Town in the South-East designated in 1947, and about 25 miles from Central London. Harlow's population peaked around 1980, fell to 75,000 in 1991, and had risen again to nearly 80,000 in 2001. The original population moved into Harlow between the early 1950s and the late 1960s, attracted by the twin offers of a job and a house. The number of people of pensionable age in the Harlow population is on a steep upward trend, from 5 per cent of the population in 1971, to 16 per cent in 1991 and 21 per cent in 2001.

Harlow attracted the growth industries of the 1960s, including printing, electrical and mechanical engineering, and distilling. Like the rest of the UK, Harlow has experienced a decline in manufacturing industry, although this has been much more rapid than elsewhere. As recently as 1985, the split between manufacturing and service employment was about 50:50, a much higher emphasis on manufacturing than in the UK in general, but by 1993 manufacturing had fallen to 28 per cent, and by 2000 to 24 per cent (still higher than in the UK generally). By 1993, service employment had risen to 68.5 per cent, and to 72 per cent by 2000.

The biggest employers in Harlow today are in research and development, in the pharmaceutical and electronics/telecoms industries, and in the NHS. However, there is a mismatch in skills between the resident Harlow population and the growing employment sectors. Nearly half of all those employed in Harlow live outside the town. Conversely, there is considerable commuting from Harlow into London.

In 1989 unemployment in Harlow was roughly half the national average, but by 1993 this had increased to slightly above the national average. Although unemployment in Harlow is now about the national average, large areas of Harlow are defined as socially deprived, and Harlow is the third most deprived community in the East of England.

Sources: Harlow 2000 Initiative (1993) and *Harlow Baseline Study 2002 (2002), Harlow District Council.*

How would you explain the changing economic and social structure of Harlow? In particular:

- The delayed collapse in manufacturing (Harlow manufacturing was barely affected by the 1981–82 recession, but was hard hit by that in the early 1990s
- The changing patterns in unemployment – from below the national average to above the average, to equal to the average
- The extent of in-commuting
- The extent of social deprivation.

WORK ORGANISATION

The flexible organisation

The typical organisation in the 1950s and 1960s was large, monolithic and rigid, typified by the nationalised industries like the National Coal Board and British Railways – businesses employing tens of thousands, even hundreds of thousands, with many levels of management and a bureaucratic culture. Status was all-important, and the objective of a manager was to climb up the ladder of the hierarchy. The ethos was male, and based on conformity.

This rigid type of organisation was faltering by the 1970s, although in Japan it was to survive until the depression of the 1990s. By the 1970s, the dominant form was the conglomerate, with groups of disparate businesses held together by a small strategic headquarters. The view had developed that a successful manager could manage anything, hence it did not matter that the activities of the conglomerate bore little relation to each other. There was also slightly more flexibility, as a career could develop across the conglomerate. Again the conglomerate structure survived longer in Japan than anywhere else, where it formed the basis of the *keiretsu* system.

By the 1980s, conglomerates were going out of fashion, and the new orthodoxy was that expressed by Peters and Waterman in *In Search of Excellence* (1982) – 'stick to the knitting'. The spread of computers and IT-based management techniques also lessened the importance of economies of scale, and made smaller businesses economically viable. 'Stick to the knitting' was pushed further and further, as organisations started to outsource their non-core functions, leading in the ultimate to the concept of the 'virtual corporation'. Here advanced IT and communication techniques permit the organisation to become totally fluid, consisting of individuals who come together to perform particular tasks, and then separate again.

Changes in the external environment have increased the pressure on organisations to become more and more responsive. Not only have organisations become smaller; they have changed their internal organisation. The old 'smokestack' structure of large monolithic vertical departments, each with its own hierarchy, and little contact with each other, has proved too unresponsive, and increasingly has been replaced by a more flexible and fluid matrix type of organisation, based around teams, which can form, dissolve and reform to tackle particular problems. The result has been a de-layering within organisations, with many fewer layers of management. Either a manager has to adjust to this new paradigm, and settle for a series of lateral moves, or he or she must change organisations.

The idea of the flexible firm was first identified by Atkinson (1984), and the concept was refined by Handy (1991). Atkinson identified the following four types of flexibility.

1 numerical flexibility, achieved by altering working hours or altering the number of workers employed through part-time working, etc.
2 functional flexibility, achieved by training workers to perform a wider range of tasks (multiskilling) and breaking down barriers to deploying workers on different tasks (demarcation)
3 distancing, replacing employees with sub-contractors
4 pay flexibility, switching from centralised collective bargaining and rigid pay scales to individually negotiated pay and benefits.

The result is a segmentation of the workforce into core and peripheral workers. Core workers are those key workers who are central to the organisation's core functions. They will be long-term employees, possibly with guaranteed employment, and highly trained. They will be committed to the organisation, and the organisation will be committed to them. Peripheral workers will be those performing non-core services, often as sub-contractors. They will be hired and fired as required, and will serve as a buffer protecting the core workforce from fluctuations.

Handy developed the core–peripheral concept into his Shamrock concept. This type of organisation has three interlocking leaves consisting of three distinct groups of workers who are treated differently and have different expectations: specialist core workers; a contractual fringe, who may or may not work exclusively for the organisation, and who are paid a fee based on results rather than a wage based on time taken; and a flexible workforce, who are likely to be employed on a temporary or casual basis.

Remember, however, that what Atkinson and Handy are discussing is a theoretical model of organisations. Although many organisations have moved towards this kind of structure, many have not. As with other new management techniques, British management tends to be conservative and reluctant to adopt new ideas (Marchington and Wilkinson 2000).

ACTIVITY 7.6
The challenges of flexible working

What problems are posed by the movement towards more flexible ways of working?

The future of the workplace

Moynagh and Worsley (2001) put forward three possible scenarios for the future development of the workplace by 2020. They identify the following two key variables.

1 The degree to which organisations must adapt to their workers, and conversely the degree to which workers must adapt to organisations. Tight labour markets will shift power to workers, while more intense competition in the product market will shift power to organisations.

2 The stability of networks. Will employers favour stable networks that allow them to retain knowledge in the organisation, or will rapid change lead to virtual teams which change so frequently that long-term relationships between their members become unsustainable?

On the basic of these two variables, they identify three possible scenarios for 2020:

1 Fragile communities – workers forced to adapt, but networks stable

Individualised contracts are widespread, and workers are contracted to perform specific tasks and paid by results, but skills shortages encourage employers to retain knowledge workers. However, this model is unstable, because competitive pressures are forcing rapid change, which puts pressure on networks.

2 Stable communities – organisations adapt, and networks are stable

Competitive pressures are lessened as organisations merge or collaborate, and organisations must adapt to the needs of their workers through measures such as work-life balance. However, this may not be viable because of the pressures of globalisation.

3 Disposable communities – workers forced to adapt, and networks are fragile

Labour is seen as a commodity, and employers tap into a global pool of skilled labour. Knowledge is stored electronically, so there is no pressure to retain workers as the corporate memory of the organisation. Workers are insecure and stressed, and may respond to this by opting out of the labour market, through downshifting or self-employment. In the long run, this may make the model self-defeating.

All three of these models are plausible, but all three contain the seeds of their own destruction. The result may be a labour market that oscillates between them.

The psychological contract

All employees have a legal contract of employment, but for the employee this is usually presented as a 'take it or leave it' situation. The employee has to accept it or leave. The psychological contract is different. It is implicit rather than explicit, individual rather than collective, tacit rather than written (although elements of it may be incorporated into a social partnership agreement with a trade union) (CIPD 2003a). There are dangers in making it too explicit, as organisational and environmental changes may make it impossible to deliver on an explicit contract. (Briner and Conway, 2001). It can be defined as 'the perceptions of the two parties ... of their mutual obligations towards each other' (Guest and Conway 2002). By its very nature, the psychological contract is dependent on trust between the employer and the employee.

One view of the psychological contract is that it has changed from an 'employment security' contract to an 'employability' contract. This reflects the shift from the monolithic to the flexible organisation, which we discussed above. Under the employment security contract, the employee offered time and loyalty in return for security of employment and the possibility of promotion (Kimberly and Craig 2001). As redundancy and downsizing became more common, employers could no longer guarantee their side of the bargain, and gradually it was replaced by the employability contract – employees would still offer time and loyalty, but in return the employer would ensure that they received the work experience and training that would enable them to get another job elsewhere. This has been described as the 'new deal' at work and as producing a 'free agent' mentality among workers.

If this model is correct (and there is some doubt about this – the 'old' psychological contract often still exists, and where it has gone, it has not necessarily been replaced by an employability contract), loyalty may not be enough to keep the free-agent employee on board. The organisation may have to offer more, including possibly empowerment. If workers are to be trusted, they expect trust back from the organisation.

Other implications of the new psychological contract suggested by the CIPD include the following:

- process fairness: employers need to set up processes which ensure that employees see the way in which decisions are made is fair
- communications: communication mechanisms have to be set up to ensure that employers are aware of the employee 'voice' (this is reflected in the EU information and Consultation Directive)

- management style: employees expect to know what is going on – management style needs to change from 'top-down' to 'bottom-up'
- managing expectations: managers must be seen to be fair, honest and open
- measuring employee attitudes: managers need to know what their employees are thinking.

The employability and free-agent approaches in many ways put a lot of pressure on employees. They are forced to take responsibility for their own future in a way which, while attractive to many, does not suit everyone. Many people want security rather than opportunity. Those who really crave opportunity may well have shifted to self-employment already (the self-employment rate in the UK is currently around 12 per cent of the workforce – Philpott *op cit*). Increasingly employers have to offer something else as part of their side of the psychological contract. This is work-life balance, which we discuss in the next section.

Work-life balance

Changes in social structure have increased pressure on people in work.

- In the 1950s and even into the 1960s, women routinely gave up work on marriage, and so were at home to care for children. People married young, and had children young, with most families being completed by the age of 30. At the time when children were dependent, many parents also had an extended family to draw on and relatively young grandparents, who probably lived nearby.
- In the 1990s and 2000s, over half of all married women were in work, whether or not they had children, and families had come to expect and need two incomes. The age of marriage had risen, and many women had not had their first child by age 30. The extended family had broken down, and by the time the family needed support, grandparents were too old, did not live locally, and increasingly needed care themselves.
- The increase in the rate of marriage breakdown meant that increasing numbers of single parents with children, particularly women, needed to work to support their families, but had no external support networks to draw on. In 1991, 20 per cent of dependent children lived in single-parent families.
- Millions of women in their 50s have to care for an elderly dependent parent.
- There is an increased desire on the part of employers as well as employees for a more flexible workforce.

An Institute of Management survey in 2001 highlighted the extent of the problem (*Professional Manager* 2001):

- 46 per cent of female managers have children.
- 20 per cent care for others such as elderly parents.
- 27 per cent cite family commitments as a career barrier (up from 17 per cent in 1992).

In 2003, 9 per cent of males and 33 per cent of females had, at some time, given up work to care for somebody (*Social Trends* 2004).

In addition, people without caring responsibilities also feel that they are entitled to a life outside work. One in five people take work home almost every day, and one in ten work more than 48 hours a week (CIPD 2003b).

There are some legal requirements on employers to meet the needs of their employees for work-life balance. These are mainly concerned with the right to time off to cope with one-off situations or emergencies, and full details are given in the *CIPD Factsheet, Work-life balance* cited above. In addition, from 2003, (under the Employment Act 2002), employees with children under age six (18 if disabled) can request a change in their hours, time or place or work. The employer must consider such a request, and can refuse it, but only after following a detailed procedure and basing their decision on specified business grounds.

Although only parents of young children have the right to request flexible working, any other employee can ask for flexible arrangements, and many employers have granted this. The latest figures (for 2003) are that 18 per cent of men and 27 per cent of women working full time have some kind of flexible working arrangements, but the most common arrangements as follows (Table 7.5):

Table 7.5 *Flexible working arrangements (%)*

	Males	Females	All
Flexible working hours	9.7	14.9	11.6
Annualised hours	4.9	5.1	5.0
4 1/2 day week	1.8	1.1	1.5
Term-time work	1.2	5.8	2.9

There are similar patterns for part-time workers, with flexible working hours and term-time working being the most used options. Twenty-six per cent of males and 47 per cent of females had changed their hours or working arrangements to look after someone.

ACTIVITY 7.7

Work-life balance

1 Our discussion above has been in terms of flexible working hours or time off. What other family-friendly arrangements could employers offer?

2 What business case could you put to your employers to persuade them to adopt family-friendly policies?

3 Among your workforce are two workers, Anne, who is a single parent with a daughter aged four, who has asked to work school hours only, and Peter, who is the sole family carer for his elderly mother, who has Alzheimer's disease. He has asked to work a 30-hour week, instead of the normal 35, and to leave work one hour early, in order to get home before his daytime carer leaves. What response would you make to each worker?

Equal opportunities and diversity

The UK is a very diverse society: diverse in terms of race, sex, sexual orientation, religion, age, disability and life experience. Equality of opportunity is based on legislation, and has as its main aim assimilation – that whatever people's backgrounds are, they should all have the opportunity to achieve the same outcomes. Diversity is much more about difference. The differences between the two are illustrated in Table 7.6.

Table 7.6 *Differences between equal opportunities and diversity*

Equal opportunities	Diversity
Externally imposed	Internally driven
Groups	Individuals
Assimilation	Diversification
Systems	Total culture
Responsibility of personnel/Human resources	Responsibility of all, permeates the culture

Source: Adapted from Ross and Schneider (1992)

Kandola and Fullerton (1994) identify three key elements of diversity.

1 Diversity is a source of real value to the organisation.

2 Diversity is not only about obvious visible differences, but is about all the ways in which people can differ.

3 The aim of diversity is to enrich the organisational culture and working environment.

All of these points are illustrated in the following case study.

CASE STUDY 7.1

Diversity and the war against crime

The Metropolitan Police has set up a Cultural and Communities Resource Unit, headed by a (black) detective chief inspector, Keith Fraser. The unit maintains a database of the range of backgrounds, lifestyles and specialisms in the Met and the City of London Police. The unit has 800 people on its books, and has located experts who have helped with 700 criminal enquiries all over the country. Examples of the work of the unit include the following.

■ Investigating the murder of an elderly Bengali woman, white police officers were getting no co-operation from the community. Bengali officers immediately got co-operation.

■ A Chinese person had been missing in the North of England for two weeks. A Chinese policeman from London found him in a day and a half.

■ Tamil officers are investigating violence between rival Tamil gangs.

■ A voodoo expert helped interpret seemingly innocuous but actually sinister objects sent to a Bangladeshi man.

As DCI Fraser says, 'the unit highlights the true meaning of diversity and the fantastic opportunities and benefits it gives policing'

Source: Cowan (2004)

Trade unions

So far in this section on work organisation we have concentrated on the position of individuals. We conclude by analysing the collective – the role and position of trade unions.

Trade union membership peaked in 1979, at more than 13 million. Since then it has nearly halved, to around 7.5 million in the late 1990s. It has since stabilised, helped by legislation on union recognition in 1999. The nature of trade union membership has also changed. Union density (the proportion of workers who are union members) fell from 54 per cent in 1979 to 29 per cent in 2003, but for women it has only fallen from 37 to 29 per cent.

Density is also affected by age. Density among the over-50s is 33 per cent, while for the age group 25–34 it is 25 per cent (*Social Trends* 2004). Density among full-time workers is 32 per cent, among part-time workers only 21 per cent. Density among professional and associate professional workers and personal service workers is higher than among manual workers. Density in the public sector is 60 per cent, while in the private sector it is only 20 per cent.

In 1979 the typical union member was a male manual worker in heavy industry – a miner or a steelworker. By 2003, the typical union member was a female teacher or an NHS worker.

Many reasons have been put forward for the decline in union membership. These include:

- the decline of traditional highly unionised sectors of industry
- the anti-trade union legislation of the Conservative Governments between 1979 and 1997
- the recessions of the early 1980 and 1990s
- the growth of a flexible workforce, which is more difficult to unionise
- the growth of pay review bodies in the public sector
- the spread of performance-related pay and individualised HRM systems
- the fall in the size of firms
- defeat in highly publicised set-piece disputes like the Miners' Strike.

The response of the trade unions, led by the TUC, was to change their orientation. The traditional perspective taken by unions was a pluralist one – that management and unions have some common aims, but many more conflicting aims, within the employment relationship. Collective bargaining was seen as managing the balance between the interests of management and workers, and would frequently be adversarial. Many individual union leaders took a more radical Marxist perspective, and saw the management–labour relationship as an exploitative one.

In the early 1990s, unions in America developed a different approach, known as New Unionism, based much more on a co-operative relationship, recognising that management and unions have basic agreement in wanting the employment relationship to work more smoothly, and that both sides benefit from a high-wage high-productivity environment. New Unionism also recognised that the approach of union members and potential members is an instrumental one – they want a union to protect their individual interests. They buy union membership like they buy a foreign holiday – they want value for their money.

CASE STUDY 7.2

Social partnership at Vertex

Vertex is an outsourced services company, part of United Utilities, formed in 1996 when North West Water merged with North West Electricity. In five years, it has moved from collective bargaining to union derecognition to non-union consultation to collective bargaining based on partnership.

The head of employee relations, Tony Stark, said 'I'd had a bellyful of trade unions after working in the car industry and the docks in Liverpool.' However, he was to lead negotiations with Unison which led to partnership. Even when the union was derecognised, union officials were elected onto the company-wide employee consultation forum, and proved constructive partners.

After the passing of the Employee Relations Act, Unison applied for a ballot on recognition. Rather than fight the request, Vertex set up a working party with the union, which produced agreement on recognition and social partnership. The company and the union put in a successful bid to the DTI's Partnership Fund, which aims to make organisations aware of best practice in partnership. This funded six months of workshops, facilitated by Ruskin College.

The partnership has produced tangible results, including a pay progression agreement, which has helped the company to achieve a retention rate much higher than that prevalent in the call centre industry. The partnership has also helped the company to win contracts with the public sector.

Source: Walsh (2001)

In 1996, the TUC adopted New Unionism. The emphasis in future was to be on developing social partnerships with willing employers, and on stressing casework for individual members (Barber 1998). To further New Unionism, the TUC set up an Academy in 1998 to train union representatives. The typical Academy student was female and from an ethnic minority.

New legislation introduced by the Labour Government supported the new approach. Under the Employment Relations Act 1999, all workers have the right to be accompanied by a fellow worker or union official to disciplinary proceedings. The Employment Act 2002 set out the statutory rights of union learning representatives, who have a key role in helping to promote learning and development within organisations which recognise unions (CIPD 2004a).

Perhaps most important, the 1999 Act introduced a statutory right to union recognition through ballot, so long as 50 per cent of workers vote in favour of recognition, and at least 40 per cent of those eligible to vote are in favour. This ensures that a small minority of the workforce cannot force through recognition.

Crucial recognition agreements were those with Honda and Sheerness Steel in 2001. Honda is a classic example of the 'good' company which feels that because it is a good company, unions are not needed (Clement, 2001), while Sheerness Steel was the scene of a bitter derecognition dispute in 1992 between the ISTC and the then owners, CoSteel (Gall, 2001).

ACTIVITY 7.8

Union recognition

What do you think are the advantages and disadvantages to employers of recognising trade unions?

SUMMARY AND CONCLUSIONS

This chapter has analysed Marxist and Weberian theories of social stratification, and has examined the major socio-economic classifications used in the UK. It has examined the nature and extent of social mobility in the UK, and the social effects of a slowdown in the rate of mobility, including its impact on inequality and poverty. Changes in the industrial and economic structure of the UK have been analysed, and the flexible firm has been identified as a major developing form of organisation. The psychological contract has been examined, with particular reference to employability and work-life balance. Finally, the changing nature and extent of trade unionism in the UK has been analysed.

KEY LEARNING POINTS

- Marxist theories of social class are related to ownership of the means of production, whereas Weberian theories are wider, and consider status and power as well as class.

- Throughout most of the twentieth century, social mobility in the UK was high, as the absolute size of the middle class rose considerably at the expense of the working class, but these trends have slowed in recent years.

- There are considerable inequalities in both income and wealth in the UK, and these inequalities have been widening in recent years.

- Inequality is closely related to relative poverty, which has persisted in the UK, and which leads to an impairment of the life chances of the poor.

- Since the 1970s, manufacturing has declined rapidly in the UK, along with a growth in employment in services. This has helped to lead to an increasing feminisation of the UK workforce. Globalisation and computerisation have also led to the growth of flexible forms of work organisation.

- The psychological contract has evolved from an emphasis on job security, to employability, and to work-life balance.

- Equal opportunities is about assimilation, while diversity is about celebrating difference.

- Trade union membership in the UK has almost halved as a result of changes in social and industrial structure. The response of the unions has been to develop the concept of New Unionism.

FURTHER READING

Social class and social mobility are discussed in any good sociology textbook. Poverty and inequality are covered in Vic George and Paul Wilding, *British Society and Social Welfare: towards a sustainable society*. Excellent overviews of the evidence on social trends are given in two papers by Stephen Aldridge, an economist in the Prime Minister's Strategy Unit (formerly the Performance and Innovation Unit), listed in the References, and in John Philpott's CIPD pamphlet *HRH – A Work Audit*, published for the Queen's Golden Jubilee in 2002. The CIPD has also published a series of excellent Factsheets relevant to this chapter, including 'Managing the psychological contract' and 'Work-life balance'. On trade unions, the TUC website (www.tuc.org.uk) is invaluable.

Technology

OBJECTIVES

By the end of this chapter, readers should be able to understand, explain and critically evaluate:

■ **the key technological developments in information technology and other fields**

■ **the direct impact such changes have had on organisations**

■ **how technology has influenced goods, services and the labour markets**

■ **the concept of knowledge management**

■ **some of the reasons why technology has not always been seen as a beneficial influence.**

INTRODUCTION

No one doubts that massive technological advances have changed the world, as set out in the causes of globalisation in Chapter 3. The developments in information and communication technologies, biotechnology, energy supply and transportation have altered the world beyond recognition over the last 50 years. To put it more accurately, technological change enables massive changes to take place – changes in organisation, communication, products, marketing and distribution together with associated ways of managing people. The uniqueness of technology is that, once it has been invented, it cannot be 'un-invented'. Other resources can be used up (oil), can suddenly disappear (chief executives), or be replaced (buildings) but the technological knowledge will always survive. In fact, once one organisation uses that technology and gains competitive advantage, then it needs to be adopted in some form by all the competitors to ensure survival.

The speed of technological advance is increasing, prompting even speedier changes in society. In fact, writing about examples is quite difficult because, by the time this text is printed, most of the examples will be out of date and because the most influential changes of the next 10 years are only known about by small cliques of researchers in multinational research and development labs and their counterparts in leading universities.

PAUSE FOR THOUGHT

Recognising the importance of new technology can sometimes be tricky. In 1979, the medium-sized organisation I worked for as head of HR bought its first word processor, set up in its own specially designed room. I was tasked to recruit an operator internally and expected to have to fight off the wave of applicants. Surprisingly, nobody applied; they did not want to be 'sidelined' onto specialised work. They liked the routine and variety of being a secretary and the kudos of being accurate including getting letters out with only the occasional mistake. At last, I was approached by one of the newest and youngest (and brightest) employees to take the job on. Within two years, she was working for the chief executive with a doubled salary and a guaranteed career. Her knowledge was unique in the organisation and she had to be adequately rewarded to prevent her leaving.

PATTERNS OF TECHNOLOGICAL DEVELOPMENT

The common differentiation between man and other animals is the ability to design and use tools so primitive technologies have been utilised for many thousands of years. However, the beginnings of the Industrial Revolution in the mid-seventeenth century saw the early stages of fundamental technological growth where machines replaced hand operations.

Although technological invention appears to follow a continuous and unrelenting line, a pattern has been identified by, among others, Hall and Preston (1988). Named K-waves, after the Russian Kondratiev who first developed the concept in the 1920s, a 50-year cycle for each wave has been identified (see Table 8.1).

Table 8.1 *K-waves and their cycles*

K1	1770s to 1830s	Early mechanisation in textiles and water power with the construction of canals which led to the first large-scale factories and companies
K2	1830s to 1880s	Invention of steam power used in railways and machines which led to vastly improved communications and location independent of water sources
K3	1880s to 1930s	Inventions of electricity, steel, chemicals and synthetics creating new industries with reliable and powerful energy leading to very large scale production and control (Trusts and cartels) and opening up of transportation and communication through cars and aircraft. Technologies were integrated to create assembly line techniques
K4	1930s to 1980s	Explosion of development of cars and aircraft together with petrochemicals and consumer durables. Controlled through integrated manufacturing processes and by multi-national organisations
K5	1980s to current	ICT developments producing ability to source and manufacture flexibly across the world, creating global brands, communicated by television, radio and internet technologies. Robotics allows complex manufacturing and medical processes

There can be much debate about the timing of these waves and the overlapping feature of new technologies, but an economic pattern emerges that shows four stages. First, the invention and diffusion of the technology produces prosperity, especially for the organisations leading the way. However, after a period, demand slackens or competitors catch up leading to a recession where new investment falls. After such a period, the third stage is that of outright depression arising from reduced activity and restructuring with mass unemployment before the final stage – recovery – appears, when the economic conditions improve sufficiently for the next wave of technological development.

ACTIVITY 8.1

There is some evidence that the current technological cycle is swinging towards a down phase. Set out the reasons why this down phase might be occurring and also explain why the contrary may be true – that the current technological phase is gathering more steam.

TYPES OF TECHNOLOGICAL CHANGE

Freeman (1987) identified four different types of technological change:

1   Incremental innovations – these are small-scale changes made at a local level. For example, a quality circle might come up with a new way to calibrate existing equipment in a factory.

2   Radical innovations – they change the way things are done. For example, the development of semi-conductors rather than valves in the 1960s changed the ways in which computers could operate.

3   Changes of technology systems – these often involve linking together two existing technological systems to form a new system. For example, multimedia entertainment systems bring together computer and TV technologies.

4   Technology revolutions – these occur about every 50 years or so and revolutionise our approach to technology. One was the development of the steam engine in the 1770s, another, the growth of the railways in the 1830s. The development of the computer in the 1940s and the creation of the World Wide Web/Internet have been the latest two.

Information technology

In all technological developments, it is in the field of information technology that the speed of development has been the greatest, as has the effect upon society. A stream of inventions has followed the arrival of the first commercial computer in the 1950s. In *hardware*, integrated circuits have become increasingly powerful through the invention of optical chips and biochips paralleled by the improvements in data storage systems. The price of PCs continues to decline while ever more powerful laptops allow work to be carried out at any location and on the move. S*oftware* has offered the ability to network information so it is available to multiple organisational users and to operate real-time systems so that leisure activities, such as flights or theatre tickets can be booked electronically; in banking, money markets around the world are linked with instant access to information and market changes, programmes can control tools to perform any task previously carried out by hand such as cut, weld or burn and controls can be programmed into complex machinery which determine the output and the quality of the process.

All these developments have led to the computer being at the heart of business and, increasingly, private lives. Production, sales, distribution, finance and human resources are all aided by computer systems which increase the speed of operation, while providing reliable operations, communications and storage. Recent developments, badged as 'Business Intelligence', aim to transform large numbers of data, often scattered across the organisation, into the key information that drives informed decision-taking, and delivering it in an easily read form through the computer screen to anybody wherever and whenever they need to know. So essential is this intelligence that the estimated worldwide market for BI systems in 2008 is around £20 billion.

Communication technologies

Supporting the development in information technologies have been two major technological developments in communication. First, satellite communication, starting in the mid-1960s, has increased exponentially resulting in there now being over 100 geo-stationary satellites in orbit facilitating cheap and instantaneous communication and data transmission.

Secondly, the invention and development of optical fibre technology has provided a competitor in huge capacity handling at great speed. FLAG Europe-Asia, for example, is a 27,000 km system servicing half the world at lower and lower costs. An example (*Economist* 2000) is that the cost of transmitting the Encyclopaedia Britannica electronically from New York to Los Angeles cost $187 in 1970 but by 2000, the entire contents of the Library of Congress could be sent the same distance for less than $40.

Both these developments have led to the creation of mass markets, allowing consumers to be aware of the goods and services on offer. Even if incomes are low, the spread of multinational advertising and brand creation produces images that people can aspire to with the result that they become future consumers. Television has had the most dramatic effect because it makes no demands on standards of literacy, unlike the printed word. The technological development improvements since its invention in the 1930s, which have consistently reduced the price and increased the quality and reliability, have had two effects on the mass markets. The first effect is direct, in that most television channels are commercial so the products and services are directly communicated to the consumer. The second effect is more elliptical in that television programmes show styles of life that create the aspirational effect. This was most pronounced in Eastern Europe under communism where the nightly broadcasting of western European TV channels indicated clearly how far behind the communist economic model was compared to the West, and contributed to its eventual collapse.

Transportation technologies

The 'shrinking world' is a simplistic but accurate description of the rapid technological change since the 1940s, heralded by the invention of the jet engine and its development into the *commercial jet liner*. The time difference in travel by air compared to boat and train has been so substantial that it has created two linked mass markets. First, for the traveller, whether business or pleasure, for whom the swiftness and pleasure of the journey is joined to the associated activities it allows. Secondly, for the tourist where the travelling is a means to take holidays in other countries and where a vast supporting infrastructure has been built up – hotels, holiday complexes, leisure activities. The break-up of the nationalised, non-competing flag-carrying airways has allowed the creation of a flood of low-cost carriers, bringing regular travel to the mass market. A weekend flight to Paris can be cheaper than a taxi journey across London.

Another less publicised development but of considerable importance has been *containerisation* for the movement of freight across land and sea. It is such a simple and obvious development that it tends to be overlooked that it only started in 1956 and, before that time, loading and unloading cargo could be a slow, hazardous and wasteful activity. It was also associated with a strong union presence in the ports of most developed countries, threatening strike action against developments that might reduce labour costs or employment. By the 1980s, union power had been broken in both America and the UK and, today, the container can be 'stuffed' on the factory site and loaded and unloaded quickly by crane, and enjoys protection against weather and theft throughout its routes of shipment.

The Internet

There has been an astonishingly quick development of Internet technology since its origins in the US Defence department in the mid-1970s and its commercial usage since the mid-1990s. It now affects all aspects of work and leisure at a steadily reducing cost and therefore its utilisation is now within the grasp of most citizens in the developed world and many in the developing world. Society communicates through e-mails while hard-copy communications (such as letters) are used only in specific situations. Some organisations, such as easyJet, have attempted to become completely paper-free by scanning all the in-coming post and insisting on all correspondence, internal and external, being carried out through e-mails. The Internet provides a huge range of information that is relatively simple for anybody to access (although, surprisingly, having little effect on book sales). It also facilitates buying and selling transactions to take place at the work station.

ACTIVITY 8.2

Not all organisations have been enthusiastic about implementing online buying and selling. What is holding them back from gaining advantages in this area?

Biotechnology and medical technologies

Biotechnology is the process of altering life forms, essentially through genetic modification. Arising from the fundamental discovery of the structure of DNA in 1953 by Crick and Watson, modification of biological processes allows such interventions as the introduction of new genes into organisms, so permitting the breeding of organisms to form new variants or treating organisms with new compounds.

One example of biotechnology is the creation of genetically modified organisms (GMOs). Here, plants, animals and micro-organisms (bacteria, viruses) have had their genetic characteristics modified artificially in order to give them new properties. This could include a plant's resistance to a disease or an insect, or the improvement of a food's quality or nutritional value or a plant's tolerance of a herbicide.

The implications for food production and medical advance are astounding. The biotechnology industry has promised a vast increase in food production which would be sufficient to eradicate all forms of undernourishment world-wide. In medicine, applications promise the eventual eradication of genetic diseases, such as cystic fibrosis, as well as better understanding and treatment of common diseases and conditions, such as cancer and Alzheimer's disease. Governments around the world have co-operated in the massive genome project to map all human genes, which was successfully completed in 2004.

However, the outcomes in recent years have proved problematical. In food production, there has been considerable opposition to the acceptance of GM foods in many countries, especially the UK, to the extent that all UK trials of GM cereals were halted in 2004. There have also been very few signs of medical developments. In cystic fibrosis, for example, the discovery of the errant gene in 1984 has not led to any improved treatment owing to technical problems of gene therapy processes and similar problems have occurred in other treatments as shown in Case Study 8.1.

CASE STUDY 8.1
Gene therapy

In 1999, Jesse Gelsinger, a 19-year-old with a rare liver disorder, participated in a voluntary clinical trial using gene therapy at the University of Pennsylvania. He died of complications from an inflammatory response shortly after receiving a dose of experimental adenovirus vector, a new device to direct the new gene to the appropriate location. His death dealt a blow to the confidence of scientists and halted all gene therapy trials in the USA.

Source: Subramanian (2004)

EFFECTS ON BUSINESS STRATEGIES AND OPERATIONS

The impact of new technology can be seen in two main developments: in business strategies and the method of operation on the one hand and in new products and services on the other.

The biggest effect is for organisations to have the ability to be *flexible* and to be *eager to change*. New developments put old technologies out of business very quickly. For example, in the 1990s, only luxury cars had air conditioning; in the twenty-first century, few cars, except those at the very cheapest end, will sell without it. Given the extended period of design and development, manufacturers need to build in the ability to alter the standard product quickly and effectively to within a very tight budget. In reality, the product must combine extreme reliability that new technology has brought with design obsolescence to ensure the customer continues to purchase a company's new products.

Associated with this trend is the need to *mass-customise* products, perhaps something of a contradiction. Mass production is needed to produce a cost saving, but varieties are required to meet customers' diverse needs. A good example in services is provided by Compass Plc, which has thousands of catering contracts across the world, every one different but with some essential sourcing, marketing and administration systems in common. IT systems allow control and monitoring of every detail despite a setup becoming more complex. The customised feature has altered manufacturing approaches to assembly lines, many of which have been abandoned in favour of *cell production systems*, where groups of multi-skilled employees work in teams to meet the differing production contracts, taking responsibility for quality, waste reduction and innovation.

The vast improvements in efficiencies in production, brought about through robotics and other IT processes, and the ability to manufacture on a global basis has led to a growing *decline in manufacturing in developed countries* as the technology has been transferred to developing countries, together with using the sources of cheap capital and labour.

Technology has offered two additional *marketing opportunities*. Better knowledge of an organisation's customers through manipulation of a vast amount of purchasing data, allows much closer targeting of their requirements, a process that retailers, such as Homebase and Tesco have developed through loyalty cards. This quantity of information is only available to large organisations but the second opportunity, the Web, can be used by a business of any size. In fact, the Web has allowed many niche organisations to market, sell and distribute their products and services at low costs, many without the overheads of retail premises. Web-based business activity has expanded exponentially since the mid-1990s, especially business-to-business where sourcing can be fixed through Web-based tendering or even a quasi-auctioning system. Jupiter research (epaynews.com) have forecast that US on-line purchases will reach 5 per cent of all retail sales by 2008.

ACTIVITY 8.3

It is evident that some forms of technological development provide organisations with a competitive advantage. One example is the invention by St Helens glassmaker Pilkingtons of the float glass process in the 1950s. This brought huge competitive advantages in both the quality of the sheet glass and the productivity levels.

Think of a further THREE examples of this process and explain why such an advantage was gained in this way.

Specific products

The implications arising from the recent rapid developments in information technology and communications for the market-place are substantial. Here are just a few examples, with more shown in Case Study 8.2.

■ Increasing offering by subscription of movies, music and television/radio programmes by operators such as Disney, Comcast and Rhapsody will mean that programming-on-demand will take the place of normal TV and radio schedules. It is likely that the BBC will eventually set up a subscription service for all its huge archive of programmes. This will allow the viewer to choose, say, a set of 1970s 'Play for Today' or exactly which episodes of 'Hello, Hello' they want to watch, when they want to watch them.

- Flat-screen, computerised TVs will consistently drop in price and become essential furniture of the networked home, with users demanding ever more bandwidth to fill the high-definition screens used.

- Myriad websites compete with TV, music and video producers and distributors. Individuals can beam up their own productions onto the Web and become their own publishers.

CASE STUDY 8.2

The cellphone business

A new wave of innovative services is about to revolutionise the cellphone business, spreading into such areas as video-conferencing, Internet radio, purchasing and home movies. Here are a few examples:

- Grocery giant Kroger Company allows shoppers to instantly purchase their Wheaties from a store shelf by waving a cellphone equipped with an infra-red port over the side of the container. Instead of going through the checkout with a cashier, the customer can simply pass the phone over another scanner near the store's exit, confirming the goods have been paid for.

- With faster networks in place, four-way video calls can be made, making it easier for people to work while they are travelling.

- Yahoo is planning to make 100 channels of Internet radio services available to cellphone users.

- The cellphone will be an alternative to carrying cash or credit cards, making payments to scanners on cash registers and vending machines.

- It is possible to watch video-clips from football games and news clips, having followed the game live on radio using the cellphone.

- A video of a house can be sent by an estate agent to a potential buyer through their cellphone and the phone can be used to record houses seen for later comparisons. A 3-minute maximum is available at the time of writing but technological advances will increase this substantially within one or two years, perhaps less.

- Hearing an unfamiliar song at a restaurant, a phone owner can record an extract and wire it to a wireless service to identify the artist and singer in seconds. (Yes, they could ask the restaurant owner but he'd be busy!)

- As satellite systems can pinpoint the location of a phone to within a few hundred yards, phone owners can be informed of great offers from stores close by or be helped if they are lost..

Source: Adapted from Business Week *(2004)*

EFFECTS ON LABOUR MARKETS AND HUMAN RESOURCES

Technology both eliminates jobs and creates them. The introduction of railways in the nineteenth century eliminated most jobs in the canal transport industry but created a substantial net increase in jobs in total, both in the rail industry itself and in the suppliers to the industry, and in the associated expansion of industry and commerce that fast rail transport provided.

The same is true for today's technological changes. The IT software industry has created a huge number of jobs around the world, while the outcomes of their labour have reduced jobs selectively in manufacturing, distribution and administration. Introducing robotics into paint-spraying operations in car production, for example, has reduced the labour requirements in this function by 95 per cent. On the other hand, this technological change, among others, has reduced the price of the finished car to the extent that it is affordable to a greater mass market and employees in car manufacturing around the world continue to show a small overall increase.

It is the nature of the labour force that has changed with technological innovation. A polarisation has occurred with an increased demand for highly trained professional and technical employees and, at the same time, a reduced demand for low-skilled assembly and production operatives on the other. An even bigger decline has occurred in the demand for semi-skilled employees or those with traditional apprentice-served skills, most of which have been replaced by automation. This is also reflected geographically with most of the employees in Silicon Valley and other high-tech clusters in America and Japan in the high-skills category while the actual production of semi-conductors, printers and other hardware is carried out in East Asian countries and Mexico with largely low-skilled employees.

The perceived need for a reservoir of highly skilled employees has been the driving force for advanced countries, including the UK, to lay greater stress on achieving an increased percentage of the population to be qualified through higher education (the current target is 50 per cent) or through education programmes of skills achievements.

INCREASE IN TEMPORARY LABOUR

Information technology can provide information in a more reliable form and at a much more rapid rate. This allows organisations to respond far quicker to variations in consumer demand which, in turn, requires the labour market to become far more flexible.

Employers have responded in their employment model by making much greater use of non-standard employment, such as part-time or temporary employees. Supermarkets, for example, use their sales data to forecast precisely the number of checkouts required every hour of the year, and use part-time employees to resource the varying needs. The need for temporary staff for Christmas and holiday periods can also be precisely pinpointed through the accurate data provided. This allows supermarkets to reach their business target of queues of no greater than one or two people.

Case Study 8.3 shows a micro example of this process.

The direct implications for human resource practitioners of new technologies can be seen in the fields of recruitment and selection, teleworking and call centres, and in the way the human resource operation is structured.

CASE STUDY 8.3

Lettuce leaves and the labour market

It has become clear in recent years that consumers are steadily reducing their purchases of whole lettuces and increasingly purchasing packages of prepared lettuce leaves in a variety of forms. For supermarkets, this has provided an excellent opportunity with Tesco Plc selling over £150 million-worth a year, with a very high mark-up (as applies to most ready-prepared foods). But such packs have a very short shelf-life, despite the chemical methods applied during their preparation. In addition, the purchase of such packs (often on impulse) varies very much in line with the weather.

The supermarket response to this scenario is to assemble incredibly accurate information on purchasing trends, adjust for forecast weather conditions and put in their orders with a very short delivery time – usually no more than a day in advance, sometimes shorter. The suppliers, who are dealing with large orders they cannot afford to lose, in turn need to adjust their labour requirements flexibly. Most cannot afford to operate a system of on-call labour so they turn to labour service providers. One pack-house, for example, has contracted in 2004 for 2.7 million hours of temporary labour for lettuce and other convenience salad packs. The providers, now known as 'gangmasters', have large groups of itinerant labour, mostly from overseas, whom they call on a daily basis to meet heavily fluctuating demand in preparing lettuce packs and other highly seasonal goods.

The estimate of the number of immigrant (legal and otherwise) engaged in such work varies greatly but it continues to rise by every report. Provista, a major player, recruits regularly from Eastern Europe, which goes some way to explain the increase of 70,000 in reported work permits from that area since the accession of the new EU member states in 2004.

Source: The Economist (2004)

RECRUITMENT/SELECTION PROCESSES

Most organisations use the Web to post their current job vacancies and require applicants to complete their application online, saving considerable costs. Technology also enables telephone screening of applicants to take place, as shown in Case Study 8.4.

A further example of automated short-listing is the use of equipment to **electronically read CVs** using OCR (optical character recognition) software. The system's artificial intelligence reads the texts and, by using search criteria such as qualifications, job titles and companies where the applicant has worked, will produce a ranking list of applicants against the mandatory and optional aspects of the person specification.

This system is quicker and more consistent than if it were carried out manually but will only be efficient as the search engine and will certainly miss many potential candidates, let alone the difficulty the technology faces in trying to understand poor handwriting.

CASE STUDY 8.4

Telephone screening at Standard Life

Applicants for vacant positions advertised online called a dedicated telephone number and then went through an automated telephone screening interview. The company sorted through 561 candidates before taking on 15 recruits and claimed that the screening system saved 143 work days. The phone lines were open 24 hours a day, seven days a week. The system, developed by Gallop, was tested on 100 existing staff and looked for six generic performance attributes: achiever, conscientiousness, responsibility, agreeableness, numeracy and stability.

Source: People Management (1998)

 Originally published in *People Management* 28 May 1998, and reproduced with permission

ACTIVITY 8.4

What are the advantages and disadvantages to employers and employees of online recruitment?

TELEWORKING

The development of the World Wide Web and associated technological innovations has facilitated the process of working at a distance from the employee or main contractor. The process allows a variety of models, ranging from the ability to work one or two days at home with a lap-top to being a fully fledged teleworker hundreds of miles away where physical contact with the office site is restricted to an annual conference visit. As phones merge with computers, video calls will become far more common with far-flung teams working on shared documents in virtual meetings.

Advantages of teleworking

■ Productivity gains – employees working from home are often more productive. They get away from the frequent interruptions and distractions that pepper the working day. In is also in their interests to show they are more productive, so ensuring the continuation of the teleworking arrangement.

■ Employees can work out a work-life balance much more easily with more time spent at home. Caring responsibilities can be balanced with work to be completed, so long as the will and the self-discipline is present.

■ Time saving – for mobile teleworkers, the ability to complete tasks at remote locations, rather than returning to a central office, saves considerable time and expense. Time is saved on regular commuting to work.

■ Reduced accommodation costs – most organisations sell teleworking to their boards through setting out the huge savings in accommodation costs, especially where these are in central city locations.

Difficulties that could arise

- Teleworking can be difficult to manage without daily face-to-face contact. Managers often want prompt answers to questions or a special task performed quickly. This is far more difficult to achieve with remote workers. Supervisors and managers need specialised training to manage the remote worker. Contact has to be regular but not too intrusive.

- Performance management systems need to be carefully devised. They have to be based much more on outputs and outcomes rather than traditional measures such as attendance. Regular meetings need to be held to discuss the employee's performance.

- Employees may not have office work distractions but they may have home ones instead – children, other family members, friends, callers, etc. can all disrupt a steady workflow. Relationships with family members can suffer if the borders between work and home are not drawn tightly to everybody's satisfaction.

- Health and safety in the home needs to be carefully monitored.

- Dealing with confidential documents in the home setting has to be addressed.

- Some teleworkers feel too remote from the workplace. They miss the comradeship of the office and lose out on the regular gossip and social activities. There is also a general concern that teleworkers lose training and promotion opportunities because of their low visibility.

An example of the benefits of teleworking is shown in Case Study 8.5.

ACTIVITY 8.5

Research has shown that teleworkers often suffer from social isolation. Can you suggest ways that these effects can be mitigated?

CALL CENTRES

The invention and development of the automated call distribution (ACD) system which both released the need for a switchboard operator and provided detailed call information, have promoted the introduction of a growing number of call centres. It is estimated that over 500,000 employees were employed at UK call centres in 2003, a number that is increasing despite the dispersal of many such jobs to the Indian sub-continent where labour rates are cheaper.

Operators work with the required database to answer customer queries or process sales and service agreements and most centres build in an interactive instruction guide for the employee to follow, which reduces the time and cost for training. The technology also allows management to monitor calls to identify process glitches, training needs and earnings through any incentive scheme. Call centres can take a distributed form, allowing calls to be channelled to teleworkers at distant locations, with the technology allowing access to all necessary data.

CASE STUDY 8.5

Teleworking at Baxter International

Baxter International is a leading US manufacturer and supplier of technology relating to the blood and circulatory systems, employing over 40,000 worldwide. In the late 1990s, as part of their close technological relationships with Nortel Networks, they implemented Nortel's HomeOffice 2 system, which connects remote workers to the corporate phone system and intranet as if these workers were still in the office. This system matched their need for increased flexibility owing to the following.

- The global and distributed nature of the business meant staff had to go to the office regularly in the early hours for audio conferences.
- Many of their offices, including the UK base at Compton in Berkshire, were in rural settings, leading to substantial driving involved for staff to get to and from work.
- The life-critical nature of the business meant that some staff need to be available at all hours to the hospitals and to be able to direct the action required through the organisation's systems. This had previously meant 24-hour rotas in the workplace, which was unpopular.
- Similarly, call centre staff at the dialysis equipment supplying subsidiary, cover the period from 8.00am to 10.00pm with every patient having a named agent. Working early and late was, again, not very popular.

Introduced in 1999, the scheme has become so popular that around 20 per cent of non-manufacturing staff now work from home, working out with their manager how often and when they come into the office. World-wide, over 3,500 employees use the teleworking system.

The set-up cost per employee was around £3,000, including the Nortel system installation, a fax, copier, printer and scanner, a desk and ergonomic chair, fire extinguisher and a smoke detector. There are also on-going costs as the company paid for ISDN costs and personal calls. Most employees concerned had already been issued with lap-tops.

The organisation has gradually changed its culture in response to its distributed system of operation. Performance management is now almost totally related to outputs. Managers with homeworkers have needed to be trained in target-setting, measurement and relationships with their staff, for example.

A number of additional benefits have arisen since the scheme began. Retention of existing employees has improved but so has the ability to trawl through a relatively small pool of crucial specialists who no longer will necessarily have to relocate to the company's main centres. This ability to avoid family disruption can be crucial in the decision as to whether to accept a job opportunity, as well as saving a large amount of re-location costs.

In addition, the proportion of staff returning from maternity leave has risen as many have joined the teleworking loop and take part in audio-conferencing to keep themselves up to date.

Overall, the scheme has been seen as very successful indeed, not just for the speed of take up by staff but by the hard-nosed measures of increases in productivity – estimated at around 30 per cent on average. Alongside this has been the substantial saving in office space.

Source: Flexible Working. October 2000, pp11–14

The implications for human resource practitioners are quite complex here, where there has been much debate about the high staff sickness and turnover, quality of job design and the ethical nature of the job requirements.

ACTIVITY 8.6

Call centres have some of the highest staff turnover rates (average over 40 per cent) and absenteeism rates (over 6per cent) of any UK employment sector. Can you suggest why this has happened and what should be done about it?

EFFECT ON THE STRUCTURE OF HUMAN RESOURCE OPERATIONS

Sparrow *et al* (2004) have set out the way that technology has facilitated new and developing human resource systems, as follows.

Shared services – this is the system adopted by many large organisations, such as Lloyds TSB, Whitbread and HSBC, to extract the routine HR processes from operating units and place them in a central service, not necessarily anywhere near a head office. Activities include payroll, record keeping (attendance, starters and leavers, pensions), the operation of recruitment, job advertising and short-listing together with advice on company HR systems and employment law. Technology allows the access to the databank of information held at the centre that can be drawn upon by local managers and video-conferencing arrangements for wider discussion of action on, say, a difficult disciplinary situation. Many shared services have access to a network of experts for areas such as reward and benefits or selection testing.

The savings that are made by using this system involve the cutting back of duplication of HR support at each operating unit (averaging 20-40 per cent), moving the work to low-cost locations, savings on purchasing of technology and services at one point rather than many and a near certainty that consistent decisions will be made, avoiding litigation in discrimination and other legal areas (Reilly 2000).

E-enablement of HR processes – the ability to get HR information to and from, and support onto, line managers' desks without a formal HR intervention allows far more time for the HR department to focus on more strategic areas. The early stages of developments here of access to policy documents and routine statistical processes has moved on to empowering line managers to take greater control of their HR responsibilities. They can access external information on pay and benefits, authorise pay increases, select the appropriate standardised terms and conditions to go in an offer letter, process key data on an individual's performance management and manage their staff and training budgets.

Outsourcing of HR – service centres and e-empowerment can be organised in-house or it may be outsourced to firms that have the technological expertise to offer such services at low cost. For example, Arinso Corp have contracted with Shell to produce a shared services system utilised by over 100,000 employees across 45 countries (Glover 2004). HR departments may therefore be reduced in capacity with interesting implications for career planning. The normal stepped climb up the organisation may instead become leaps between service providers and organisations, not unlike the current career path of senior management.

An example of shared services is shown in Case Study 8.6.

CASE STUDY 8.6

Shared HR services at Standard Chartered Bank

In the early 1990s, Standard Chartered Bank decentralised its decision-making processes to regional centres around the world. However, this led to a patchwork of different approaches, duplication of effort, myopia, constant reinvention of the wheel and a large increase in costs.

In 2001, the company decided to revert to centralising standard transactional processes and delivering them to its 32,000 employees in 56 countries through Web technology from Chennai in India. This location was picked because of its technology infrastructure availability, well-educated workforce and low costs. Here 45 staff will handle routine enquiries, supporting the standardised HR systems and processes available on the Web. Eighty-five local HR jobs were eliminated in the process, with substantial cost savings.

The local HR teams will lose much of their autonomy with the driving force the concept of 'a single recruitment and reward process so that everybody does it the same way time and time again' (p36). The menu on offer includes development planning, scheduling of training courses, talent management tools and e-learning.

Routine calls will be handled by staff with a call-centre background. If they cannot solve the query, it is referred to a 'case analyst', who has postgraduate HR qualifications. The remaining HR structure consists of a 12-strong organisational effectiveness team based at head office responsible for formulating HR strategy and working with the business to improve its performance. The next level down consists of centres of excellence: small, geographically dispersed groups of specialists in resourcing, reward and organisational learning.

Source: Arkin (2002)

 Originally published in *People Management* 24 January 2002, and reproduced with permission

---

KNOWLEDGE MANAGEMENT

So great is the speed of technological innovation and so dominant are the changes that it brings in the form of new products, services or the way we live and work, that commentators have expressed the view that we now live in the 'knowledge economy'. Furthermore:

> ** A firm's competitive advantage depends more than anything on its knowledge, or, to be slightly more specific, on what it knows, how it uses what it knows and how fast it can know something new. **
>
> **Prusack (1997), ix**

Having the knowledge can be regarded as even more important than possessing the other means of production – land, buildings, labour and capital, because all the other sources are readily available in an advanced global society while the right leading-edge knowledge is distinctly hard to obtain. Linked to this thinking is the concept of 'intellectual capital', which can be bought (and, if appropriate, stored securely) either through purchasing patents or intellectual property rights or through employing the highly skilled/intelligent employees/consultants who possess that capital (Stewart 2001).

This capital is not necessarily discoveries and processes that can be patented. Society is developing in such a way that services are becoming the dominant commodity over manufacturing. This means that skilled services in areas such as advertising, design, leisure and even sport can command very high fees – just look at the prices paid for the world's top hundred footballers, film stars or music performers. So wealth created in the economy is increasingly perceived as derived from knowledge and intangible assets (Storey and Quintas 2001).

ACTIVITY 8.7

Do you see knowledge as a source of competitive advantage in the market-place? If so, how?

Because it is such an important asset, organisations are starting to assess their own collection of knowledge bases and ensure they are available for use. This is not just about sorting patents but analysing the knowledge gained through the experiences of their skilled staff. In HSBC, for example, a senior manager has been appointed to identify banking expertise among staff and ensure this knowledge is not lost when they retire or leave the organisation and to organise ways that critical knowledge can be shared across the organisation. Part of the role is to develop 'tacit knowledge', such as the intuitive approaches to problem-solving in a particular work context or vague ideas about a new product or service into 'explicit knowledge' that can be written down and communicated (Stredwick and Ellis 2005).

ISSUES IN TECHNOLOGY

Although technological developments generally lead to improvements in standards of living, not all are seen as universally benign. For every five citizens who welcome new products, job opportunities, improved quality and variety of services, better healthcare and ease of transportation, a sixth will see a darker side with bleaker effects. This can be examined by looking at each of the three short case studies illustrated in this chapter.

Case Study 8.1 Gene therapy. In itself, this is a dispiriting case of shaken expectations but there are further difficulties in this area. One of the success stories has been the development of devices to allow accurate screening for genetic disorders. This can be carried out at any age and even for unborn babies. The main benefit is that such disorders can be treated at an early stage so that the prognosis improves. However, this presents a number of problems. First of all, insurance companies (and employers who provide and pay for life insurance of their employees) are very interested in carrying out such tests before accepting insurance risk. For those citizens with no disorders and long life expectancy, life insurance costs would be cheap but pensions expensive. For those with a disorder, the opposite would apply with life assurance virtually impossible to obtain. There is considerable debate currently as to whether such tests should be compulsory, the outcome of which would leave vulnerable citizens uninsurable and regarded as second-class citizens. A second problem is the dilemma faced by the parents where pre-natal tests show up genetic disorders. They provide the opportunity for the birth to be aborted and some of the life-long pain averted, but such an irreversible decision is a very hard one to take and most parents (except those who already have one disabled child) choose to avoid taking such tests.

Case Study 8.3 Lettuce leaves. There are a number of ethical and regulatory issues surrounding this case. First, it is becoming very difficult to challenge the power of the largest supermarkets in demanding such tight schedules on suppliers and, subsequently, their employees. In America, Wal-Mart, with over 25 per cent of the huge US market, virtually writes the rules with suppliers being unable to match its negotiating power. The situation in the UK is somewhat better with a competing group of supermarkets matched against, in certain product areas, a similar group of large producers, but the growing dominance of Tesco is creating some worries for regulators. This issue is discussed further in Chapter 5 on Regulation. The second issue is whether it is ethical for so many migratory labourers, living in poor conditions, to provide fresh food for the community in the twenty-first century. It is hoped that they are protected by the Minimum Wage Act, but many will slip through the net and the rules concerning deductions for accommodation are very complex with such situations being rarely investigated. Added to this are some safety issues, which was shown graphically by the death of 20 illegal Chinese immigrants working as cockle-pickers in Morecambe bay in 2003. Consumers may demand fresh produce at affordable prices but it may come at an indefensible cost.

Case Study 8.6 Shared HR services. There are experiences of 'one product fits all' which may not apply in fast-moving, customer-orientated businesses. The quality of the service provided by unqualified staff can be questionable with a background in call centre work rather than human resources. Many opportunities for seriously effective HR interventions and innovations can arise through regular discussions about routine issues, often in informal settings, which are far less likely to happen under formalised shared services environments. Moreover, services that are shared across countries run the risk of cultural confusion.

WHAT OF THE FUTURE?

'The horse is here to stay!'

Forecasting the effects of new technology is very tricky and many serious and well-respected forecasters have got their forecasts very wrong. In an excellent article by Smith (2004), which details truly awful forecasts, he quotes pioneers in the IT industry from whom we would have expected a clearer vision. For example, IBM forecast in 1952 that their worldwide sales of mainframe computers would be 52 and, 30 years later, had raised this figure to 200,000, roughly what they now ship every week. Even Bill Gates made gaffes, such as stating in 1981 that '640k should be enough for anybody'. Going further back, the President of Michigan Savings Bank advised people in 1901 against investing in the Ford Motor Company, quoting the statement at the beginning of this section.

There was a better performance by Kahn in his 1967 book *The Year 2000* where he predicted computers, mobile phones, video recorders and satellite dishes. But he, like many forecasters since, seriously misjudged the effect of technology on working lives. Almost everybody had forecast that we would all be working far fewer hours (30 a week at most, according to Kahn), have much more holiday and retire very early. This was because technology would take away jobs, which it clearly does. What almost all futurologists failed to grasp is that, while some jobs disappear, more arise in their place. Production jobs have disappeared either through automation and robotics or to developing countries with lower wages. In their place have arisen industries that provide services – business services, such as IT, financial services and many consultancy services, or those that provide personal services, such as leisure, health and beauty and personal finances. At the same time, services that used to operate for the few, such as hotels, eating out, travel and tourism, are now used by everybody in increasing numbers.

What is just as significant is that such new and developing industries are generally very labour intensive (automated hairdressing is still not with us) so technology has released employees from the grind of heavy production but provided instead the more sociable but equally routine (and absolutely vital) tasks involved in such activities as 'housekeeping' in hotels and 'care working' in hospitals and old people's homes. This explains why the average working week has decreased only marginally in the last 25 years and why unemployment in flexible societies, such as the UK and America, remains very low.

KEY LEARNING POINTS

- Technological development can occur through incremental innovation, radical innovation, change in technological systems or technological revolution (Freeman 1987).

- 'Business Intelligence' is a key concept where the aim is to transform large amount of data, often scattered across the organisation, into the key information that drives informed decision-taking, and to deliver it in an easily read form through the computer screen to anybody where and when they need to know.

- Technological developments provide the capacity for organisations to be *flexible* and to be *eager to change,* in fields such as product design, advertising and marketing (especially on the Web), customer relations and quality development.

- Technology has had a profound effect upon labour markets through facilitating novel flexible working practices, such as annualised hours, complex shift systems and multi-skilling, together with the development of sophisticated recruitment and selection processes.

- Human resource systems have been affected by the technological changes that allow systems of shared services, outsourcing and e-enablement of HR processes.

- It has been recognised in recent years that Knowledge management is a vital process to ensure that organisations can collect, store and distribute key areas of knowledge that help create competitive advantage.

Social Responsibility and Ethics

INTRODUCTION

This chapter examines the nature of ethics, and different approaches which can be taken to ethical problems. It discusses professional and business ethics, stakeholder theory, values, and codes of ethics. The second half of the chapter analyses corporate social responsibility (CSR) and sustainability, the role of businesses, HR and the Government in promoting CSR, and the extent of compatibility between CSR and profit.

ETHICS

The theory of ethics can be extremely complex, and in order to be of use in a day-to-day work situation, it must be made practical. Here we immediately run up against a problem. To philosophers, ethics is about the theory of right and wrong, not about the practical application of those principles. This is the area of morals. Ethics involves the values that a person seeks to express in a certain situation, morals the way he or she sets out to achieve this (Billington 2003).

A wider definition of ethics is given by Connock and Johns (1995). This includes the following three elements:

1   fairness

2   deciding what is right and wrong

3   the practices and rules which underpin responsible conduct between individuals and groups.

Billington (Billington 2003, pp20–25) lists five distinctive features of ethics:

1   Nobody can avoid ethical decisions. We all make ethical decisions every day.

2   Other people are always involved in ethical decisions. There is no such thing as private morality.

3   Ethical decisions matter – they affect the lives of others.

4   Although ethics is about right and wrong, there are no definitive answers. The philosopher can put forward principles which should guide decisions, but the ultimate decision is always down to the individual.

5   Ethics is always about choice – a decision where the individual has no choice cannot be unethical.

ACTIVITY 9.1

Can you think of any situations where an individual has no choice about what action they should take – in a work environment, or any other situation?

Ethical principles

Billington identifies three different approaches to ethics:

1   Absolutism – ethics are underpinned by absolute values, which apply in all societies and to all situations: the Ten Commandments. The problem here is that an absolutist might make decisions which could be seen as morally repugnant. For example, a pacifist who believes literally in the absolutist statement 'Thou shalt not kill' would logically have found himself refusing to fight the evil of Nazism.

2   Relativism – ethics depends on the situation, and on the cultural mores prevalent at a particular time or place. Thus for example, racism in Victorian England, or child labour in present-day Pakistan must be seen as reflecting the mores of those societies – the 'When in Rome' principle. This approach has been criticised on two grounds: that it freezes the status quo and is therefore inherently conservative, and that in practice every major religion (Buddhism, Christianity, Confucianism, Hinduism, Judaism, Islam and Sikhism) subscribed to the absolutist Golden Rule (see below) (Snell 1999).

3   Utilitarianism – as Jeremy Bentham put it in the early nineteenth century, 'The good of the greatest number is the criterion of right or wrong' (Billington 2003, pp35–40, 119). This begs the question of what does 'good' mean.

Archie Carroll widened out these principles into eleven ethical guidelines (Carroll 1990).

Table 9.1 *Carroll's ethical guidelines*

Name of principle	Description
Categorical imperative	You should not adopt principles of action unless they can be adopted by everyone else
Conventionalist ethic	Individuals should act to further their self-interest as long as they do not violate the law
Golden rule	Do unto others as you would have them do to you
Hedonistic ethic	If it feels good, do it
Disclosure rule	You should only take an action or decision if you are comfortable with it after asking yourself whether you would mind if all your associates, friends and family were aware of it
Intuition ethic	You do what your 'gut feeling' tells you is right
Means-end rule	You should act if the end justifies the means
Might-equals-right ethic	You should take whatever advantage you are powerful enough to take
Organisation ethic	Be loyal to your organisation
Professional ethic	Do only that which can be justified to your professional peers
Utilitarian principles	The greatest good of the greatest number

Source: adapted from Carroll (1990)

The three most popular among managers were the Golden Rule, the Disclosure Rule and the Intuition Ethic.

Ethical dilemmas

Managers face ethical dilemmas at work every day of their working lives. Some typical ones are examined in Activity 9.2 below. On the basis of interviews with managers in Hong Kong, Snell (1999) identified a number of typical sources of dilemmas (Table 9.2).

Table 9.2 *Sources of dilemmas*

Sources of dilemma	% incidence
Subordinates' perceived deceit, incompetence or disobedience	18
Policy, or request by superior, that is mistaken	25
Policy, or request by superior, that is ethically suspicious, exploitative or unfair	13
Improper, suspicious or unfair request from client, supplier or colleague	6
Conflicting instructions, ,decisions or directives from above	9
Caught in the middle of a direct conflict between other parties	5
Direct dispute with another party	6
Aware of another's misconduct, neglect or unfairness, but not directly responsible	8
Other	10

Source: Snell (1999), p347

Snell's interviews also suggested four possible responses arising from requests by a superior to do something they knew to be wrong (Snell 1999, p348):

1 'little potato' obedience (quiet, fearful, humble, deferential conformity)
2 token obedience (following orders half-heartedly and semi-incompetently)
3 undercover disobedience (only pretending to obey, and keeping disobedience hidden)
4 open disobedience (conscientious objection).

ACTIVITY 9.2
Ethical dilemmas

■ You are a personnel manager for a medium-sized company, and you are faced with what you see as a series of ethical dilemmas Consider how you would approach each scenario, and what ethical principles you would apply.

Scenario 1 It is the custom in your industry for customers to be lavishly entertained. Your company gives each customer's sales manager a bottle of very good quality malt whisky on his or her birthday, his or her partner's birthday, and at Christmas. Your purchasing manager expects similar perks from his suppliers.

Scenario 2 Your organisation is undertaking a number of redundancies. You decide who is to be made redundant. The production manager asks you to add a particular worker to the list. This worker does not meet any of your criteria for redundancy, but he is well known for not getting on with the production manager. You point out that if you sack this worker without justification, he will take you to an employment tribunal and will win a claim of unfair dismissal. The production manager's response is, 'Fine, It'll be worth it to get rid of him'.

Scenario 3 You are responsible for training, and you have used an old friend of yours to run a recent training programme. Your friend met all your criteria, and had adequate if not glowing references. However, the feedback from the programme is strongly negative. You are about to repeat the programme, and your friend has asked you if he or she will be given a repeat contract.

■ How far do you think Snell's identified responses to ethical dilemmas are likely to be universally valid, and how far do you think they reflect the culture of Hong Kong?

Professional ethics

If one is thinking of words to describe a professional, one probably comes up with words like:

■ qualified
■ objective
■ impartial
■ honest
■ competent
■ accountable.

These words all imply ethical principles, and one main role of a profession is to set and maintain ethical standards for its members. Rosemary Harrison (2002), p139, stresses two aspects:

1   qualified advice
2   standing by the integrity of that advice.

This implies two ethical responsibilities:

1   to the organisation for which one works (organisational ethics) and
2   to impartial integrity (an absolutist ethic, which lies at the heart of professional ethics).

Most professions lay down ethical standards for their members to follow through a Code of Ethics, and the Chartered Institute of Personnel and Development is no exception. Its *Code of Professional Conduct and Disciplinary Procedures* (2003a) can be downloaded from www.cipd.co.uk.

Lawton (1998), p88 suggests 10 functions for a code of professional ethics:

1   to promote ethical, and deter unethical behaviour
2   to provide a set of standards against which to judge behaviour
3   to act as guidance to decision-making
4   to establish rights and responsibilities
5   a statement indicating what the profession stands for
6   to create a contract between professionals and clients
7   to act as a statement of professional development
8   to legitimise professional norms and justification for sanctions
9   to enhance the status of the profession
10   a statement of professional conduct.

Business ethics

We have now moved some distance from our original concern with individual ethics. As we have seen, professions can impose ethics on their members. We now go one step further, and consider whether there is, or should be, a distinct field of study called business ethics – in other words, does a business, organisation or public body have any ethical responsibilities over and above the ethical responsibilities of the individuals who work for it?

Peter Drucker argues that ethics is, by its very nature, a code of individual behaviour. As a result, a business has no ethical responsibilities separate from those of every individual. An act which is not immoral or illegal if done by an individual cannot be immoral or illegal if done by a business. For example, if an individual pays money to an extortioner under threat of physical or material harm, that individual has in no way acted immorally or illegally. However, Drucker quotes the case of the Lockheed aircraft company, which gave in to a Japanese airline which extorted money as a prerequisite for purchasing its L-1011 airliner, and was heavily criticised for doing so. He says, 'There was very little difference between Lockheed's paying the Japanese and the pedestrian in Central Park handing over his wallet to a mugger' (Drucker 1990, p236).

CASE STUDY 9.1

The disciplinary powers of the CIPD

In an article in *Personnel Today* in October 2001, Paul Kearns argued that the CIPD should be prepared to 'strike off' negligent, incompetent or dishonest members, in the same way that the General Medical Council strikes off doctors, or the Law Society, solicitors. He argued that this was essential for the CIPD to have credibility as a profession, particularly given its new Chartered status. The implication was that such a striking-off should be public, and that a person who had been struck off should be prevented from practising the profession.

In response, the Secretary of the CIPD, Kristina Ingate, made three points. First, a comparison with professions such as medicine or the law is not appropriate. Personnel is not a statutory closed shop, unlike medicine or law, and CIPD membership is not a requirement to work in the personnel field. Secondly, the CIPD has a disciplinary procedure, and, as a last resort, members in breach of its Code of Professional Conduct can be expelled from the Institute, although admittedly this is likely to be for misconduct rather than for incompetence. However, she urges caution. By its very nature personnel is about human relationships, frequently in stressful situations. As a result, a complaint about a personnel practitioner will frequently either be totally unwarranted, or in reality a complaint against the policies or practices of the employer, rather than the individual practitioner. Thirdly, CIPD members have high standards of both conduct and competence, and members are expected to keep their competence up to date through continuing professional development.

Source: Kearns and Ingate (2001)

It seems to me that Drucker's example is a poor one. The mugger can do the pedestrian a great deal of physical harm if the wallet is not handed over. On the other hand, the airline could not positively harm Lockheed by not buying its plane. I would regard the Lockheed case not as extortion by the airline, but as bribery by Lockheed, and a clear case of breach of business ethics.

In contrast, Michael Hoffman argues that companies can be held morally responsible (Hoffman 1990, p250). Companies can be morally good or bad according to the consequences of their actions. They espouse values, and individuals coming into the corporation are subject to those values. These values are maintained and reinforced by the culture of the organisation. As a result, it is quite legitimate to talk of business ethics as separate from individual ethics.

Stakeholders

Stakeholders are 'those individuals or groups who depend on the organisation to fulfil their own goals and on whom, in turn, the organisation depends' (Johnson and Scholes 1997). Stakeholders can be inside the organisation, like shareholders or employees, or outside, like customers or suppliers. In some cases, the relationship is legal, as with statutory regulatory bodies or lenders, or moral, as with the local community, or a mixture of the two, as with employees (to meet the requirements of the contract of employment and to respect legal employment rights [legal], and to fulfil the expectations of the psychological contract [moral]). In the case of the public sector, there are no shareholders, but a wide range of client stakeholders.

Note that the CIPD has a narrower definition of stakeholder. It includes only those parties who have a legal or financial relationship with the organisation. All others are defined as 'other interested parties' – the CIPD specifically mentions the media and the local community (CIPD 2003b, pp6, 30). However, this narrow definition ignores the moral and ethical dimensions of stakeholder theory. For example, a local community may have no legal claim on a company that routinely but legally pollutes its environment, but few would deny its moral claim on the company.

Stakeholder theory states that organisations have responsibilities to a wide range of stakeholders. This can be contrasted with the stockholder theory of corporate governance, which states that the organisation's only responsibility is to its shareholders ('stockholders' in American). Stockholder theory has been defended from several different angles. One is the agency approach associated with Milton Friedman. He argues that managers are legally the agents of the organisation's owners (its shareholders), and under agency law are thus legally obliged to serve only their interests, so long as they keep within the law. Another is the logical argument put forward by John Argenti, who argues that it is logically impossible for an organisation to pursue multiple objectives – ie it cannot simultaneously serve the interests of a range of stakeholders. In times of prosperity, the organisation might be able to deal out rewards in such a way as to keep all the stakeholders quiet, but, in hard times, shareholders will take priority, if only because, in the last resort, shareholders can sack the board of directors (Argenti 1993).

Company law in the UK supports the stockholder approach, although UK corporations do have legal responsibilities to other stakeholders, as noted above. Other countries take a different approach to corporate governance. In Germany, companies have two-tier boards, a supervisory board and a management board. The management board runs the company, but is answerable to the supervisory board, which has shareholder, employee and third-party representatives on it (Farnham 1999, pp300–301).

Big business in Japan is organised through large integrated corporations called *keiretsu* (Mitsui, Mitsubishi, etc.). These are both vertical, where manufacturers, suppliers and sub-contractors are members of the same *keiretsu*, and horizontal, where the *keiretsu* companies operate in different markets. Mitsubishi, for example, is involved in gas, chemicals, plastics, steel, aluminium, cement, butter, brewing and paper (Charkham 1994, p77).

Customers and suppliers are thus frequently within the same *keiretsu*, and relationships with them are thus much closer than in the West (as a corollary, customers and suppliers outside the *keiretsu* might find themselves much more harshly treated). Japanese society is also heavily based on the concepts of family, consensus and *wa* (harmony). This leads naturally to a heavy reliance on the stakeholder approach. The hierarchy of interests tends to be customers first, employees second, managers third, and shareholders last. The controversy over excessive 'fat cat' rewards to top management which is so prevalent in the UK would be impossible in Japan.

Not all stakeholders are equal. Some are much more important to the organisation than others. The relative importance of stakeholders can be analysed using stakeholder mapping (Johnson and Scholes 1997, pp197–203. Stakeholder mapping classifies stakeholders by the power which they have over the organisation, and the degree of interest which they have in it. These can be plotted on a two-by-two matrix (Figure 9.1).

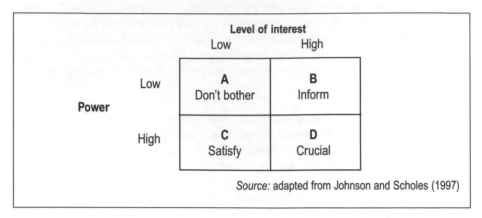

Figure 9.1 *Stakeholder mapping*

Stakeholders of type A can effectively be ignored. They are not interested in the organisation, and have little power to affect it anyway. Conversely, type D are critical, and their interests must be taken into account at all times. Type B are interested in the organisation, but do not have the power to affect it significantly. They need to be kept informed, particularly as they may in turn be able to influence other stakeholders. Type C are passive stakeholders. They have great potential to influence the organisation, but at present little interest in doing so. They need to be kept quiet, so that they do not suddenly take an adverse interest in the organisation, and shift into type D.

The implication is that stakeholders have to be actively managed. They can be crucial in mobilising support for the organisation, or, if things go badly, they can cripple it.

ACTIVITY 9.3

Edexcel

Edexcel is one of three major examination boards in England, Wales and Northern Ireland. It awards 1.5 million qualifications a year, which include GCSEs, A levels, BTEC qualifications, NVQs and GNVQs. Its annual turnover is £112m. The other major examination boards are AQA (turnover £128m) and OCR (turnover £77m).

Edexcel was formed in 1996 as a result of a government-inspired merger between BTEC, a quango (quasi-autonomous non-governmental organisation), which specialised in vocational qualifications, and the University of London Examinations and Assessment Council, owned by London University, which specialised in GCSE and A level qualifications. At this stage Edexcel had charitable status.

Edexcel and the other exam boards are answerable to the Qualifications and Curriculum Authority (QCA), the regulator for the industry, and ultimately to the Department for Education and Skills.

Running an examination board is a high-risk activity. GCSE and A level results are issued in a blaze of publicity each summer, and any mistakes made by the exam boards are picked up by the media in a blaze of adverse publicity. Exam boards always seem to get the blame, even for things which are not their own fault. .

An extreme example occurred in the summer of 2002. Edexcel had already endured a wave of bad publicity in the winter of 2001–02, which culminated in a threat by the Education Secretary, Estelle Morris, to strip Edexcel of its licence, condemnation by Number 10 as 'sloppy' and 'unacceptable', and a public apology by Edexcel's chief executive John Kerr. Then in the summer of 2002, there was a row over late changing of grade boundaries for A levels, which led to many A level grades having to be changed, and hundreds of university places being put at risk. Ironically, Edexcel was not at fault – the main culprit was OCR – but all the exam boards suffered from the resulting media storm. The chairman of QCA, Sir William Stubbs, was sacked, and eventually the Education Secretary herself resigned.

In 2003, Edexcel was taken over by the media giant Pearson, an FTSE 100 company with wide interests, including the *Financial Times*, and the publisher Pearson Education. Pearson already had interests in examination systems overseas, and saw it as its aim to 'globalise the marking process'. It is investing heavily in order to computerise the examination system, including online testing and marking.

Ken Boston, the new chairman of QCA, said at the time of the takeover, 'I see no reason why we should blanch at private sector companies'. However, other commentators were less complacent. Martin Ward, deputy general secretary of the Secondary Heads Association, said, 'the entry of a commercial organisation...has the potential for less accountability', while Ted Wragg, emeritus professor of education at Exeter University, said, 'I feel alarmed about the future ... People want to feel that an examination board is focused on standards, not profit'.

Sources: Lewis (2002) and Curtis (2004)

- Identify and map the stakeholders (including 'other interested parties' of Edexcel as at the summer of 2004.
- Do you think that the public service role of Edexcel is incompatible with its private ownership?

CASE STUDY 9.2

Stakeholding in reverse: Huntingdon Life Sciences

Huntingdon Life Sciences is an organisation in Cambridgeshire which carries out drug tests on behalf of the pharmaceutical industry. Many of these tests involve experiments on animals. This is legal, but is regarded as immoral by the animal rights pressure groups. Co-ordinated by Stop Huntingdon Animal Cruelty (SHAC), the pressure groups have carried out a long campaign to force Huntingdon to close down.

The animal rights groups have used tactics, including physical violence against employees, which are themselves morally questionable, but this case study is not concerned with the ethics of the situation (do the ends justify the means?) but with the involvement of Huntingdon's stakeholders. Pressure has been put not only on Huntingdon, but on its stakeholders, including its bankers, its insurers and the market maker which dealt in its shares. In industrial relations, this is known as secondary picketing, and was banned by the Conservative Government in the 1980s.

The technique has been partly successful. The Government has been forced to supply banking and insurance services to Huntingdon itself, and the company has delisted its shares in London, and transferred its legal domicile to Maryland, USA, where company law enables it to operate in much more secrecy than in London.

However, the research facility is still operating, and the company and its stakeholders have found a way to use the law against its opponents. Using the Protection from Harassment Act 1997, which was originally designed to protect individuals against stalkers, both Huntingdon and some of its stakeholders (including in one case the landlord of a stakeholder (tertiary picketing?) have obtained injunctions placing exclusion zones around their premises and the homes of their employees.

Sources: Williams (2001) and *Tait (2003)*

ACTIVITY 9.4

The child labour dilemma

You are personnel manager for a UK clothing retailer. In addition to your personnel duties, you are also the company's ethics officer, responsible for implementing the Code of Ethics. One of your successful clothing lines are T-shirts, which are assembled in Pakistan and imported into the UK.

Opening your e-mails today, you find a report from one of your buyers of his recent visit to Pakistan. He reports that in a plant in Lahore, he has seen girls who look no older than 10, sweeping the floor between the rows of sewing machines the other women work on. Your code of ethics does not specifically mention child labour, but it does contain a clause about treating all workers, both directly employed and employed by suppliers, with dignity and respect.

Your first action is to e-mail Mansur Khan, your agent in Lahore, and to ask him to investigate. He reports back that working conditions aren't bad. The girls concerned are aged from eleven upwards, and are the daughters of female production workers. He also says that child labour below the age of 14 is illegal in Pakistan, but there is widespread evasion of the law, which is not generally enforced.

Your first reaction is to tell your Purchasing Department to insist that the supplier stops employing the children, or your contract with it will be cancelled. However, a friend then brings to your attention the view of the International Confederation of Free Trade Unions (ICFTU), which has called for clauses on labour standards to be incorporated into World Trade Organisation (WTO) agreements, despite claims by developing countries that they could be used to prevent Third-World goods competing against Western products.

The ICFTU is concerned by employers that pay low wages, use child labour, ignore health and safety standards and deny staff union representation. Some argue that free trade is exacerbating exploitation by allowing companies to relocate to wherever production costs are lowest, regardless of local employment standards. But NGOs and developing countries argue that if Third-World countries are to compete in the global economy, they cannot afford to pay the same levels as Western employers, because their productivity levels are much lower. Developing countries should not be denied the competitive advantage they gain from lower wages.

You are now thoroughly confused. Do you have the right to impose Western moral principles on the factory in Lahore, if there is a risk that as a result the girls and their mothers will lose their jobs?

You decide that the best way forward is use Archie Carroll's ethical principles.

Using in turn the Golden Rule, the Disclosure Rule, the Intuition Ethic and the Utilitarian Principle, think about what your response to this problem would be.

Values

Values underpin ethics, and the values of an organisation underpin its business ethics. Organisational values answer the question 'What do we stand for?' – 'What are the key principles that matter to us?'. This is the second of three questions which organisations must ask themselves as they evolve their mission statement (see BITC 2000).

1 What are we here to do? (purpose)

2 What do we stand for? (values)

3 What would we like to see ourselves become? (vision)

Values, so long as they are shared, help to bring together the people in an organisation, and get them working for a common aim (purpose and vision). Successful companies place a high emphasis on values, and share the following three characteristics (Deal and Kennedy 1990, p108).

1 They stand for something.
2 Management fine-tunes their values to conform to the environment of the organisation.
3 The values are known and shared by everyone in the organisation, and are also known, understood and supported by key stakeholders.

A value-driven company is likely to be more consistent in its decision-making, to be single-minded, and not to be deflected from its long-term vision by short-term expediency. Its staff are also likely to be more committed and motivated, so long as they have ownership of the values. However, values can be counter-productive if top management behaviour is not consistent with their stated values. For example, one of the long-standing values of Marks & Spencer was support of suppliers, and the company lost a great deal of public sympathy when it axed long-standing suppliers in the UK in order to buy more cheaply abroad.

Codes of ethics
One definition of a code of ethics is 'a written, distinct, formal document, which consists of moral standards which help guide employee or corporate behaviour' (Schwartz 2001, p27).

Codes can be of three different types (Brinkmann and Ims 2003, p266):

1 educational – aimed at increasing moral awareness and behaviour within the organisation.
2 regulatory – detailed rules for behaviour, which recognise moral conflicts and help with resolving them.
3 aspirational – laying down general values, and communicating ideals to individuals within the organisation.

Poor codes of ethics tend to be inward-looking, and to ignore external stakeholders, and they tend to be regulatory and over-detailed. Many companies do not make their codes of ethics available to external stakeholders, and some do not even make them easily available to their own staff (which would seem to make them totally counter-productive).

Good codes of ethics recognise the importance of relationships with all major stakeholders, both internal and external, and involve stakeholders in their preparation. They are also clearly communicated to all stakeholders, and training is provided for stakeholders in order to ensure that they are understood and effective.

Even a good code of ethics is no guarantee of ethical behaviour. The existence of codes of ethics did not prevent the scandalous collapse of Enron and WorldCom in the USA, or the deliberate over-statement of oil reserves by Shell. Just as with values, top management must live the code of ethics at all times. If they do not, all respect for the organisation is likely to collapse.

Finally, an American survey in 1987 measured opinions on codes of ethics among American businesspeople. Respondents were asked to comment on a number of statements, with responses coded from 1 (strongly agree) to 4 (strongly disagree) (Table 9.3).

Table 9.3 *Opinions on codes of ethics by US businesspeople*

	Mean response
Professionals consider codes as a useful aid when they want to refuse an unethical request impersonally	1.8
Codes raise the ethical level of the industry	2.1
A code helps managers in defining clearly the limits of acceptable conduct	1.9
In cases of severe competition, a code reduces the use of sharp practices	2.7
People violate codes whenever they think they can avoid detection	2.5
Codes are easy to enforce	3.3
Codes protect inefficient firms and retard the dynamic growth of the industry	3.3

ACTIVITY 9.5

Multigenome and its code of ethics

Multigenome is a US-based multinational research company. Its code of ethics is reproduced below.

Critically evaluate this code of ethics.

'Because we are separated – by many miles, by diversity of cultures and languages – we need a clear understanding of the basic principles by which we will operate our company. These are:

- that the company is made up of individuals, each of whom has different capabilities and potentials, and all of whom are necessary to the success of the company
- that we acknowledge that individuality by treating each other with dignity and respect
- that we will recognise and reward the contributions and accomplishments of each individual
- that we will continually plan for the future so that we can control our destiny instead of letting events overtake us
- that we maintain our policy of providing work for all individuals, no matter what the prevailing business conditions may be
- that we make all decisions in the light of what is right for the good of the whole company, rather than what is expedient
- that our customers are the only reason for the existence of the company
- that we must use the highest ethics to guide our business dealings to ensure that we are always proud to be a part of Multigenome
- that we will discharge the responsibilities of corporate and individual citizenship to earn and maintain the respect of the community
- as individuals and as a corporate body we must endeavour to uphold these standards so that we may be respected as persons and as an organisation'.

Corporate social responsibility

Corporate social responsibility (CSR) is the way in which an organisation expresses its values in behaviour towards stakeholders. The European Commission defines it as 'a concept whereby companies decide voluntarily to contribute to a better society and a cleaner environment' (European Commission 2001), while the DTI defines it as an organisation which recognises that its activities have a wider impact on society; takes account of the economic, social, environmental and human rights impacts of its activities, and works in partnership with other groups and organisations (DTI 2002).

Several key points come out of these definitions, as follows.

■ CSR is voluntary. Mere compliance with legal requirements is not CSR.
■ An organisation's CSR behaviour must go beyond the law.
■ CSR is active. It involves behaviour, not just good intentions.
■ CSR involves environmental as well as social responsibilities.
■ CSR is often carried out in partnership with others.

Although the EC mentions companies only, CSR extends to all organisations, public and private, profit-making and not-for-profit.

Corporate social responsibility can take a number of forms. These include:

■ community involvement, frequently in partnership with other organisations; this can include sponsorship of worthy bodies, or direct involvement of the organisation's employees in community activities
■ socially responsible investment, which can include ethical banking, and refusal by pension funds to invest in companies making, for example, armaments or cigarettes
■ corporate governance, concerned with the behaviour of a company towards its shareholders, and including elements like the appointment and responsibilities of non-executive directors
■ fair trade – buying goods produced by suppliers who are, for example, organic, or non-employers of children, or not based in human-rights-abusing countries such as Burma
■ sustainability – acting in such as way as to assist the long-term survival of the planet.

Several of these are illustrated in case studies below, derived from winners of Business in the Community's *Awards for Excellence 2004*, (www.bitc.org.uk/resourdes/case_studies).

Corporate social responsibility has been criticised as often being little more than a PR stunt, designed to boost sales rather than to benefit society. This is particularly true of community involvement activities – it has been called 'cause-related marketing'. For example, Vodafone sponsors the England cricket team, but in return gets endless exposure of its logo on players' shirts during Test Matches. Tesco runs its Computers for Schools project, which supplies computers to schools, but only after customers have collected vouchers to verify their spend in Tesco stores. (For a spirited condemnation of cause-related marketing, see Monbiot, 2001.)

CASE STUDY 9.3
The Co-operative Bank

The Co-op Bank launched its ethical policy in 1992, after consultation with customers. It launched its partnership approach in 1997, identifying seven groups of stakeholders, or partners, and pledging to deliver value to them in a socially responsible and ecologically sustainable manner. It published its first triple bottom line (profit, society, environment) independently verified Partnership Report in 1998. The 2002 Partnership Report sets out 77 targets, along with the names of the individuals in the organisation who are charged with their achievement.

It is the UK's biggest provider of financial services to the Credit Union movement, which tackles financial exclusion. Its community investment, at 2.7 per cent of pre-tax profits, is among the best in the UK. Its campaigns mobilise its customers to protest on international human rights issues, for example, against the illicit trade in conflict diamonds – a source of finance which has fuelled civil wars and human rights abuses in Africa – and against the use of cluster bombs.

CASE STUDY 9.4
Marks & Spencer

Marks & Spencer has pulled together its wide range of community involvement programmes into a more focused approach called Marks and Starts. This runs the biggest work experience programme in the UK, designed to help people who face the biggest barriers to obtain sustained employment.

It also takes responsibility for the total footprint of its business through the manufacture, use and disposal of its products. It is rated number 1 by Greenpeace on avoiding GM food, and by Friends of the Earth on pesticide reduction. It is supporting an innovative approach to fisheries management called Invest in Fish, which brings together stakeholders (fishermen, fishing communities, NGOs and the fish trade), to develop a fishing industry which is successful economically, and socially and environmentally responsible.

Early in 1999, Industrial Relations Services carried out a survey of ethics in the workplace (*IRS Employment Trends* 675 March 1999). The survey asked why organisations were involved in community activities. Respondents could choose as many of six responses as they chose. The results were as follows.

		%
1	Enhancement of corporate image	82
2	Moral obligation	62
3	Employee satisfaction	59
4	Develop staff potential	51
5	Promote the business	46
6	Improve profitability	15

Short-term profits (no. 6) were mentioned by only a small minority of respondents, while long-term profitability (nos 1 and 5), employees (nos 3 and 4) and moral obligation (no. 2) were seen as much more important. Perhaps community involvement is a rare example of a true win-win situation. (See also Kelly 1999, 'Corporate citizenship costs more than cash'. *Professional Manager*, January.)

ACTIVITY 9.6

Is your own organisation involved in the community?

Find out what community activities (if any) your own organisation is involved in. If possible, also try to find out why the organisation chose these particular activities. Was the primary motive short-term profits, long-term profits, employee benefit or moral obligation (or a mixture of several of these)?

Sustainability

Sustainability is about our responsibility to the ultimate stakeholder: our own future, and the future of the planet. We are using up the resources of the earth and degrading the planet at an increasing rate, and this can only be at the expense of future generations. 'To operate sustainably, an organisation must ... [be] supportive of the survival of the physical environment and also the communities and economies in which it operates' (*Accountability Primer: Sustainability* (nd) (www.accountability.org.uk).

At the macro level, we have the problem of global warming and the associated climate change, the result of the excess of greenhouse gases, particularly carbon dioxide, in the atmosphere, caused at least in part by our excessive burning of fossil fuel. This can only be tackled at global level (global social responsibility). The Kyoto Treaty in 1999 committed industrialised countries to large reductions in carbon emissions, but this effort has been frustrated by the refusal of the Bush Administration to ratify the treaty. The UK is fully committed to the Kyoto principles, and has introduced a Climate Change Levy on polluting industries.

At a micro level, sustainability concerns us all, organisations and individuals alike. At an individual level, it is as basic as composting our garden waste, rather than sending it to landfill sites, and turning off our television sets at night, rather than leaving them on standby. At an organisational level, it can be about energy conservation, and also about the kind of activities highlighted in the following Case Study and Activity.

CASE STUDY 9.5

Carillion Plc

Carillion is one of the UK's leading construction companies. Its sustainability activities include:

- Self-sufficient materials strategy – when building the M6 toll road, much of the required building materials were sourced from within the construction site, so saving on vehicle movements. Pulverised fuel ash was used to replace cement in concrete mixture, so saving on extraction activities.

- Waste management – Carillion is responsible for hospital waste disposal, and better training on the nature of clinical waste has led to a considerable fall in the volume of material going into clinical waste bins.

- Energy management – consumption of energy in head office buildings was reduced by 19 per cent.

- Sustainable construction – working with its supply chain, Carillion has developed new construction methods which save energy, produce less waste and lower long-term running costs.

Source: adapted from a Business in the Community case study (www.bitc.org.uk)

ACTIVITY 9.7

Explore Worldwide and responsible tourism

In 1999, Richards and Gladwin put forward their definition of a socially sustainable enterprise (Richards and Gladwin 1999).

'The characteristics of a socially sustainable enterprise are that it would:

1 return to communities where it operates – selling as much as it gains from them

2 meaningfully include stakeholders impacted by its activities in associated planning and decision-making processes

3 ensure no reduction in, and actively promote, the observance of political and civil rights in the domains where it operates

4 widely spread economic opportunities and help to reduce or eliminate unjustified inequalities

5 directly or indirectly ensure no net loss of human capital within its workforces and operating communities

6 cause no net loss of direct and indirect productive employment

7 adequately satisfy the vital needs of its employees and operating communities

8 work to ensure the fulfilment of the basic needs of humanity prior to serving luxury wants'.

Explore Worldwide is a UK tour company, specialising in small group exploratory holidays. Its brochure stresses its commitment to sustainability.

Respecting our planet

Our commitment to responsible tourism

Explore's dedication to Responsible Tourism is the driving force behind our Environmental Policy. Far from being an abstract ideal for us, Responsible Tourism shapes all our major decisions – from the concept that 'Small Groups Leave Fewer Footprints' to the choice of local agents and suppliers.

Here are our guidelines in a nutshell:

By operating in small groups, we minimise the impact on the local culture and resources, whilst blending in more easily

We issue our travellers with clear guidelines on responsible tourism. These cover a variety of issues from littler and waste disposal in remote areas, to begging and artefacts. We encourage customers to buy local crafts and support local skills, but never to buy products that exploit wildlife or harm the habitat

We use locally owned suppliers wherever viable to provide and run services. This ensures that the local economy benefits directly. We also expect local suppliers to meet our standards, with particular consideration for the environment

When recruiting Tour Leaders, we assess their environmental credentials and then train them to our own standards. They are also required to complete a Responsible Tourism Audit on each tour

Throughout a tour, the Leader will encourage the education of our customers on the social workings of a region. And part of their role is to make sure that the local communities benefit from our visit, ensuring that we will always be welcome.

Explore's passion for travel goes beyond the yearning for discovery. Ours is a reasoned, tried and tested approach to the enjoyment of a truly amazing planet.

Source: Explore Worldwide 2004–2005 Brochure Reprinted with permission

Critically evaluate Explore's Responsible Tourism policy against Richards and Gladwin's principles.

CORPORATE SOCIAL RESPONSIBILITY AND HR

Who should be responsible for directing an organisation's policy on ethics and corporate social responsibility? There are three leading contenders, each reflecting a particular perception of ethics and CSR:

1 marketing/PR, if CSR is primarily seen as a marketing tool, and the key relationship is that with customers

2 the Company Secretary, if CSR primarily is seen as a matter of regulation, and the key relationship is the corporate governance one with shareholders

3 HR, if CSR is primarily seen as a cultural issue and about human behaviour, and the key relationship is that with all stakeholders.

The theory on ethics and CSR would strongly suggest that the policy can only be meaningful if it permeates all the activities of the organisation, and if everyone in the organisation truly internalises the policy, rather than merely paying lip-service to it. This would suggest that HR should be the lead department. However, of even greater importance is that, whichever department is in day-to-day charge, top management, in the form of the CEO, should at all times behave ethically him- or herself. Just as quality entails Total Quality Management, ethics/CSR requires Total Ethical Management.

So what in detail should be the role of HR in ethics/CSR?

- Helping to identify the values of the organisation. HR should have experience with values, and is well placed to canvass opinions on values across a wide range of stakeholders. Here HR has a clear strategic contribution to make.

- Drawing up a code of ethics. HR should be used to draft policies, many of which themselves have a clear ethical content.

- Behaving ethically in its own relationships with a key stakeholder, the organisation's own staff. Here the concept of the 'psychological contract' is important (CIPD 2003b, pp18–19). This defines the implicit deal between employer and employees, as distinct from the formal deal contained in the contract of employment. It is an understanding about what each side can expect from the other. This has two implications for HR in the context of ethics/CSR: the psychological contract should itself be an ethical one, and the concept of the psychological contract can be extended to relationships with other stakeholders.

- Managing the culture of the organisation. A culture which fully supports ethics does not just happen – it has to be nurtured, maintained and communicated.

- Development. If staff in an organisation are presented with a CSR policy and a code of ethics, it will mean nothing to them until they are thoroughly trained in what they mean and how they should be implemented. This presents HR with a crucial development role, at all levels of the organisation. Some help here is likely to come from the launch of the DTI's online CSR Academy in July 2004 (see 'CSR help is at hand', *Personnel Today*. 27 July 2004).

- Maintaining the 'employer brand'. Increasingly companies want brand values to be reflected in everything that the organisation does. An ethical brand value has clear marketing advantages and recruitment/retention advantages (see CIPD 2003b, p23).

ACTIVITY 9.8

Institutional racism

In 1999 the Macpherson Report on the murder of Stephen Lawrence identified the principle of institutional racism. The report defined this as 'The collective failure of an organisation to provide an appropriate and professional service to people because of their colour, culture or ethnic origin. It can be seen or detected in processes, attitudes and behaviour which amount to discrimination through unwitting prejudice, ignorance, thoughtlessness and racial stereotyping which disadvantages minority ethnic people' (Home Office 1999).

Macpherson argued that because of its ingrained culture (the so-called canteen culture), the Metropolitan Police was institutionally racist. This does not mean that every Met officer is racist, or that there is a deliberate policy of racism in the organisation, but that the organisation is unthinkingly racist in its attitudes and behaviour.

After the publication of the Report, the Met pledged itself to eliminating institutional racism, as did other police forces.

What actions could the police take to eliminate institutional racism?

CORPORATE SOCIAL RESPONSIBILITY AND THE GOVERNMENT

The Government has two main roles in CSR. First, the Government is itself a major employer and a major purchaser and supplier of services. In this role, it can and should behave ethically just like any other organisation.

However, the Government also has a role in the promotion of CSR (Cowe 2004). In March 2000, the first minister for corporate social responsibility was appointed, within the Department for Trade and Industry. The current minister (2004), Stephen Timms, makes it clear that the Government takes its role seriously: 'What we are talking about here is beyond philanthropy. CSR is not an add-on. It must be about the very way we do business, both at home and overseas'.

The main interest of the Government has been in securing greater transparency. The Pensions Act of 2000 requires pension fund trustees to make a statement of investment principles, disclosing their policy on social, environmental and ethical issues. Its Company Law Review will lead to the introduction in 2005 of a requirement on all public companies to include an Operating and Financial Review in their annual report to shareholders. In addition, the Government set up a new CSR Academy in 2004.

However, locating the responsibility for CSR within the DTI has inevitably led to an emphasis on the corporate governance aspects of CSR. Other departments clearly also have an involvement in CSR – the Department of Work and Pensions in pensions, the Department for International Development in trade and aid aspects of CSR, and the Department of the Environment in issues of pollution, sustainability and climate change. The involvement of the Government is likely to increase.

THE BOTTOM LINE

Do corporate social responsibility and ethical behaviour increase a company's profits? A series of studies suggests that they do.

First, corporate social responsibility seems to benefit an organisation's reputation. In 2002, Business in the Community carried out a survey on what the public thought of corporate responsibility (BITC 2002). Business leaders in general are not trusted. Only 25 per cent of respondents trusted them to tell the truth – only ahead of politicians and journalists, and well below doctors and teachers. This suggests that business has a lot of ground to make up. The public wants business to be responsible. Only 2 per cent think that companies should maximise their profits, regardless of society or the environment. Eight times as many thought companies should make a major contribution to society, regardless of cost.

Responsible behaviour also affects peoples' purchases. 86 per cent in 2002 thought it very or fairly important that an organisation show a high degree of social responsibility, up from 68 per cent in 1997. One in six people have actively boycotted a product on ethical grounds in previous years.

Is this evidence conclusive? No. It is suggestive, but little more. If you were interviewed by Business in the Community, you might have a shrewd idea of the kind of answers which the interviewer would like! It is also unfortunately true that there is often a gap between what people say they do, and what they actually do.

The second piece of evidence is a report written by the management consultants Arthur D Little in 2003, again for Business in the Community (BITC 2003), *The Business Case for Corporate Responsibility*). This identifies a number of benefits from CSR.

- It offers a means by which companies can build the trust of their stakeholders. This is supported by the American strategy guru Michael Porter, who is reported as saying that how a company is perceived by its stakeholders is becoming a source of competitive advantage (Golzen 2001).

- CSR offers more effective management of risk. CSR encourages firms to understand and empathise with society and the environment, and this makes it more likely that they will be proactive about social and environmental risk.

- CSR helps to attract and retain a talented and diverse workforce.

- CSR stimulates learning and innovation within organisations.

- CSR facilitates access to capital. Over half of analysts and two thirds of investors believe that a company that emphasises CSR is attractive to investor.

- CSR improves competitiveness, market positioning and profitability. The report quotes from Collins and Porras' *Built to Last*, a pioneering study in the 1990s, which compared successful companies which had been in business for at least 50 years, with a control group who had been less successful. It was found that a key characteristic of the successful 'visionary' companies was that they had a core purpose beyond making money (Collins and Porras 2000).

CASE STUDY 9.6

Case studies of ethical companies

Friends Provident

The 200-year-old insurance company is convinced that its Quaker origins and ethical reputation have served to differentiate it from its competitors.

Centrica

After Centrica developed an employee community involvement programme at its Cardiff call centre in 2000, it found higher retention rates among volunteering employees, increased levels of job satisfaction, and lower absenteeism.

The Beacon Press

The Beacon Press has demonstrated that higher standards of quality in printing can be achieved through environmental best practice. This has led it to push the boundaries of technology.

Is the Arthur D Little evidence conclusive? It is certainly very strong. Although some of the findings are based on opinion, others are based on hard evidence of changes in behaviour (see the Case Study on Centrica above).

The third study was carried out by the Institute of Business Ethics in 2003. This examined a sample of FTSE 350 companies which were perceived as being ethical (they had had a code of ethics in operation for at least 5 years, they scored highly on *Management Today*'s annual league table of 'most admired companies', and they were rated highly by the specialist ratings agency SERM on their 'socio-ethical risk management'). These ethical companies were compared with a control sample.

The ethical companies were found to score more highly on three measures of financial performance – market value added, economic value added and price/earnings ratio. On a fourth measure, return on capital employed, they did less well until the stock market collapse of 2000, but have performed better since then, suggesting that their profits are more stable (Caulkin 2003 and Maitland 2003).

Is this evidence conclusive? Again, it is very strong, but unfortunately it is not conclusive. There is clearly a strong correlation between ethical behaviour and profits, but this does not prove that the ethical behaviour causes the profits. The link may be the other way round – profitable companies may be more likely to be ethical – or both may be the result of some unknown third factor.

A more theoretical approach was taken by Reitz, Wall and Love (1998). They concentrated on the relatively narrow area of business negotiation, and argued that taking an unethical stance in negotiation has the following four major costs.

1 Rigidity. Unethical negotiators will tend to stick to the patterns of negotiation which have paid off in the past. They will thus trap themselves in a rigid bargaining position which can be matched and exploited by their opponents.

2 Damaged relationships. If a bargaining partner feels that it has been manipulated through underhand tactics, it is likely to feel embittered and to seek revenge.

3 Sullied reputation. Success in business frequently depends on reputation. If you get a reputation for cheating or other unethical behaviour, this will harm your future business prospects.

4 Lost opportunities. Negotiation is about finding a win-win situation, whereby both sides gain. A reputation for sharp dealing may lead potential partners to avoid making concessions to you, for fear that you will not make concessions in return.

Their conclusion is that ethical negotiation is not only morally desirable; it is good business.

ACTIVITY 9.9

CSR and profits – the contrary view

A strong case against CSR has been made by David Henderson (Henderson 2001). He makes the following points:

■ CSR involves organisations in higher costs, and, in so far as it means that they may forego some activities seen as non-responsible, lower revenue. The result will be lower profits (although he admits that in some cases, this could be offset by gains as a result of enhanced reputation). This argument is supported by evidence that, in 2003, the

Dutch insurance company Aetna spent 20 million euros in order to comply with the US Sarbanes-Oxley regulations, introduced after the Enron scandal (Targett 2004).

■ Some of the leading CSR companies have gone through spectacular collapses in profits. He cites the US jeans manufacturer Levi Strauss, but the same point could be made about Body Shop and Ben and Jerry's ice cream.

■ The CSR agenda is frequently set not by 'society', but non-governmental organisations (NGOs) such as Greenpeace, which he sees as anti-capitalist pressure groups, and as unrepresentative of society as a whole.

Critically evaluate these arguments.

SUMMARY AND CONCLUSIONS

In this chapter has been analysed the nature of personal and professional ethics, whether or not it is possible to see business ethics as a distinct ethical area, the principles and application of stakeholder theory, the use of values and codes of ethics, and the nature and importance of corporate social responsibility.

KEY LEARNING POINTS

■ Three main approaches can be taken to ethics, and these lead to a larger number of ethical guidelines. The most commonly used of these are the golden rule, the disclosure rule and the intuition ethic.

■ All managers face ethical dilemmas on a daily basis in their work.

■ Professionals have an ethical responsibility both to their organisation and to impartial professional integrity.

■ There is a considerable argument over whether a separate business ethic exists.

■ Stakeholder theory holds that organisations have responsibilities to a wide range of stakeholders.

■ Values underpin ethics, and an organisation's values underpin its business ethics.

■ Codes of ethics, unless they are internalised in the organisation's culture, do not guarantee ethical behaviour.

■ Corporate social responsibility is the way in which an organisation expresses its values through its behaviour towards stakeholders. It involves making contributions towards both a better society and a cleaner environment.

■ HR has a key role to play in promoting CSR.

■ The Government has an important role in promoting CSR.

■ Although the evidence is not totally conclusive, it appears extremely likely that there is a positive correlation between CSR and profit.

FURTHER READING

Stephen Connock and Ted Johns' *Ethical Leadership*, published by the CIPD in 1995, is a useful summary of ethical issues from an HR standpoint. The CIPD also published a useful Factsheet on *Corporate Responsibility and HR's role* in 2003 (available on the CIPD website www.cipd.co.uk). Another useful website is Business in the Community (www.bitc.org.uk), which contains a number of useful reports on ethics and CSR.

Strategic Management

INTRODUCTION

This chapter will analyse the nature of strategic management, and identify different models of strategy. It will analyse the stages of strategic decision- making – analysis, choice and implementation. The last part of the chapter will concentrate on the nature and practice of change management.

WHAT IS STRATEGIC MANAGEMENT?

The origins of strategy are military, and concern the art of war. A *strategos* was a general in commend of a Greek army. Quinn (1980) identifies the following three elements of strategy:

1 *Goals or objectives*: what is to be achieved, and when it is to be achieved. Major goals which affect an organisation's overall direction are strategic goals.

2 *Policies* are guidelines which set out the limits within which action should occur. Major policies are strategic policies.

3   *Programmes* lay down the sequence of actions necessary to achieve objectives. They set out how objectives will be achieved within the limits set by policies.

In other words:

- Where do we want to get?
- What actions should we take to get there?
- How can we carry out these actions?

The essence of a strategy is to build a position so strong that the organisation will achieve its objectives no matter what unforeseeable forces attack it (ie How can we win, whatever the enemy does?). Effective strategies should:

- contain clear and decisive objectives – sub-goals may change in the heat of battle but the over-riding objective provides continuity over time
- maintain the initiative
- concentrate power at the right time and place
- have built-in flexibility so that one can use minimum resources to keep opponents at a disadvantage
- have committed and co-ordinated leadership
- involve correct timing and surprise
- make resources secure and prevent surprises from opponents.

Strategic decisions have a number of characteristics, as follows.

- They are concerned with the scope of an organisation's activities – the boundaries which an organisation sets to its activities.
- They are concerned with matching the activities of an organisation to its environment.
- They are concerned with matching the activities of an organisation to its resource capability.
- They often have resource implications for an organisation – if current resources do not permit a particular strategy, can the necessary resources be acquired?
- They affect operational decisions – a whole series of implementing sub-decisions must flow from the making of a strategic decision.
- They are affected by the values and expectations of those who have power in an around the organisation – its stakeholders.
- They affect the long-term direction of an organisation (Johnson, Scholes and Whittington 2004).

Strategy can be seen at the following levels:

- corporate level, concerned with the overall scope of the operation, its financial performance, and the allocation of resources to different operations

- competitive or business unit level – how to compete within a particular market at the level of a strategic business unit (SBU)

- operational level – how the different functions of the organisation contribute to the overall strategy; this level is often seen as tactical rather than in any real sense strategic, but it can equally be seen as the implementation stage of strategy.

Strategic management is about doing the right things. It is:

- ambiguous
- complex
- non-routine
- organisation-wide
- fundamental
- inclusive of significant change
- environment- or expectations-driven.

Operational or tactical management is about doing things right. It is:

- routinised
- operationally specific
- inclusive of small-scale change
- resource-driven.

ACTIVITY 10.1

The Second World War

Each major participant in the war had a different strategic approach to the war, which reflected their resources situation.

UK

- Avoid war if possible.
- If war was inevitable, plan for a long war, and to involve the USA (UK resources were limited, but the UK could draw on the human and technological resources of the Empire, and hopefully of the USA).
- Use the navy to keep supply routes open.
- Build up the defensive capacity of the RAF (fighter planes).

Germany

- Blitzkrieg – go for quick, knock-out blows, exploiting the superior fighting ability of the German army.
- Avoid a long war, because of Germany's limited supply of raw materials, particularly oil.
- Avoid a war on two fronts – this made it essential that the USSR was knocked out of the war in 1941–42.

USSR

- Buy space and time (through the pact with Germany in 1939 which gained the USSR half of Poland and the Baltic States).
- Retreat into the interior of Russia to stretch the German lines of communication (just as in 1812).
- Exploit the USSR's vast reserves of manpower.
- Avoid war on two fronts – hence no declaration of war on Japan until August 1945.
- Press the Western Allies to open a second front in Europe.

USA

- Avoid war.
- Exploit the mass production capacity of American industry to out-produce the Axis powers.

Japan

- Pre-emptive strike – to destroy the US navy at Pearl Harbour.
- Blitzkrieg.
- Seize oil supplies in Indonesia to make up for Japan's shortage of oil.
- Avoid war on two fronts – hence no declaration of war on the USSR.

Once the USA had entered the war in 1941, the Anglo-American allies made the crucial corporate-level strategic decision that the war in Europe was to have first priority. In Asia, Japan was to be contained, particularly at sea.

Another corporate-level (but unsuccessful) strategic decision was to attempt to knock Germany out of the war through strategic bombing, exploiting the West's technological and material advantages, while leaving the USSR to defeat the German armies, using their manpower advantage.

Examples of business unit level decisions were the decision to invade Sicily rather than the Balkans in 1943, and Normandy rather than the Pas de Calais in 1944.

Operational tactical decisions were those to deploy particular national allied armies to particular beaches in the Normandy landings.

How far do the strategic decisions and approaches used in the War fit the characteristics of strategic decisions listed earlier?

MODELS OF STRATEGY

Corporate planning

This was a product of the 1950s and 1960s, a period with a largely placid environment. Detailed corporate plans covering the whole organisation were drawn up by a central planning team and then agreed by top management. The details of the plan were extremely complex, as were the models used, but the planning process itself was relatively simple as the corporate future was seen as programmable because the future was expected to be a continuation of the past. The role of line management was to implement the plan. The main exponent of corporate planning was Igor Ansoff, although he has since modified his views on strategy (Ansoff 1965). There are clear parallels with the system of central planning as used to run the Soviet Union.

The strength of the corporate planning approach is its rigour, and the vital information which is collected in the course of drawing up the plan. However, it has a number of weaknesses. It is inflexible – the plan is too vast and complex to cope with rapid change in the environment. However, some of the best corporate planners – those at Shell – coped with this by developing a range of scenarios about the future environment. One of these forecast exactly the huge rise in oil prices which happened in 1973, with the result that Shell could react very quickly to the new situation.

Centralised corporate planning is also demotivating. Nobody owns the plan except for the planners – the line managers who have to implement it have no commitment to it. At worst, corporate planning was an academic exercise, and the plan was put away in a drawer and quietly forgotten.

Strategic management

This model emphasises adaptability in the face of a turbulent environment. There is no rigid long-term plan, although there are long-term visions and values. Strategy becomes bottom-up, as line managers react to or anticipate changes in the environment. The organisation has to be very responsive to changes in the environment, which requires managers at all levels constantly to monitor the environment. The organisation becomes a learning organisation in the fullest sense of the term, as it is constantly scanning and learning from its environment.

Leading exponents of the strategic management concept are:

Tom Peters. *In Search of Excellence* in 1982 (Peters and Waterman 1982) stressed the importance of a number of attributes for excellence, which emphasised values, simplicity, quick reactions and understanding the customer:

- stick to the knitting
- close to the customer
- productivity through people
- autonomy and entrepreneurship
- hands on, value driven
- bias for action
- simple form, lean staff
- simultaneous loose–tight properties.

He followed this up with *Thriving on Chaos* in 1985 (Peters 1985), wherein he argued that the organisation should cope with chaos by becoming chaotic itself – being in a continual state of flux. He also stressed that chaos provides marvellous opportunities for the fleet of foot.

Michael Porter. Porter approached strategic management as an economist. He stressed the importance of the competitive position of an industry (the Five Forces) (1980), the nature of generic strategies, and the importance of the organisation's value chain in identifying its competitive advantage (1985).

Ralph Stacey. In *The Chaos Frontier* (1991) and *Strategic Management and Organisational Dynamics* (1993), he developed the application of chaos theory to strategic management. The environment facing organisations is one of chaos – multiple and ultimately unpredictable reactions follow from a single event – the classic example of the fluttering of a butterfly's wing ultimately leading to a hurricane. The environment facing an organisation is like that facing a weather forecaster – modelling permits the patterns of weather to be forecastable several days ahead, but the further the forecaster looks into the future, the more outcomes become possible. As a result the organisation must be highly responsive and reactive. The role of top management is to develop and support creativity and innovation.

Gary Hamel and **C K Prahalad**. In *Competing for the Future* (1994), they stressed that the key role of management is to manage the organisation in such a way that it is flexible and able to respond to a changed environment. This means identifying and developing the core competencies of the organisation. We will return to this later. Hamel later developed the *10 principles of revolutionary strategy* (Hamel 1996), given below.

1 *Strategic planning isn't strategic* – it assumed that the future will be more or less the same as the present.

2 *Strategy-making must be subversive* – strategy is about breaking rules and assumptions.

3 *The bottleneck is at the top of the bottle* – top managers are most resistant to change.

4 *Revolutionaries exist in every company.*

5 *Change is not the problem, engagement is* – senior managers fail to give people responsibility for managing change.

6 *Strategy-making must be democratic* – senior managers must recognise that creativity is spread throughout an organisation.

7 *Anyone can be a strategy activist* – senior managers must see activists as positive, not as anarchists.

8 *Perspective is worth 50 IQ points* – organisations have to use all their knowledge to identify unconventional ideas.

9 *Top down and bottom up are not the alternatives* – both are necessary.

10 *You can't see the end from the beginning* – strategy can often throw up surprises.

James Quinn. In *Strategies for change: logical incrementalism* (1980), Quinn developed the concept of logical incrementalism, that strategy does not consist of a big bang, but rather of a series of small steps (incrementalism).

Say an organisation wants to get from A to E. It does not set out to go straight from A to E, but instead identifies intermediate steps on the road, B, C and D. It then concentrates first on getting from A to B, and experiments with ways of getting there. This may involve several false starts and blind alleys, but eventually the firm gets to B. Then it follows the same process to get to C, and so on.

HENRY MINTZBERG AND STRATEGIC MANAGEMENT

One of the most trenchant critics of corporate planning has been the Canadian guru Henry Mintzberg. His writings include *The rise and fall of strategic planning* (1994). He argues that old-style corporate planning was all about left brain activity – numbers, linearity, analysis. Strategic management is right brain – ideas, patterns, relationships, intuition. He talks of crafting strategy, rather than planning strategy. Strategy emerges as a result of a whole series of decisions throughout an organisation.

Mintzberg is famous for his Five Ps of Strategy:

1 Strategy as a **plan** for action. Here the strategy is made in advance of the actions which are relevant to it, and it is applied consciously and purposefully. However, as we will see later, outcomes may not be as expected.

2 Strategy as a **ploy**, a manoeuvre to outwit opponents.

3 Strategy as a **pattern**. A pattern of behaviour becomes a strategy. If a particular course of action tends to lead to favourable results, a strategy emerges. The strategy is the result of events, rather than the cause of them. A variation on this he calls the umbrella strategy, where top management lays down broad principles, and line managers have autonomy to act within these principles. Here strategy is both planned and emergent.

4 Strategy as **position**. Strategy here is about finding a niche in the market, a position which balances the pressures of the environment and the competition.

5 Strategy as **perspective**. Here the strategy reflects how the organisation views the world and its place in it. A classic example is Hewlett-Packard's 'H-P way', where the whole approach of the organisation is based on engineering excellence and innovation. The important thing here is consistency in behaviour.

CASE STUDY 10.1

The Egg McMuffin

One innovation introduced by McDonalds was the Egg McMuffin, basically an egg in a bun, the classic American breakfast. Mintzberg posed the question of whether this was a strategic change for McDonalds. Some students argued that it was – McDonalds was moving into a new market, the breakfast market. Others argued that nothing had changed – all that had happened was that an egg had replaced a burger.

Mintzberg argued that both were right, and both wrong. McDonald's position had changed by moving into breakfasts, but the perspective was exactly the same – the product was classic McDonald's. The position could be changed easily because it was consistent with the perspective. Mintzberg suggested that a change in perspective would involve McDonald's entered the sophisticated evening dining market with a product like a 'McDuckling à l'Orange'

Source: Mintzberg (1998)

Planned strategies often require modification as they are implemented, as environmental or organisational factors change. It is very rare that a long-term strategic plan can be implemented over a period of years without modification. The intended strategy may not be realised in practice, and, even if it is, it may not achieve the desired results.

There are six possible combinations of intended strategy, realised strategy and results, as follows.

1   What is intended as a strategy is realised with desirable results.

2   What is intended as a strategy is realised, but with less than desirable results.

3   What is intended as a strategy is realised in some modified version because of an unanticipated environmental and/or internal requirement or change. The results are desirable.

4   What is intended as a strategy is realised in some modified version because of an unanticipated environmental and/or internal requirement of change. The results are less than desirable.

5   What is intended as a strategy is not realised. Instead, an unanticipated environmental and/or internal change requires an entirely different strategy. The different strategy is realised with desirable results.

6   What is intended as a strategy is not realised. Instead, an unanticipated environmental and/or internal change requires an entirely different strategy. The different strategy is realised with less than desirable results.

ACTIVITY 10.2

Honda and the US motorcycle market

When Honda established an American subsidiary in Los Angeles in 1959, its intended strategy was to push the sales of motorcycles with 250cc and 350cc engines, despite the fact that the much smaller 50cc model was a top seller in Japan. Honda's top managers believed that the American environment and the US consumer would prefer bigger models. However, Honda's 250cc and 350cc bikes did not sell well.

At this time, Honda's executives were using their own 50cc motorbikes to commute in traffic-congested Los Angeles. The convenience and appearance of the bikes began to be noticed. Orders for the 50cc model began to come in from motorbike retailers, but Honda was reluctant because it did not want its image in the USA to be associated with a small, no-frills motorbike. When the major US retailer Sears Roebuck expressed an interest, Honda management changed its mind. The move was overwhelmingly successful

Honda's success in selling its 50cc bikes gradually convinced the firm to try again at developing a market for its bigger bikes. This was successful from the late 1960s to the mid-1980s. Honda's success was partially based on its reliable and sturdy products, but also on the weakness of the competition. With the exception of a lethargic Harley-Davidson, Honda did not face any serious threat from American companies, and European and Japanese competitors had not matched Honda's investment in the US market.

This scenario began to change during the mid-1980s. Foreign competitors became more aggressive in the US market, particularly for small- and medium-sized bikes, while, following a management-led leveraged buyout in 1981, Harley-Davidson began to reassert its dominance in the large-bike market. Harley-Davidson increased its market share for the largest bikes from 23 per cent in 1983 to 60 per cent in 1990. Honda's overall share of the US market plunged from 58 to 28 per cent between 1985 and 1990. Hence, as the competitive situation changed rapidly, Honda's results deteriorated.

Identify episodes in the Honda experience which fit the intended and realised strategies outlined above

THE ELEMENTS OF STRATEGIC MANAGEMENT

The analysis so far may seem extremely complex, but the important thing to remember is that the essence of strategic management is very simple. It consists in getting answers to the following four questions.

1 Where are we?

2 Where do we want to get?

3 How can we get there?

4 What do we have to do to get there?

From this we can derive the three elements of strategic management.

1 *Strategic analysis* – this tackles the first two questions: What is our current position and Where to do we want to go?

2 *Strategic choice* – this is the third question: How can we get there, ie What strategy should we choose?

3 *Strategic implementation* – What do we have to do to implement our chosen strategy?

Strategic analysis

Strategic analysis is concerned with the strategic position of the organisation. What are the key characteristics of the organisation, what changes are going on in the environment, and how will these affect the organisation and its activities? The aim is to form a view of the key influences on the present and future well-being of the organisation.

- Expectations of stakeholders, the culture of the organisation, and, most important, the organisation's vision and values.

- The environment, as identified through a STEEPLE analysis (and other techniques). Many of these variables will give rise to opportunities, and many will pose threats. The main problem is to distil out of the complexity the key environmental impacts for the purposes of strategic choice. I'm sure you will be delighted to hear that we have already covered the necessary techniques for this part of the analysis – the principles of STEEPLE and SWOT in Chapter 1, and Porter's Five Forces and portfolio analysis in Chapter 2, plus the detailed impact of the various elements of the environment throughout the book.

■ Resources. Strategic capability is about identifying strengths and weaknesses by considering the key resource areas of the business such as physical plant, management, finance, products, etc.

Classical corporate planning saw environmental analysis as the key element in strategic analysis, while strategic management sees culture and values as most crucial.

Gap analysis

The extent to which there is a mismatch (a gap) between current strategy and the future environment is a measure of the strategic problem facing the organisation. As the diagram below shows, over time the current strategy is likely to get more out of line with the environment, and a planning gap will grow.

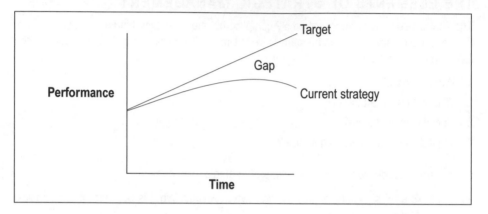

Figure 10.1 *The planning gap*

The organisation needs to choose a new strategy which will ensure that this gap is filled.

Strategic choice

Strategic choice involves the following three steps.

1 Generation of strategic options. Three levels of analysis are involved here: what fundamental or generic strategy should be followed; within this generic strategy, what strategic directions are needed; and then what methods of strategic direction are most appropriate?

2 Evaluation of strategic options. This involves testing options for suitability (do they fit the generic strategy, and will they provide the desired results); feasibility (are resources available or obtainable; and acceptability (do they fit the values of the stakeholders)?

3 Selection of strategy – either logically, using some kind of weighting criteria, or politically.

Strategic implementation

Strategic implementation involves resource planning, organisational structure, systems, change management techniques, etc.

STRATEGIC ANALYSIS

Vision, mission, values and objectives

- Vision, mission, values and objectives are closely linked, and often confused. However, they are clearly distinguished by Peter Senge in *The Fifth Discipline* (1990).

- Vision is the *what* – the picture of the future we want to create, or the desired future state of the organisation (where do we want to get?).

- Mission is the *why* – the over-riding purpose of the organisation, its scope and boundaries (what business are we in, why do we exist?).

- Values are the *how* – the underlying beliefs and ethical stance which drive how the business behaves (how are we going to behave while we are getting there?).

- Objectives operationalise all the other three – a precise statement of where we want to be and when, which turns the vision, mission and values into concrete quantifiable terms. It is frequently said that objectives should be SMART:

  Stretching
  Measurable
  Achievable
  Relevant
  Time limited

The mission and objectives of the organisation are constrained by four main factors (Johnson, Scholes and Williamson, *op cit*), as shown in the box following.

Corporate governance	External constraints on the organisation, set by company law; reports of investigations such as the Cadbury Report on non-executive directors or the Greenbury Report on directors' pay; regulatory bodies such as the Financial Services Authority, and targets and controls Imposed by the Government on public bodies (ie Best Value for local authorities)
Stakeholders	The rights and power of various stakeholder groups were discussed at length in Chapter 9, but basically stakeholders can influence the organisation's strategic direction through their power and/or their interest
Business ethics	Again this was discussed at length in the previous chapter, but ethics can impact on an organisation at three levels: general ethical policy; how the organisation interprets its corporate social responsibility when it formulates its strategy; and the ethical behaviour of individuals within the organisation. Clearly ethics is all about values, particularly the values of top management
Culture	Culture in organisations operates at three levels: ■ Values, often written down as part of the mission statement, but often vague, like 'service to the community' ■ More specific beliefs, often expressed as policies ■ Taken for granted assumptions – the organisational paradigm – the 'way things are done here'. At grass roots level, these may often be in conflict with the values and beliefs officially expressed at a higher level. For example, the police force in the UK is totally committed to eradicating 'institutional racism', but at the level of 'canteen culture' there are still racist PCs.

ACTIVITY 10.3

London Zoo

In 1993 *Management Today* published an article on the strategy of London Zoo. Although the case is an old one, it still deals with some fundamental issues in strategic management.

The Zoo, owned by the learned society, the Zoological Society of London (ZSL) had been going through hard times. By 1992, it had lost money for a decade, and had only survived through drastic cost cutting, including redundancies among keepers, which many felt had reduced staffing to dangerous levels. The turnaround led to a small profit in the year ending March 1993.

However, the turnaround plan was only the start of a bitter battle for the soul of the Zoo, between the Zoo's commercial staff and their supporters – the 'suits', who wanted the Zoo to become much more commercial, using high-tech computer displays and interactive technology, and a militant group on the council of ZSL, the 'beards', who thought that the Zoo should stick to its original aims of breeding and conserving endangered species. The suits were led by a property developer, David Laing, and the beards by a left-wing journalist, Colin Tudge. The centrepiece of the suits' plan was a giant interactive aquarium to be built at the Zoo.

Each side was vitriolic about the other. The beards referred to the suits' plan as 'animal prostitution', and said that the animals would be reduced to 'bit part actors on a stage', while the suits described Tudge as 'that breeding fanatic' and his supporters as 'Leninists with their heads in the clouds'. However, both sides genuinely thought that their plan would make the Zoo more attractive to visitors.

The job of resolving the quarrel fell to Jo Gipps, the director of the London Zoo. His business plan, revealed in 1993, was a compromise, but leaning more towards the beards.

Crucial to the argument was the mission statement of ZSL, which read:

> **'To achieve and promote the worldwide conservation of animals and their habitats'.**

Both sides could argue that this supported their argument. The beards pointed to the word 'conservation', while the suits pointed to the word 'worldwide' – in their view the Zoo should be fully commercial, and raise money which could be used to support conservation elsewhere in the world, rather than specifically at London Zoo.

Sources: Hugh Sebag-Montefiore, 'Who's who at the Zoo?'. Management Today. July 1993. ZSL Mission Statement (www.zsl.org)

What does this case tell you about the importance of vision, values and mission?

The mission statement

This is the most generalised statement of organisational purpose. It sets the direction of the organisation, and provides a benchmark against which policies can be evaluated.

An effective mission statement should achieve the following.

- It should be visionary and long-term. It is meant to inspire and drive the organisation.

- It should clarify the main intentions and aspirations of the organisation and the reasons why the organisation exists.

- It should describe the organisation's main activities and the position it wishes to attain in its industry.

- It should contain a statement of the key values of the organisation in relation to its stakeholders.

- It should be taken seriously within the organisation.

- It should be a focus for activity, which can serve as a continual guide, rather than a closed aim which can be fully achieved.

However, there are two great dangers with mission statements. The first is a risk that they can appear grandiose, or even ridiculous. Too many overblown mission statements have tended in the past to lead to the whole concept being treated with ridicule. Typical is the *Dilbert* website (www.dilbert.com); this contains a mission statement generator, which will produce randomly generated mission statements.

The other danger is that the mission statement may become set in concrete. The external environment may change in a way that renders the mission statement obsolete, and a hindrance rather than a help to strategy formulation (see Case Study 10.2).

CASE STUDY 10.2

Komatsu

Komatsu produces earth-moving equipment, in an industrial sector where the market leader is the American company Caterpillar. In the 1950s, it was a small company serving only its Japanese home market. In 1964, Kawai became president of Komatsu, and announced the company's new mission statement – 'Maru C' or 'encircle Caterpillar'. This was to be the driving force of the company's strategy for the next 20 years.

The statement served Komatsu well – by the 1980s, it was the world's second-largest producer of earth-moving equipment, although it had failed to overtake Caterpillar. Unfortunately, while Komatsu had been focusing all its attention and energy on Caterpillar, it had ignored changes in the environment. Demand for basic earth-moving equipment was falling, and new competitors in different but related industries were becoming a threat (albeit an unseen one).

Fortunately, the new company president, Katada, spotted the danger in time. He decided that the company's new emphasis should be as a 'total technology enterprise', with the new mission statement 'Growth, Global, Groupwide'. Komatsu's sales decline was reversed, thanks entirely to an explosive growth in its non-construction equipment business.

ACTIVITY 10.4

The WEA (Northern Ireland)

The Workers' Educational Association (WEA) in Northern Ireland publishes its Mission Statement and WEA Values on its website (www.wea-ni.com), as follows.

The WEA Mission Statement

We will make learning accessible to all men and women, especially those removed from the educational experience. As well as offering opportunities to individuals we will assist those who wish to work collectively for the benefit of their communities and for the good of society as a whole.

The Value Base of the WEA

The WEA has been a catalyst for social change since it began in Belfast in 1910. The following values underpin our commitment to social change.

- Social inclusion – we make special efforts to reach those most removed from the learning experience.

- Voluntarism – we provide opportunities for people to volunteer to work both individually and collectively for the betterment of our society.

- Active citizenship – we equip people to play a full role in the social, economic, cultural and political life of our society.

- Building alliances – we work closely with others to improve opportunities for learning.

- Sharing experience – we share good practice to promote mutual learning.

- Equality – we promote equality of opportunity through learning.

Evaluate the WEA mission statement against the six characteristics of an effective mission statement listed above.

Reprinted with permission

Resource analysis

Resource analysis is internal to the organisation. It is concerned with the Strengths and Weaknesses parts of SWOT analysis, and measures the efficiency and effectiveness of an organisation's resources, and their degree of fit with the external Opportunities and Threats also identified through SWOT. Ideally Strengths should support Opportunities, and be able to counteract Threats. Resources should be seen in the widest sense, to include the organisation's competitive position, as identified through techniques such as Five Forces and portfolio analysis. However, SWOT analysis has severe limitations. The most important of these is that it is subjective – different analysts will identify totally different strengths and weaknesses. Stevenson (1989) found no consensus among the managers in the companies he studied on the strengths and weaknesses of their companies. Higher-level managers tended to be more optimistic about the balance of strengths and weaknesses than lower-level managers.

Prahalad, C. and Hamel, G. (1990) in 'The core competence of the corporation', *Harvard Business Review*, May–June, identify the concept of the core competencies of the organisation – those factors which give the organisation its key competitive advantages. Unlike resources, which are tangible, tradeable and easily replicable, competencies are based on the accumulated knowledge and skills of the organisation, are unique to it, and are difficult to copy. They are based on people rather than things. Examples are the way in which Dell Computer builds all computers individually to order, or the reputation of Body Shop as an ethical crusader. Other analyses have suggested that the crucial competence needed by all organisations is the ability to be nimble, flexible and responsive to rapid and unpredictable changes in the external environment.

Core competencies can be based on the following.

- Cost efficiency. Many advantages based on cost efficiency are not really core competencies, as they can relatively easily be copied by other organisations. One which may lead to a core competence is cost efficiency based on experience – the more experience an organisation has, the lower its costs tend to be.

- Value added. Is the organisation more effective than the competition? In the early stages of the quality movement in the 1970s and 1980s, quality could be a core competence. Now it is a given – it is expected of all organisations and it does not in itself give a competitive advantage. Value added is more likely to be experienced by the customer through service than through the product itself – Dell does not necessarily sell a better computer, but it gives the customer a flexible computer configured to his or her requirements.

- Managing linkages, between different stages of production, or through alliances with other organisations. For example the low-cost airlines like easyJet and Ryanair pioneered the use of Internet-based ticket-booking systems and paperless tickets, giving them both a cost and an effectiveness advantage, as well as allowing a very flexible pricing system. They also offer web links to suppliers of hotels and car hire.

- Robustness. How easy is it to ensure that the competencies are difficult to copy?

If it can develop a number of core competencies, an organisation can greatly strengthen its strategic position. However, there is the danger that over time the core competencies may no longer match the external environment. If computing becomes based on mobile phones rather than PCs and laptops, Dell's core competence may prove to be a weakness rather than a strength.

STRATEGIC CHOICE

Generic strategies

The concept of generic strategy was introduced by Michael Porter (1985 *op cit*). He identified the following possible strategies.

- Cost leadership. An organisation will succeed if it can achieve lower costs than its competitors, but sell its products at or near the industry average price.

ACTIVITY 10.5

WH Smith and Ottakar's

WH Smith was founded in 1792. It is now a diversified retail and wholesale operation, which describes itself as 'the number one family retailer'. Its retail operations include WH Smith High Street, with 553 high street stores, WH Smith Travel Retail, with 220 stores, located at main railway stations and airports, and open 365 days a year, and an Internet sales site. WH Smith Retail had a turnover in 2003 of over £1.5bn and an operating profit of £90m. Its products include books, newspapers, magazines, maps, greetings cards, videos, CDs, stamps, batteries and lottery tickets. The group also includes wholesale distribution of newspapers and magazines (the publisher Hodder Headline was sold in September 2004), and operations in France and North America.

The company sees its core skills as offering the very best in service, quality and value for money, and as providing an environment that is easy to shop in and where recommendations, innovative products and services inspire the customer. Its strategy is based on store development and increased efficiency. It prides itself on its HR policy. Training and development are seen as vital to the company's success, along with communication to ensure every employee feels an integral part of the company's structure.

However, WH Smith is in trouble. Sales and operating profit for the retail operation both fell between 2002 and 2003, and in January 2004 the company issued a profits warning. It is under pressure from rivals in the following two areas:

1 from online bookselling, in the form of Amazon
2 from the big supermarket chains, who sell many of the goods sold in WH Smith, and who offer best-selling books at big discounts.

Ottakar's is a very different operation. It was founded in 1987 by the present managing director, James Heneage, who spotted the opportunity to establish a chain of bookshops offering high levels of range and service across the market towns of England. It expanded slowly in the early 1990s, and floated on the stock exchange in 1998. Since then it has expanded rapidly, through both organic growth and acquisition and now has 120 branches. It refuses to open stores in big cities, where rents are much higher and competition is more intense. Consistent with this policy, it has closed its original outlet in Brighton.

Head office policy is to offer uniform excellence in range and service across all branches. However, the company is a collection of intensely individual bookshops. Branch management are given a great deal of autonomy to provide a service tailored to their local community. Key to the company's success is its recruitment and development policy. All staff must have a love for and a knowledge of books, and be able to pass that passion on to the customer. All sales staff are known as Booksellers. The company is developing its own in-house Bookselling Diploma. Most branch managers are promoted internally from Booksellers, and all who are recruited externally must have a bookselling background.

Its strategy is summed up by the acronym PRISM:

Physical expansion

Range development

Innovation

Staff welfare

Margin growth

The company does not see Amazon as a threat. It is convinced that the knowledge and experience of its staff counterweigh any price advantage which Amazon (or the supermarkets) can offer.

The model seems a successful one. Like-for-like sales in 2003 were up by over 6 per cent on 2002 to around £150 million, and growth has continued into 2004. Profit margins also improved. Operating profit in 2003 was £7m, 20 per cent higher than in 2002.

Ironically, there is a link between Ottakar's and WH Smith. Early in 2004, WH Smith recruited a new manager to take charge of bookselling, Trevor Gould-Wheeler, previously the managing director of Hammicks (taken over by Ottakar's in 2003).

Identify strengths, weakness and core competencies of WH Smith and Ottakar's.

- Differentiation. An organisation will succeed if it can produce a differentiated product which commands a premium price, but at the same time keep its costs to the industry average.
- Focus. An organisation will succeed if it concentrates on a niche market, in which it can achieve either cost focus or differentiation focus.

Porter's generic strategy concept has been further developed by Bowman (1996), who proposes the strategy clock, based on a combination of price and perceived added value. He identified eight possible strategies, listed below:

1 low price/low added value – not likely to be feasible in the long term unless the organisation operates in a protected niche
2 low price/standard added value – equates to Porter's cost leadership
3 low price/high added value (hybrid) – the strategy pursued by Japanese companies in the 1970s and 1980s, when they were gaining a foothold in European markets
4 standard price/high added value (differentiation) – this would be a sensible strategy as a progression from the hybrid strategy
5 high price/high added value (focused differentiation) – likely to be a niche strategy, similar to Porter's differentiation focus
6 high price/standard added value – not a long-term viable strategy; why should customers pay more if they are not gaining added value?

7   high price/low added value – only feasible for a monopoly in a market which is not contestable

8   standard price/low added value – not viable in the long term; what is in it for the customer?

Selection of strategies

This is concerned not with what strategies should be chosen, but how they should be chosen. Johnson, Scholes and Whittington (2004) propose four models.

Formal evaluation

Here the choice is based solely on analytical techniques. The decision process is impersonal and rational, and appears to be objective. This avoids the risk of taking decisions solely on gut feeling, but it should be remembered that many of the analytical techniques are themselves in practice subjective.

Enforced choice

Here choice is imposed on the organisation from outside. This may be because of the dominant influence of an external stakeholder – for example, a supplier to Marks & Spencer has very little control over its own strategy. However, in the long term, even a firm in this situation does have some strategic choice – to widen its customer base, for example.

Learning from experience

The emphasis here is on incremental change on a pilot basis with operating units, and then the application of the experience learned from this throughout the organisation. This method is increasingly used by government, which trials new policy initiatives through a pilot study before going for a national launch, and by many manufacturers, who test market new products before attempting a national launch. It is similar to Quinn's concept of logical incrementalism, which we discussed earlier. The advantage is that it pushes responsibility for strategic development down the organisation, but there is the possible disadvantage that there is never a fundamental strategic rethink – the organisation can suffer from strategic drift.

Command

Here the dominant stakeholder (who may be the CEO, the biggest shareholder, or a government department) selects the direction of strategy, and imposes it on the organisation. This has been the experience of the National Health Service, which has had fundamental strategic change imposed on it by successive governments at regular intervals.

Evaluation of strategies

Possible strategies should be evaluated on three levels, suitability, acceptability and feasibility.

Suitability

Is this a strategy which will produce a sound fit between the organisation and its environment?

- Will it exploit opportunities in the environment and avoid or neutralise threats?
- Will it capitalise on the organisation's strengths and core competencies and avoid or neutralise weaknesses?

Various analytical techniques can be used to help answer these questions:

Life cycle analysis
The consultants Arthur D Little have identified the life cycle/portfolio matrix (see Johnson, Scholes and Whittington 2004). Here the strategies which should be adopted depend on the stage of the product/industry life cycle (embryonic, growing, mature or ageing), and the competitive position of the organisation (dominant, strong, favourable, tenable or weak). For example, the prescribed strategies for a strong firm in a growing industry are: fast growth, catch up, and attainment of cost leadership or differentiation, while for a weak firm in an embryonic industry they are: find niche, catch up or grow with industry. The model is open to criticism, as the definition used is subjective (what is a favourable position in one environment may be a weak one in another) and, because, like all models, it ignores all variables except those actually built into the model (stage of maturity and competitive position). For example, it ignores speed of technological development.

Portfolio analysis
We discussed the Boston Matrix in Chapter 2. Briefly, this categorised product lies on a matrix of market share and market growth rate, as shown in the box below.

Cash cows:	Low market growth, high market share
Stars:	High market growth, high market share
Question marks:	High market growth, low market share
Dogs:	Low market growth, low market share

Here the preferred strategic options would be to attempt to balance the portfolio between stars and cash cows. Stars are profitable, but they do not generate much cash, while cash cows may be less profitable but are highly cash-generative. Hence use cash cows to finance stars. As with the life cycle model, this is superficially attractive, but again it ignores other variables.

Value chain analysis
Value chain analysis is yet another model developed by Michael Porter. He says that the activities of an organisation should be seen as a sequence of primary events, as follows:

- inbound logistics, deliveries, storage, etc.
- operations
- outbound logistics (warehousing, wholesalers, deliveries, etc.)
- marketing and sales
- service

while underpinning all of these were support activities. These are:

- the firm's infrastructure
- human resources management
- technology
- procurement (purchasing, raising capital, recruitment).

All of these serve to add value for the organisation and form the value chain. The greater the synergies between the various elements, the greater the added value. Conversely, the whole value chain is only as strong as its weakest link. The aim of strategy should therefore be to strengthen the value chain as a whole, by building on existing strengths, or correcting weaknesses.

For example, the primary part of the chain might be strong, but the organisation might have problems caused by high turnover of staff. The strategic choice here would be to concentrate on improving staff turnover using HR techniques. Alternatively, the product might be strong, but its reputation is let down by poor after-sales service. After digging deeper, it might be discovered that the IT systems supporting service are inadequate.

The strength of the value chain technique is that it forces an analysis of how the organisation actually functions, and it avoids over-concentration on some of the more obvious strategic possibilities like merger or takeover. The weakness is that it is exclusively inward-looking. It should be combined with a rigorous analysis of fit with the environment.

ACTIVITY 10.6

Churchill China

In 1990, Churchill Pottery in Stoke on Trent was one of the companies investigated by Sir John Harvey Jones, former chairman of ICI, for his *Troubleshooter* series on BBC television. At the time, Churchill was coming under pressure from rising imports in its traditional markets. The company was family owned and had limited access to investment funds and no expertise outside the china and pottery industry, but had a good reputation for design. Two strategies were seriously considered in the programme. These were:

1 invest in cost reduction and concentrate on 'commodity' sectors of the market

2 launch a new upmarket range.

More radical strategies such as diversification, expansion into retailing or an export drive were rejected at this time.

The company opted for a move up-market, and launched a number of new ranges. This was successful (aided by national exposure on the TV programme), and the company went public in 1994 as Churchill China Plc, with a controlling interest still held by the Roper family. By 1997, it was producing profits of around £6 million a year, and had developed significant export markets in Europe and North America. However, a slump in the ceramics industry in 1998, and growing imports, particularly from China, led to a crisis in 1998–99. Profits in 1998 fell to £1.5 million, and in 1999 the company made its first loss, nearly £5.5 million.

The company responded to the crisis by cutting capacity, and by restructuring into two divisions:

1 Dining In – aimed at the retail market

2 Dining Out – aimed at the hotel and restaurant market.

By 2001, profits had recovered to over £3 million, but since 2001, they have fallen again, to just over £1 million in 2003. The company's return on capital employed in 2003 was just over 4per cent – poorer than an investment in many building societies. The bulk of the losses came in the Dining In division, as Dining Out has increased its share of both turnover and profit, selling to many four- and five-star hotels. Sales for the company have been static for a number of years, at around £50 million.

This reflects the performance of the industry, where sales have been static for the past 5 years, and where no growth is forecast for the next 5 years. A market research report on the industry in 1994 characterised it as suffering from 'overcapacity, inadequate training, high stocks and inefficient management' (Key Note 2004b). There was growing competition from imports from China, and although market sales have been static, manufacturing output has fallen by 28 per cent in the last 5 years. The market leaders are Wedgwood and Royal Doulton, with half of the output of the tableware segment of the industry. Churchill's market share is less than 5 per cent.

What strategic options do you think were open to Churchill in 2003–04?

Acceptability

Strategies have to be acceptable to internal and external stakeholders. This can be assessed in three ways: return, risk and stakeholder reaction.

Return can be assessed using a range of standard accounting techniques, including profitability analysis (discounted cash flow, etc.), shareholder value analysis (looking at the overall increase in value for the shareholder, using techniques such as Economic Value Added), or cost–benefit analysis (looking at non-financial as well as financial factors).

Risk can be assessed using techniques including:

- Break-even analysis – if the break-even point for the new strategy is a very high percentage of capacity, the project is highly risky.
- Ratio analysis – if the new strategy will result in very low levels of liquidity, as measured by standard ratios, it is high risk.
- Sensitivity analysis – how sensitive is the profit of the project to a shortfall in any of the key financial variables?

Stakeholder reactions can be assessed using techniques such as stakeholder modelling (discussed in the previous chapter). Stakeholders may well have strong views on risk, and these should be taken into account.

Feasibility

Strategies have to be feasible in terms of resource availability. Techniques to measure this include the following.

- Funds flow analysis – what is the implication for future cash flows? If sufficient cash is not currently available, can it be acquired on reasonable terms?

CASE STUDY 10.3

Stakeholder acceptability

An acceptable strategy – Ben & Jerry's and Unilever

Ben & Jerry's ice cream was one of the leading lights of the ethical business movement. It was not only concerned to trade ethically; it wanted to change the world. It donated heavily to radical causes, and was deeply involved in the anti-globalisation movement. These values were fully supported by its staff and customers, both key stakeholders.

In April 2000, Ben & Jerry's was taken over by the strait-laced Anglo–Dutch conglomerate Unilever, a classic representative of the globalisation that Ben & Jerry's had opposed. Although it had a good ethical reputation, Unilever was in no sense radical. Ben Cohen, the joint founder of Ben & Jerry's, forecast that the takeover would lead to the destruction of the company.

However, when Unilever appointed a 25-year Unilever man, Yves Couette, to run Ben & Jerry's, he was given the license to be a 'grain of sand in the eye' of Unilever. He abandoned his suit and tie, and followed a deliberate policy of empowerment and delegation. Tough profit targets were set, but Couette pointed out to staff that this would mean that more money would be donated to charity through the Ben & Jerry Foundation, which would continue to have a free hand to support any charity or movement that it chose (including the anti-globalisation movement).

An unacceptable strategy – Marconi

Throughout the 1980s and 1990s, GEC was seen as a safe, rather solid company, dominated by the safety-first philosophy of its long-time chairman, Arnold (Lord) Wienstock. The company prospered in household electrical goods and defence electronics, and built up a bank balance of several billion pounds. It appealed to risk-averse shareholders.

In the late 1990s, new management, headed by George Simpson, decided on a radical new strategy. The defence electronics business was sold to British Aerospace, most of the domestic electrics businesses (Hotpoint, etc.) were sold, and the company, now renamed Marconi, began a dash for growth in the exciting new world of Internet electronics. The rationale was that Marconi would benefit from the dot.com boom which was raging at the time. The bank balances, plus several billions more, were used to buy up American Internet companies.

Unfortunately, the purchases were made right at the peak of the dot.com bubble, and when the bubble burst, many of the new acquisitions were effectively worthless. Marconi's share price plummeted, and when the company eventually went through a financial restructuring, shareholders effectively lost all their money.

Like all shareholders, the Marconi shareholders should have realised that any share investment is by its very nature risky, but they could legitimately argue that they had originally bought their shares in GEC precisely because it was seen as a low-risk company.

- Break-even analysis – what is the break-even point given the present cost structure? If the break-even point is too high, can the cost structure be improved?

- Resource deployment analysis – what are the key resources and competencies required for each strategy; does the organisation already possess them, and, if not, can it reasonably acquire them?

Strategic option screening

Several methods can be used to screen options to see whether they meet criteria on suitability, acceptability and feasibility. These include:

Ranking

Here options are assessed against key factors in the environment, resources and stakeholder expectations, and a score (or ranking) is established for each option. To take a very simple example, assume that a company has two strategic options, A and B, and two success criteria, profitability and stakeholder acceptability. It has established that it regards profitability as more important, and has given this a weighting of 70. Stakeholder acceptability has a weighting of 30 (producing a total weighting of 100).

Strategy A scores 50 out of 70 for profitability, but only 10 out of 30 for stakeholder acceptability. Strategy B scores less well on profitability, scoring 30 out of 70, but it scores 20 out of 30 for stakeholder acceptability.

This gives a total score for strategy A of 60/100 (50 + 10), and a total score for strategy B of 50/100 (30 + 20). Strategy A is thus the preferred option.

Decision trees

Here options are progressively eliminated by testing them against various criteria. For example, a company has two decision criteria, high growth (most important) and low cost (less important). It is considering four strategies:

Strategy W	high growth, high cost
Strategy X	high growth, low cost
Strategy Y	low growth, low cost
Strategy Z	low growth, high cost.

The first decision step would eliminate strategies Y and Z, because they are low growth, leaving W and X. The next decision step would eliminate W, leaving X as the preferred strategy.

Scenario planning

Here the options are evaluated against various scenarios for the future. For example, if the organisation thinks that the most likely future for the UK exchange rate is stability, this would favour a policy of manufacturing in the UK. If the most likely scenario is seen as a rising pound, this would favour manufacturing overseas.

ACTIVITY 10.7

Strategic evaluation

A risk-averse firm with a strong current financial position, but little access to long-term capital, has decided that it must adopt a policy of unrelated diversification, in order to reduce its dependence on a declining industry. It has evaluated a number of areas for diversification, and decided on the appropriate industry to enter. It is now considering the best way to enter the new market.

Its options are to:

- develop and manufacture a new product
- manufacture an existing product under licence
- set up a joint venture with a firm that already has expertise in this field
- buy out a firm already in the industry
- market under their brand name an existing Taiwanese product not currently imported into the UK

The firm has established the following criteria, and weighted them as follows.

	Weighting
(a) Low risk	40
(b) Speedy entry into the market	20
(c) Low capital cost	20
(d) Profitability	15
(e) Short payback period	5

- Discuss the advantages and disadvantages of each method of entry.
- Using your own judgement, assign scores to each strategy and rank them.

STRATEGIC IMPLEMENTATION

The final stage in the strategy process is implementation – having decided on the chosen strategy, how is it put into practice? Frequently this will be the most difficult phase of the whole process. It involves a key competency of all managers – the ability to manage change.

Incremental and transformational change

Most of the writers on strategic implementation distinguish between incremental and transformational change, although their terminology varies. Johnson, Scholes and Williamson (2004 *op cit*) see strategic change on a two-by-two matrix – type of change and extent of change. A small change is incremental, a large change transformational. Each is of two types, dependent on whether the change is proactive or reactive. Proactive incremental change is tuning, reactive incremental change adaptation, while transformational change is divided into planned and forced change.

Walton (1999) defines transformational change as change that results in entirely new behaviour on the part of organisational members. He sees transformational change as in its very nature strategic. However, drawing on the work of Quinn on logical incrementalism, he sees incremental change as a possible route to strategic change. He also identifies transitional change, the process of carrying out change.

Porter (1999) concentrates on the outcome rather than the process. Changes such as the introduction of re-engineering or Total Quality Management are transformational, but they are not strategic. He sees them as improving operational effectiveness rather than changing the strategic position of the organisation. They are about doing better the same things as the competition are doing. Operational effectiveness is about running the same race faster, strategy is about running a different race.

Models of change

The classic model of change was identified by Lewin in the 1950s and developed by Schein in the 1980s (Armstrong 1999; Walton 1999). They identified three stages in change management, as follows.

1 Unfreezing – creating a readiness for change, through creation of a sense of anxiety about the present situation. The sequence here is to enable those involved to be convinced of the need for change.

2 Movement – taking action that will encourage the desired new behaviour patterns. This involves doing things differently, based on access to new information, and identifying with new role models.

3 Refreezing – embedding the new ways of working into the organisation.

Lewin also developed the concept of force field analysis – analysing the restraining and driving forces within the organisation that oppose or support the proposed change, and then taking steps to encourage the driving forces and decrease the restraining forces.

Beer took a different approach. He argued that the approach that tries to change attitudes in order to change behaviour is flawed. He argued that change should be approached in an opposite way – put people in new roles that require new behaviours, and this will change their attitudes. This is similar to the theory of cognitive dissonance, which we discussed in the previous chapter in relation to ethics. Beer proposed a six-stage model of change (CIPD 2004) involving:

1 mobilising commitment to change through joint analysis of problems

2 developing a shared vision

3 fostering consensus and commitment to the shared vision

4 spreading the word about the change

5 institutionalising the change through formal policies

6 monitoring and adjusting as needed.

The Lewin and Beer models both come out of relatively placid environments. They have been criticised for their assumption that it is possible to plan an orderly transition from one static state to another static state (Burnes 1996). In a more dynamic and chaotic environment like that experienced at present, a more continuous and open-ended change process is more appropriate. They also assume that a 'one size fits all' model of change is appropriate, whereas a more modern perspective would be to take a contingency approach and to argue that each organisation has a unique relationship with its environment. Its approach to change should reflect this.

The emergent approach to change as put forward by Burnes and Shaw (CIPD 2004), stresses that change is not linear – it is not a movement from state A to state B; it is continuous and messy. Just like its environment, an organisation is in a continuous state of flux, and the forces for change emerge as the organisation engages with its environment. Change in this model is bottom-up rather than top-down, and it emerges through experimentation. What is important is to ensure that the organisation is responsive to change, and the best way of doing this is to ensure that the organisation is a learning organisation.

Managing change

Kotter (1995) proposes an eight-step plan for transformation, as listed below.

1   establishing a sense of urgency – realising that change is needed
2   forming a powerful guiding coalition – a powerful and influential group of change leaders is needed
3   creating a vision – what will things be like after the change is achieved?
4   communicating the vision
5   empowering others to act on the vision
6   planning for and creating short-term wins – a long change process that appears to be getting nowhere can be demotivating. Building in some short-term wins can improve morale
7   consolidating improvements and producing still more change
8   institutionalising new approaches – similar to Lewin's refreezing process.

Bridges and Mitchell (2000) identify the following three stages in a change programme.

1   saying goodbye – letting go of the way that things used to be
2   shifting into neutral – the in-between stage when nothing seems to be happening, but everyone is in a stressful state of limbo. In the case of a major merger, this phase might take two years
3   moving forward – when people have to behave in a new way.

They describe seven steps in managing transition.

1   Describe the change and why it musty happen – in one minute or less.
2   Make sure that the details of the change are planned carefully and that someone is responsible for each detail.
3   Understand who is going to have to let go of what.
4   Make sure that people are helped to let go of the past.
5   Help people through the neutral zone with communication, stressing the '4 Ps':

purpose – why we have to do this

picture – what it will look and feel like when we get there

plan – how we will get there

part – what each person needs to do

6   Create temporary solutions to the temporary problems found in the neutral zone.
7   Help people launch the new beginning.

CASE STUDY 10.4

Moses in the wilderness

Bridges and Mitchell discuss the change management techniques used by Moses on his way to the Promised Land.

Magnify the plagues. Moses had to convince a key stakeholder (Pharaoh) that change was needed – that he had to let the Jews go. He did this through creating problems for Pharaoh – the seven plagues. The worse the current situation seems, the greater the impetus for change.

Mark the ending. After the Jews crossed the Red Sea, there was (literally) no going back.

Deal with the 'murmuring'. Don't be surprised when people lose confidence in the neutral zone. Moses faced lots of whingeing. He dealt with it by talking to people about their concerns.

Build up change champions. Moses and his lieutenant Joshua appointed a new cadre of judges to champion the change.

Capitalise on creative opportunities. It was in the Wilderness, not in the Promised Land, that the Ten Commandments were handed down.

Resist the urge to rush ahead. Not much seems to be happening in the neutral zone, but it is where the true transformation takes place. Moses was in the Wilderness for 40 years!

Different stages need different leadership styles. Moses was an ideal leader for the neutral zone, but the Promised Land required a new type of leadership, provided by the conqueror of Jericho, Joshua.

Resistance to change

Resistance to change can be of two types:

1   resistance to the content of change – ie opposition to the specific nature of the change

2   resistance to the process of change – ie opposition to how to the change is introduced.

Each might be a perfectly rational response to change, however inconvenient to management.

Armstrong (1999 *op cit*) identifies the following eight reasons why individuals might resist change.

1   the shock of the new – people tend to be conservative, and they do not want to move too far from their comfort zones. To this I would add regret for the passing of the old

2   economic fears – threats to wages or job security

3   inconvenience

4   uncertainty

5   symbolic fears – the loss of a symbol, like a car parking space, may suggest that bigger and more threatening changes are on the way

6   threats to interpersonal relationships

7   threat to status or skill – a change may be seen as deskilling

8   competence fears – concern about the ability to cope or to acquire new skills.

ACTIVITY 10.8

Overcoming resistance to change

What techniques do you think can be used to overcome resistance to change?

The role of HR in change management

The crucial role of HR in change management can be clearly identified using Beer's model of change. HR intervention is crucial at each stage of the model, as follows.

1   Mobilise commitment to change through joint analysis of problems
    HR should play a leading role in benchmarking and other environment-scanning techniques, and so help to spot the need for change. HR staff are likely to be the organisers of the teams and workshops who are involved in problem identification and analysis. Underpinning this should be a learning organisation, in which HR should be a prime driver.

2   Develop a shared vision
    This involves an understanding of the culture of the organisation, and the ability to support and direct the visions which underpin the culture.

3   Foster consensus and commitment to the shared vision
    It is essential that those affected by the change should feel that they have ownership of it. Developing and supporting ownership is a key HR skill, as is the fostering and supporting of change champions.

4   Spread the word about the change
    Here, as noted by McCarthy (2004), communication is key. McCarthy stresses that this should involve communication *with*, rather than communication *at*, those involved. He suggests the concept of 'conversation' as being appropriate here.

5   Institutionalise the change through formal policies
    This may well include the development of new HR policies on recruitment, reward and development. It is crucial that the reward system supports the new ways of doing things, for example.

6   Monitor and adjust as needed
    HR policy will need to be proactive after the change process is apparently completed. Development policies should be responsive to the need for any new competencies which become apparent.

Armstrong (1999 *op cit*) identifies a number of 'guidelines for change management', in most of which the role of HR is key. These include:

■   commitment and visionary leadership from the top

■   understanding the culture

- development of temperament and leadership skills at all levels which support change
- an environment conducive to change – a learning organisation
- full participation of those involved, so that they can own the change
- the reward system recognising success in achieving change
- a willingness to learn from failure – a support culture rather than a blame culture
- support for change agents
- protection of those adversely affected by change.

Ridgeway and Wallace (1994) discuss the role of HR in managing a common strategic change – a takeover. Here, matching the culture of the predator and the target is key. They quote from Furnham and Gunter (1993) on how such a match should be identified. It would involve:

- identifying the culture of the acquiring company
- deciding on any changes needed to ensure that the culture supports the proposed strategy
- identifying potential acquisitions and their cultures
- isolating likely changes to those cultures
- designing a format for assessing other cultures
- establishing criteria by which to identify suitable acquisitions.

Crucial here is establishing how the senior management of the target company will fit with the acquirer's culture, and what senior staff gaps will be exposed.

The HR department of the acquiring company will also be responsible for ensuring that the procedures and systems of the two companies are compatible, or can be made compatible, including any industrial relations implications. During the takeover process, the HR department also needs to manage communication. This will involve close liaison with PR, as employees of the target company will get a lot of their information about the takeover via the media.

Change leadership

Ridgeway and Wallace (*op cit*) identify a number of competencies, listed below, required for effective change leadership:

- intellectual skills: intellectually curious and able to handle ambiguity
- influencing skills: assertive, proactive and energetic
- counselling and people skills: sensitive, flexible and adaptable, with a high tolerance of pressure.

While this list is solid, I think that it misses the true essence of change leadership. A good change leader must, above all, be driven by a vision of the future, and be able to inspire others with that vision. This involves a high sense of values, exceptional communication abilities, a sense of inspiration, and the ability to empower others with the vision. All of these qualities are illustrated in Case Study 10.6.

CASE STUDY 10.5

The Morrisons takeover of Safeway

The takeover of the supermarket chain Safeway by its rival Morrisons is an example of the most difficult type of takeover to manage – a takeover of a bigger company by its smaller rival. Safeway had three times as many stores as Morrisons, and a bigger turnover, when it was taken over in March 2004.

The cultures of the two companies were totally different. Morrisons was run as a family firm, dominated by the larger-than-life personality of Sir Ken Morrison, the son of the founder. It was aggressively northern, and prided itself on its 'call a spade a spade' philosophy – nothing subtle, pile it high and sell it cheap. Sir Ken even personally recorded all the store announcements used by the company. Safeway was very different. It had been formed from a number of mergers over the years, was impersonal and bureaucratic, and very southern. Although its stores were smaller than those of Morrisons it stocked many more lines. Its pricing policy was to draw customers in with a few drastic headline price reductions, but higher 'background' prices.

The merger also took a long time. Because of a Competition Commission investigation, the whole process took 14 months, long enough for gloom and despondency to spread throughout Safeway. Perhaps reflecting this, or even a subconscious desire to sabotage Morrisons, Safeway introduced a totally new accounting system, incompatible with that of Morrisons, weeks before the takeover was completed.

Once the takeover was finalised, Morrisons did not handle things in the most tactful of ways. Except for one very small previous takeover, they had no experience of managing this kind of situation. The attitude was very much 'we know best', and surviving Safeway management was expected to adopt the Morrisons ways of doing things. The Safeway head office in Surrey was closed, and Morrisons was surprised when only 200 of its 1,600 staff wanted to transfer to Bradford. On the other hand, staffing in the old Safeway stores was increased, as, although it stocked fewer lines, Morrisons did more in-store (bakeries, etc.). Although sales rose in the Safeway stores that were converted, they fell in those stores which were not yet converted, leading Morrisons to issue a profits warning in July 2004.

Morrisons also tended to alienate another important stakeholder, the City. The company was notoriously media-shy, and reluctant to talk to City analysts. This was tolerated before the takeover, as Morrisons was relatively small (an FTSE 250 firm), and also very successful. As it was now in the FTSE 100, it was much more in the media spotlight, and the City expected a much higher standard of communication.

The Morrisons share price has underperformed the market. From a peak of 256p in March, at the time of the takeover, it had fallen to a low of 171p in September, and had only recovered to 225p (on a rising market) by the end of November 2004. The company's woes continued in 2005. In March it issued its second profits warning in eight months. Institutional shareholders continued to complain about corporate governance issues, as well as the difficulties in integrating Safeway. The City wants to see more non-executive directors, and a clear succession plan for when Ken Morrison retires.

The verdict: a takeover performance which illustrates Morrisons' lack of experience, failure to take the HR needs of ex-Safeway staff into consideration, and over-confidence.

Sources: Finch (2004); Mesure (2004); Townsend and Webb (2004) Ryle and Wachman (2005)

CASE STUDY 10.6

Nelson Mandela

Nelson Mandela is almost universally recognised as the last, and one of the greatest, inspirational leaders of the twentieth century. His career illustrates the characteristics of a brilliant change leader.

Mandela was born in 1918, a member of a chiefly clan in the Xhosa tribe. He trained as a lawyer, and was drawn at an early age into the struggle against white domination through his membership of the African National Congress. The political struggle intensified in the 1950s after the election of the white supremacist National Party Government, and the establishment of the apartheid system of racial segregation.

In the early 1960s, Mandela was on trial for his life. His statement from the dock in his trial put forward his vision: 'I have fought against white domination. I have fought against black domination. I have cherished the ideal of a democratic and free society in which all persons live together in harmony and with equal opportunities. It is an ideal which I hope to live for and to achieve. But, if needs be, it is an ideal for which I am prepared to die.'

Mandela was sentenced to life imprisonment on Robben island, where he was to remain for 27 years. For much of this he was under a hard labour regime. A telling incident from his imprisonment throws more light on his vision. A particularly tough prison governor imposed a brutal regime on the prisoners, but when he was transferred, he wished Mandela and the other ANC leaders the best for the future. To Mandela, this illustrated the possibility of redemption. The man was brutal not because he had a brutal nature, but because he was conditioned by a brutal system. Like the Catholic Church, Mandela distinguished between the sin and the sinner. From this came his concept of redemption and reconciliation, which was to be a driving force of his presidency.

By the mid-1980s, another key player had entered the scene – F W De Klerk, the new National Party leader. De Klerk recognised that the apartheid system must go, and that a settlement must be negotiated with the ANC. In Bridges' terms (Bridges 1995), this marked the end of the old system, and a move into the neutral transition zone. After lengthy negotiations, Mandela was released from prison in 1990. A new constitution was negotiated, leading to democratic elections in 1994 and the election of Mandela as the first democratic president of South Africa.

Mandela now faced his most severe test as a leader – how to hold the new South Africa together, and forge a new multiracial democratic state. He faced threats on all sides. A right-wing Afrikaner element was threatening civil war, and there was also an undeclared civil war between the ANC and the Zulu Inkatha Freedom Party. The Zulus were one of the largest tribes in South Africa, and resented the power held by the Xhosa Mandela.

Mandela's approach was to use symbolic acts of reconciliation. He visited the widow of the architect of apartheid, Hendrik Verwoerd. He also presented the Rugby World Cup to the victorious South African team wearing a South African rugby shirt. Rugby is an Afrikaner sport in South Africa, with almost totally white support. This action helped to reconcile the Afrikaner community to the new South Africa. He also pursued reconciliation with the Zulus. The Inkatha Freedom Party leader, Mangosuthu Buthelezi, was made minister for home affairs, and number three in the government, after Mandela and the vice-president Thabo Mbeki.

Mandela also used the idea of redemption through the Truth and Reconciliation Commission, which he launched with Archbishop Desmond Tutu. The idea here was that perpetrators of political crime could confess their involvement, and receive public absolution. Mandela insisted that this should apply as much to members of the ANC as to the agents of the apartheid regime.

Mandela's last great act of leadership was to recognise that by the end of his term as president in 1999, the transition phase had ended, and that South Africa was into the new beginning. Even his greatest admirers would not call Mandela a great administrator, and he recognised that a new type of more structured leadership was now needed. He therefore retired, leaving the way for Thabo Mbeki, a less charismatic but more structured politician, to succeed him.

When the sculptor Rodin was asked how he would sculpt an elephant, his reply was that he would start with a very large block of stone, and then remove everything which was not elephant. Mandela had a similar vision. Everything which was not part of his vision of a democratic, multicultural South Africa was irrelevant, including bitterness, revenge and recriminations.

Sources: Battersby (1999); Boroughs (1999)

SUMMARY AND CONCLUSIONS

This chapter has discussed the nature of strategy, and its transition from a corporate planning to a strategic management perspective, with a greater emphasis on contingency, experimentation and learning. We have identified the crucial role of change management and of the change leader in ensuring that strategy is implemented as planned.

KEY LEARNING POINTS

- Quinn identifies three elements of strategy – goals, policies and programmes.
- Strategy can be analysed at several levels – corporate, business unit and operational.
- Approaches to strategy are connected with the nature of the environment. In the 1950s and 1960s, a placid environment encouraged the rational, logical corporate planning approach, while a more turbulent environment since the 1970s encouraged the more contingent, experimental strategic management approach.
- The leading exponent of the corporate planning approach was Igor Ansoff, while the leading exponents of the strategic management approach are Tom Peters, Michael Porter, Ralph Stacey, Gary Hamel and C K Prahalad, James Quinn, and Henry Mintzberg.
- It is important to distinguish between intended strategy and released strategy.
- Strategic analysis is concerned with the strategic position of the organisation. What are the key characteristics of the organisation, what changes are going on in the environment, and how will these affect the organisation and its activities? This involves an analysis of: the expectations of stakeholders; the culture of the

organisation; the organisation's vision and values; the environment, as identified through a STEEPLE analysis; and the key resource areas of the business.

■ The extent to which there is a mismatch (a gap) between current strategy and the future environment is a measure of the strategic problem facing the organisation.

■ Vision, mission, values and objectives are closely linked, and often confused

■ The mission and objectives of the organisation are constrained by corporate governance, stakeholders, business ethics and culture.

■ The mission statement provides a benchmark against which policies can be evaluated.

■ Resource analysis is internal to the organisation. It is concerned with the Strengths and Weaknesses parts of SWOT analysis, and measures the efficiency and effectiveness of an organisation's resources.

■ Prahalad and Hamel identify the concept of the core competencies of the organisation – those factors which give the organisation its key competitive advantages.

■ The concept of generic strategy was introduced by Michael Porter, and developed by Cliff Bowman.

■ Possible strategies should be evaluated on three levels: suitability, acceptability and feasibility.

■ Transformational change is change which results in entirely new behaviour on the part of organisational members, and is in its very nature strategic.

■ Bridges and Mitchell identify three stages in a change programme: saying goodbye, shifting into neutral and moving forward.

■ Resistance to change can be rational, and must be managed. This is one of the key functions of HR in change management.

■ The critical role of a change leader is to be inspirational and visionary.

FURTHER READING

The leading UK text on strategic management is Gerry Johnson and Kevan Scholes, *Exploring corporate strategy*. A new edition (the seventh) was published in November 2004 (with Richard Whittington). John Walton's *Strategic human resource development* is useful for the HR contribution to strategic management. Also useful is a CIPD Factsheet on Change Management (December 2004), available on the CIPD website.

Managing in a Strategic Business Context – an Integrative Case Study

OBJECTIVES

By the end of this chapter, readers should be able to understand, explain and critically evaluate:

■ **their knowledge and understanding of the external business environment to a complex situation.**

INTRODUCTION

In this final chapter, we examine a major case study of an industry which has been in a state of constant flux for the last fifteen years – the beer industry. We examine changes in the industry as a whole, and then analyse case studies of four major players in the industry, who have adopted different strategies in the face of rapid change – Whitbread, Scottish & Newcastle, Greene King and J D Wetherspoon.

CASE STUDY 11.1
The beer industry

The UK beer industry forms a fascinating case study. The structure of the industry is unlike that of the rest of British industry. Until the late 1990s, it was also very insular, with little contact with either European or world trends in the beer industry. In the last 5 years it has changed from almost exclusive UK ownership to a situation wherein more than half of the industry is owned by European or American companies. It is also an industry which has experienced enormous changes in its structure and product range over the last quarter-century, and which was thrown into turmoil by government-inspired change since 1989.

In the rest of Europe (with the exception of the Irish Republic and Belgium) beer means lager – a pasteurised product which is light in texture and colour, and drunk cold. In the UK, lager has a large and growing share of the market, but beer in the UK also means ale and stout.

The beer industry in the UK was unusual prior to 1989 in being heavily vertically integrated. Some brewers controlled their own sources of raw materials, including malt and hops, and in some cases water, but much more important was forward integration. Much beer is draught beer, sold through pubs and clubs, known as the on-trade. The remainder is sold in bottle or can through off-licences and increasingly supermarkets, known as the off-trade. The off-trade, particularly beer sold through supermarkets, has considerably increased its share of the market in recent years.

The beer industry

Of approximately 78,000 public houses in the UK in 1989, 46,000 were owned by brewers, including 34,000 owned by the Big Six companies. These were known as tied houses, because they were tied to the brewer, and obliged to sell its products, which might include spirits, wines and soft drinks as well as beer.

About 70 per cent of tied houses were tenanted, with the other 30 per cent being managed by employees of the brewery. Tenants pay rent, and take a margin on all goods and services sold. Traditionally, rents were pegged below market levels, but in return the tenant was obliged to buy his beer from the brewer at a price set by it.

Other public houses were free houses, which were owner-occupied, and normally could buy their beer from wherever they chose. However, in some cases a loan tie system operated. Here, the brewer made a low-interest loan to the publican, who in turn was obliged to sell the brewer's products.

The industry has been marked by a very considerable number of mergers, which reduced the number of companies from around 350 in 1950 to 64 in 1989. The structure of the industry was firmly established by the mid-1960s, when the Big Six brewers (Bass, Allied, Whitbread, Watney, Scottish & Newcastle and Courage) controlled 67 per cent of production. By 1989 that had increased to 75 per cent. In addition, as noted above, they owned nearly half the public houses.

Trends in the industry

Beer production in the UK peaked in the late 1970s, and has declined gently thereafter. Consumption has followed the same pattern. Average beer consumption per head in 1979 was 23 pints a month, and this has now fallen to 18 pints. Over the same period, wine consumption has risen from nine litres a year to 24 litres (BBC 2004). Both imports and exports are historically of minor importance in the industry, mainly owing to the cost of transporting a product that is mainly water. Beer which appears to be foreign is usually brewed in the UK under licence. However, in recent years the most rapidly growing segment of the market has been premium lager, much of which is imported from Europe.

The product mix decisively shifted in the period from 1960 to 1990. In 1960, 99 per cent of all beer consumed was ale, while by 1990 lager had overtaken ale, and made up 51 per cent of all sales. This has now risen to 67 per cent. The main forces behind this seem to have been that the British acquired a taste for lager on European holidays: lager was seen as a young person's drink, and also as a drink that was acceptable to both sexes; its taste and quality were totally predictable, and national brands of lager were heavily promoted by the brewers.

Another long-term trend in the market has been the success of real ale. By the early 1970s, although most beer sold was still ale, it was overwhelmingly a pasteurised 'dead' product. Real ale, or cask-conditioned ale, is by contrast a 'live' product, with the result that although its quality is much higher, it is more difficult to serve and does not keep as long as pasteurised beer. In the early 1970s, it appeared that real ale was likely to disappear from the market. It was then rescued by the activities of the Campaign for Real Ale (CAMRA), a classic example of an interest pressure group. Thanks to CAMRA's efforts, real ale revived and thrived. It is relatively easy to set up a real ale micro-brewery. Many free houses have done this, and you can more or less do it in your garden shed. Micro-breweries also have favourable tax treatment. As you will see later, real ale is central to the strategy of one of our case study companies, Greene King.

The Big Six brewers consolidated their dominant market position during the 1970s and 1980s through takeovers. They were also themselves in some cases the victims of takeovers. Watney was taken over by Grand Metropolitan, at the time predominantly a hotels group, but later a component of the wine and spirits conglomerate Diageo, while Courage passed to the Australian brewer Fosters. The third member of the Big Six to be involved in a merger was Allied, which merged with the food group J Lyons to form Allied Lyons.

A major strategic move taken by the major companies was to diversify into other areas of the leisure industry. Bass acquired Holiday Inns, Whitbread acquired Beefeater and Pizza Hut, and Scottish & Newcastle acquired Pontin's Holidays and later Center Parcs.

The overall structure of the industry was analysed by the Monopolies and Mergers Commission in 1989. They identified over 200 brewing companies, classified as follows:

- six national brewers (Allied, Bass, Courage, Grand Met, S & N and Whitbread. They had 75 per cent of UK beer production, 74 per cent of the brewer-owned retail estate (pubs), and 86 per cent of loan ties.

- 11 regional brewers, including Greene King. They had 11 per cent of beer production, 15 per cent of the brewer-owned retail estate, and 8 per cent of loan ties.

- 41 local brewers. They had 6 per cent of beer production, 10 per cent of the tied estate, and 4 per cent of loan ties.

- 3 brewers without tied estate (Carlsberg, Guinness and Northern Clubs Federation). They had 8 per cent of beer production, and 1 per cent of loan ties.

- 160 other brewers, mainly very small and local, with less than 1 per cent of beer production.

One key trend of the 1980s and 1990s was the growing internationalisation and homogenisation of the drinks industry. Throughout Europe, including the UK, the trend was towards lighter drinks, including lager rather than ale, light spirits like Malibu and Baileys rather than traditional spirits like gin or rum, and wine, fruit juices, mineral water and colas.

Pubs became less of a male, beer-drinking stronghold. More pub drinking was done by women, who were more likely to drink lighter, less alcoholic drinks, and pubs became more of a family place to eat as well as to drink, although to some extent this trend was inhibited in the UK by the restrictive licensing laws. These in theory prohibited children under the age of 14 from entering bars. Increasingly the traditional pub was replaced by theme pubs (Irish-style bars, etc.) and pub-restaurants.

An impact of the recessions at the beginning of the 1980s and 1990s was to encourage a trend towards drinking at home, rather than in pubs. This was assisted by a trend towards canned lagers rather than bottled beers, increasingly sold through supermarkets, usually at a price considerably below that charged in pubs.

The on-trade was also hit by demographic trends. The key pub drinking segment is the 18–25 age group, but from a peak of 23 per cent of the adult population in the early 1980s, this age group fell to a trough of 14 per cent in 1995.

The Monopolies and Mergers Commission Report of 1989 and the Beer Orders

In 1987, the Office of Fair Trading referred the brewing industry to the Monopolies and Mergers Commission (MMC) for investigation as a potential complex monopoly. This was legally possible although the biggest firm in the industry, Bass, only had a 22 per cent share of the market, below the single firm monopoly threshold of 25 per cent. Of particular concern was the way in which the price of beer was rising more rapidly than the general rate of inflation, and the potentially anti-competitive effects of the tied house system. The MMC carried out a painstaking investigation of the industry, and reported in 1989.

The MMC found that a complex monopoly did indeed exist, and that it acted against the public interest in three main ways.

1 Prices had been rising too rapidly.
2 Consumer choice was restricted because one brewer usually did not allow another brewer's beer to be sold in its pubs.
3 The tenant's bargaining position was critically weaker than the landlord's (the brewer).

The MMC's particular concern was with the Big Six national brewers, and their recommendations were mainly aimed at this group. After negotiation these recommendations became the Beer Orders.

The Beer Orders specified the following.

- No brewer should own more than 2,000 pubs, plus 50 per cent of the excess number owned above the figure of 2,000. This meant that the Big Six brewers had to dispose of 11,000 pubs. None of the regional brewers owned more than 2,000 pubs.
- Tenants of pubs owned by brewers with more than 2,000 pubs (but not managers) should be allowed to stock a 'guest' beer (a beer brewed by a third party).
- Abolition of the loan tie.

The clear intention was that competition in the industry should be considerably increased, by limiting the impact of the tied house system, and by opening up opportunities for smaller brewers to get a foothold in the tied houses through the guest beer concept. The hope was that many, if not most, of the pubs sold by the Big Six would be sold to their tenants, and become free houses. Events were to show, however, that the brewers were ingenious in circumventing the spirit of the Beer Orders, while obeying its letter.

Trends in the industry since 1989

Production and consumption in the UK has continued to decline since 1989. In the 1990s, overall sales fell by 9 per cent, with sales of real ale falling by seven per cent in 2002 alone, although they picked up again in 2003. Two major factors influencing the level of sales are the weather, with the hot summer of 2003 boosting sales, and major sporting events, particularly the football World Cup. Within this overall declining market, the trend towards lager has continued, with the biggest growth coming in imported premium continental lager. The share of lager in the market is now around 70 per cent.

When interviewed by the BBC in 2004, Steve Cahillane, the CEO of Interbrew UK and Ireland, saw the future hope of beer in heavy promotion of the company's continental premium lagers, including Stella Artois, Hoegarten and Leffe, each with its own designer glass. Little hope for traditional English beer there (BBC 2004)!

The trend towards a growth in the off-trade at the expense of the on-trade (pubs and clubs) has continued. The off-trade grew from 20 per cent in 1989 to around a third in 2000. This trend has been assisted by technological developments, which have enabled canned beer to be served with a head similar to that of draught beer, particularly in the form of the so-called widget, a miniature nitrogen gas cartridge built into the can. The purchasing power of the big supermarkets is as significant in beer as in other grocery products. It was reported in the summer of 1993 that Tesco was able to import Stella Artois lager from Belgium at a price which undercut Whitbread, then the UK distributor, by 25 per cent. The supermarkets also followed an aggressive pricing policy on beer, which saw its store price halve between 1998 and 2002. This policy was financed by a cut in the price which was paid to the brewers, described by Scottish & Newcastle as 'a blood bath'.

A further trend has come about as a result of the introduction of the European Single Market in January 1993. UK residents can now import alcoholic drinks from EU countries without limit, so long as the article has had duty paid on it in an EU country, and it is to be consumed by the importer him- or herself. (Importing for resale is a criminal offence, but very difficult to prove.) The result has been a stream of vans coming back from Calais full of beer and other drinks, because the duty on beer in France is about a seventh of that in the UK. Estimates of the size of the cross-Channel trade vary, but it could be up to the equivalent of a million barrels a year, or around 3 per cent of the UK market, equivalent to the output of a medium-sized brewery.

Licensing laws are being liberalised. Already all-day opening is possible, between the hours of 11am and 11pm. A children's certificate scheme, allowing under-14s to be admitted, came into force in January 1995. The Licensing Act of 2003 allows pubs to alter their opening hours to suit local demand. This may mean that some pubs will choose to operate on a 24-hour basis. Towards the end of 2004, the Government announced that smoking was to be banned in all pubs and restaurants, except for those pubs which did not supply food. Some pub chains reacted to this by threatening to abandon food altogether, as they claimed that they made a higher profit margin on drink.

The reaction of the brewing industry to the Beer Orders and other changes in the environment has been a massive restructuring. This started in October 1990 with a merger of the brewing interests of Courage and Grand Metropolitan. Under the deal, Courage acquired Grand Met's breweries, which it had originally obtained when it took over Watneys, and Grand Met ceased brewing entirely. In return Courage and Grand Met set up a joint company called Inntrepreneur, managed by Grand Met, which took over nearly all Courage's pubs and many of Grand Met's. This was the first appearance of the phenomenon which was to dominate the industry, the giant pubco, a company which ran pubs but did not brew.

In January 1993 came the launch of Carslberg-Tetley, a joint venture of Allied Lyons, Europe's seventh biggest brewer, and the Danish company Carlsberg, the European number three. Carlsberg already brewed lager in the UK, and because it had no tied estate, had built up its strength in the off-trade. Allied was strong on the on-trade, but weak on the off-trade. The deal was investigated and cleared by the MMC. Allied Lyons then merged with the wine and spirits company Domecq, and became Allied Domecq. The new company took the strategic decision to pull out of brewing. In 1996, Bass tried to acquire Allied's interest in Carlsberg-Tetley, but was blocked by the MMC. Carlsberg then bought out the Allied interest, but maintained the Carlsberg-Tetley name. Its Tetley Bitter is the best-selling cask ale in the UK.

Bass, the market leader, pursued a consolidation strategy, rationalising its production by closing three of its twelve breweries. The company sold 2,700 pubs to comply with the Beer Orders, many of them to new pubcos who agreed to take their beer from Bass. Whitbread, the long-standing number three in the industry, steadily lost ground, and fell to number five. In 1995, Scottish & Newcastle acquired Courage, immediately taking it to number one in the market.

By the late 1990s, the Big Six had shrunk to four – Bass, S & N, Carlsberg-Tetley and Whitbread. They were soon to shrink further when in quick succession the Belgian brewer Interbrew, maker of Stella Artois, acquired the brewing interests of first Whitbread and then Bass. In addition, S & N moved into a leading position in Europe with the acquisition of Brasseries Kronenbourg, the number one beer brand in France, from the French food conglomerate Danone. Interbrew was then forced to sell off many of the brewing interests which it had acquired from Bass. These were purchased by the

American number two, Coors. The American number one, and the biggest brewer in the world, Anheuser-Busch, brews a small amount of Budweiser in the UK, but is not a leading player in the UK market. The series of mergers resulted in a market dominated by Scottish & Newcastle and Interbrew, each with around a third of the market, with Carlsberg-Tetley a poor third and Coors fourth.

Bass renamed itself Six Continents, and later demerged into two companies, Intercontinental Hotels, which concentrated on hotels, and Mitchells & Butlers, a pubco, while Whitbread concentrated on its restaurant and leisure businesses (see Whitbread case study). Of the 60,000 surviving pubs in the UK, 17,000 are free houses and over 10,000 are owned by brewers, while over 30,000 are owned by pubcos.

The first pubco, Inntrepreneur, was bought by the Japanese bank Nomura, and eventually sold to the market leader, Enterprise, which now has 9,000 pubs. The Punch group now operates 8,300 pubs after its takeover of Pubmaster's 3,100 pubs in 2003, and Innspired's 1,000 pubs in 2004. Both Enterprise and Punch are thought to be aiming for 10,000 pubs. Mitchells & Butlers owns over 2,000. The biggest of the old-style integrated brewing and pub-owning companies is Greene King, which owns 2,100 pubs (see Greene King case study).

There is of course no limit under the Beer Orders on the number of pubs which a pubco can own, and the Beer Orders themselves were abolished in 2002 (*The Publican* 2002). The news was condemned by CAMRA, which saw it as restricting market opportunities for small brewers, but welcomed by Greene King, the only brewer which was anywhere near being forced to divest pubs under the Orders. The tied house system had returned with a vengeance, with the difference that rather than being forced to buy their beer from the brewers, tenants were forced to buy from the pubcos. This led to a parliamentary inquiry in 2004 by the Commons Trade and Industry Select Committee, but John Vickers, chairman of the Office of Fair Trading, in evidence to the Committee, said that he saw 'nothing intrinsically problematic' in the beer tie, and that he felt there were 'no competition or consumer law issues'.

The total turnover of the pub sector is around £14bn (2002 figures). Of this around £8bn is beer, £3bn other alcohol, and £2.5bn food. The proportion of food in total takings is rising steadily. About 85 per cent of the population visit a pub at least occasionally, but a third of all sales are to 18–25 year olds. This age group is declining as a proportion of the population. Other long-term trends include:

- the decline of the hard-drinking, teenage-orientated pub chains which were popular in the 1980s, and a movement towards pub–restaurants which are more popular with women and families
- the decline of the theme pubs (Irish, etc.) popular in the 1990s
- pubs as a venue to watch big-screen sporting events

■ the growth in wine. In 2004 a BBC Money Programme on beer carried out some informal market research, which involved showing people in the street a picture of a pint of beer or a glass of wine and asking their reactions. Reactions to beer included: 'binge drinking', 'aggressive' 'old fashioned'. 'Northerners', and 'old men', while to wine they were 'business lunches', 'delicious', 'genteel', and 'sophisticated'. This is of course not scientific evidence, as we do not know how the tape was edited, but it might be interesting to carry out a similar experiment with your own friends and relatives.

ACTIVITY 11.1

The beer industry

Carry out a STEEPLE analysis on the beer industry, analysing key drivers of change, and identifying opportunities and threats facing the industry.

CASE STUDY 11.2a

Scottish & Newcastle Plc

Introduction and history

The William Younger Brewery was established in Leith, Scotland in 1749, while The Newcastle Breweries was set up in 1890. The two merged to form Scottish & Newcastle in 1960. In 1995, S & N acquired the brewing interests of Courage, and became the leading brewer in the UK. In 2000, it acquired Brasseries Kronenbourg and Alken Maes of Belgium from Danone, thereby becoming number two in Europe, just behind Heineken. Also in 2000, it started disposal of its retail estate, a total of 2,700 pubs, restaurants, bars, hotels and nightclubs, a process which was completed in 2003.

Business activities

S & N is a specialist beer brewer, with few other interests. Through a 50:50 joint venture with Carlsberg, known as Baltic Brewery Holdings, it has a leading position in the former Soviet Union. S & N sees its future as a leading European brand, although it also has interests in India and China. Europe is the world's leading market with one third of global volumes, home to five of the world's ten biggest brewers, and generates 40 per cent of the industry's world profits. The European market is forecast to grow at 2 per cent per annum (volume) and 5 per cent per annum (profit) over the next decade.

S & N is number one in three of Europe's top six national markets – the UK, France and Russia, and is also number one in Estonia, Latvia, Lithuania and number two in Belgium, Portugal, Greece, Finland and the Ukraine. It has three of the top ten European brands – Fosters, Kronenbourg and Baltika.

Financial performance

	2002	2003
	£ million	
Turnover	4137	4278
Operating profit	421	415
Earnings per share (pence)	40.7	39.0

In 2003, the UK accounted for 42 per cent of total revenue. UK turnover was up by 0.2 per cent over 2002, and profits were down by 0.8 per cent. The company lost market share in the UK. Between 2000 and 2003, the company saw UK beer sales fall 5.4 per cent, costs rise 10 per cent and operating profit decline by 16 per cent. Its UK market share has fallen from over 30 per cent to 27 per cent. It is closing two of its major breweries, the Fountains brewery in Edinburgh and the Newcastle brewery.

Strategic objectives

The company has four strategic objectives:

1 brand growth

2 total innovation

3 most efficient operations

4 the best team.

Stakeholders

S & N is proud of its employee communications programme. This includes presentations from the chief executive and dialogue with staff across the group, to put across the message that change today ensures a long-term, successful sustainable future for S & N. New targets have been established with support from all levels of staff.

During 2004, a Technical Safety Group was developing a long-term strategy for safety management across the group, with the aim of securing 'incremental improvement through behavioural change'.

The group is aware of the harm done to individuals and society by irresponsible drinking, and, through consultation with pressure groups, politicians and other interested parties, it has developed a Responsible Marketing strategy.

The group is also committed to sustainable development and is working on the delivery of a group-wide environmental strategy which will involve the sharing of best practice.

ACTIVITY 11.2

Scottish & Newcastle

Carry out a SWOT analysis of Scottish & Newcastle.

CASE STUDY 11.2b

Greene King Plc

Introduction and history

Benjamin Greene set up Greene's brewery in Bury St Edmunds, Suffolk, still the company's headquarters, in 1799. The company expanded rapidly in East Anglia during the nineteenth century. In 1868, Frederick King set up a rival brewery in Bury St Edmunds to compete with Greene's. This proved difficult, and the two companies merged to form Greene, King and Sons in 1887. The new company quickly established a regional reputation for the quality of its beer.

By the time of the Beer Orders in 1989, Greene King was one of the leading regional brewers, with over 900 pubs, well below the limit at which it would have to dispose of pubs. Since 1989, it has acquired two other regional brewers, Ruddles and Morland, and also several pub chains. As a result of these acquisitions, by 2004 it was the biggest of the regional companies, a super-regional, with 2,100 pubs, and 11.4 per cent of the national on-trade real ale market, as well as 14.1 per cent of the premium bottled ale off-trade.

Business activities

Before its takeover of Laurel Inns in the summer of 2004, Greene King had 601 managed pubs, including the Hungry Horse branded chain, and 1,090 tenanted and leased pubs, designed to be traditional in style and aimed at the more affluent segments of the population. It is also popular in the free house segment of the market. The leading brands are Greene Abbot and IPA, Ruddles County and Old Speckled Hen. Volume sales of all its leading brands are growing at a time of general decline in the real ale market.

Financial performance

	2002–03	2003–04
	£ million	
Turnover	536	553
Operating profit	103	112
Earnings per share (pence)	71.0	80.2

78 per cent of the company's beer sales are external (ie not to the group's own pubs).

Strategic objectives

The strategy is to operate three focused, different but closely related divisions in the drinks and leisure sector – brewing, managed pubs and tenanted pubs. Each runs semi-autonomously, and is not excessively dependent on the others. However, the company does achieve synergy benefits through the close links between the three divisions.

Overall strategy is to differentiate the company from its competitors through:

- concentrating on those market sectors where competition is less intense, barriers to entry are high, and returns are more stable
- focusing on traditional drinks and pubs
- developing brands which can stand alone without excessive levels of marketing.

Stakeholders

The company is proud of its relationships with its tenants and licensees. In a national poll of licensees, it came first in each of the last 2 years in answers to the question 'How would you rate your pub company or brewer as a fair business partner?'

Many of the 650 brewery workers are fourth or fifth generation Greene King employees, and Greene King is still seen as a family company in Bury St Edmunds, where it is one of the biggest employers.

However, when the new managing director of the brewing company, Rooney Anand, arrived in 2001, he found a company which was over-focused on production, with a very traditional approach to management. Considerable effort has since been put into standardising quality, a difficult task for a real-ale brewer, as the product is still live and maturing when it leaves the brewery. Greene King is the first regional brewer to gain the ISO 9001:2000 quality standard across the whole company. Anand has also introduced the concept of a beer specially designed to be drunk with food – the 'beer to dine for'.

More than 500 of the brewing staff have completed tasting courses, which not only boosts quality but gives them a sense of ownership for the product. Training extends to deliverymen and publicans, and Greene King is the only brewer to paste handling instructions on every cask. This new emphasis on quality helped Greene King to win second place in the Champion Beer of Britain competition organised by CAMRA in 2004 with its IPA brand.

ACTIVITY 11.3

Greene King

Carry out a SWOT analysis of Greene King.

CASE STUDY 11.2c

J D Wetherspoon Plc

Introduction and history

J D Wetherspoon was founded in 1979 when 24-year-old law student Tim Martin acquired his first pub in North London, mainly because he did not like the local pubs. His strategy was to offer a range of real ales and value for money. This strategy proved successful, and the company went public in 1994, with Martin, now chairman, retaining a significant shareholding. The company has continued to grow and now owns 640 pubs throughout the UK.

Business activities

The core business of J D Wetherspoon is pub operation. Company policy is to manage rather than tenant pubs, thereby retaining total control. The pubs are larger than average, and the company specialises in converting unconventional sites – churches, post offices, banks – into pubs. All the pubs offer low prices, and all-day food, a non-smoking area and no TV or music (except for major sporting events in a few pubs). Approximately three quarters of turnover comes from bar sales, and one quarter from food. The company also operates a chain of bars, Lloyd No 1, which are aimed at the young cocktail-drinking market, and J D Wetherspoon Lodges, a chain of budget hotels.

Financial performance

	2002–03	2003–04
	£ million	
Turnover	731	787
Operating profit	75	78
Earnings per share (pence)	17.0	17.7

Although operating profits were slightly up in 2003–04, this was more than offset by a considerable increase in interest payable, leading to a fall in profits before exceptional items and a fall in taxation from £56.2m to £54.0m. Operating margins fell slightly from 10.3 to 9.9 per cent.

Strategic objectives

The strategy of the company is to operate large, low-price pubs, which appeal to the whole family. Further growth is planned, to a maximum of about 1,200 outlets. This is to be achieved through organic growth rather than takeovers.

Stakeholders

Tim Martin has firm views on what his customers want – low prices, food constantly available, no music, normally no TV, and no smoking areas. He has called for a total ban on smoking in pubs, although he says it would be 'commercial suicide' for Wetherspoons to bring in its own blanket unilateral ban. The company has strong views on responsible drinking, and feels that its policy on food inhibits binge drinking.

Martin has also criticises the general attitude to staff in the hospitality industry, which he regards as 'stone age'. The company has an extensive programme for training pub managers, including in some cases sponsoring them through university. It insists that all managers work no more than a 48-hour week, and all pub managers must ensure that all staff receive two consecutive days off a week and work no more than four late nights in each week. There is a bonus scheme for all staff.

ACTIVITY 11.4
J D Wetherspoon

Carry out a SWOT analysis of J D Wetherspoon.

CASE STUDY 11.2d
Whitbread Plc

Introduction and history

In 1742 Samuel Whitbread set up his first brewery in London. His company expanded steadily throughout the nineteenth century, pioneering bottled beer and branded beer. It went public in 1948. During the 1950s and 1960s it followed a strategy of takeovers of small regional brewers, and it was also a pioneer of lager, acquiring the licences to brew Heineken and Stella Artois. It also diversified, into wines and spirits in the 1970s and 1980s (sold to Allied Lyons in 1989), and into restaurants, setting up Beefeater, and forming Pizza Hut as a joint venture with PepsiCo. In 1995 it purchased Costa Coffee, and in 1996 the Pelican Group (Café Rouge) and BrightReasons (Bella Pasta).

Other diversifications were into hotels, with the acquisition of 16 Marriott hotels, and a licence to develop the Marriott brand in the UK. The group also operated Swallow Hotels, and the budget chain Travel Inn. The final prong of diversification was into leisure clubs, with the acquisition in 1996 of the David Lloyd Leisure business, the leading operator of health and fitness clubs.

All this diversification left the company as a rather sprawling conglomerate, and the beer business was somewhat neglected. As a result, Whitbread's share of the UK beer market fell steadily, and in 2000 the decision was taken to exit from brewing, with the sale of the brewing company to Interbrew. Pubs and bars followed in 2001. The group has completed the transition from one of the UK's oldest brewers to a leisure conglomerate.

Business activities

Whitbread operates in three main areas. Hotels contribute 50 per cent of the company's profits. Marriott is now the second-largest four-star hotel business in the UK with 62 hotels and 10,000 bedrooms. In October 2004, the company sold a number of its Marriott hotels, but with a 'manage-back' agreement, whereby Whitbread would continue to operate the hotels. This released £800 million, part to be returned to shareholders, part to reduce debt, and part to boost the pension fund. At the same time, the company sold its chain of three-star Marriott Courtyard hotels. Travel Inn, the budget hotel chain, has 29,000 bedrooms, making it the biggest hotel chain in the UK, twice the size of its nearest rival, Travelodge.

The company's restaurant brands include Beefeater, with 187 outlets, which unveiled a new format in 2003, the pub restaurant chain Brewers Fayre, with 246 outlets, aimed at relaxed family eating in an individual setting, and Brewsters, with 149 outlets, aimed at young families with children.

However, in October 2004, the company decided to abandon the Brewsters concept, and to convert the outlets to Brewers Fayre, as the emphasis on children had put off adult diners. TGI Fridays, the US-style fast-food chain, has 41 outlets, and again has updated its image in 2003. Pizza Hut has 578 units, and offers a home delivery as well as an eat-in service. Costa Coffee has 346 outlets, has developed in-store outlets with major names such as Waitrose, Ottakar's and Waterstone's, and plans to increase the number of outlets to 500. Bella Pasta and Café Rouge were sold in 2001.

David Lloyd Leisure is the brand leader in sports and leisure clubs, with 375,000 members, and an approximate 10 per cent share of the market. The total market is estimated to grow by 50 per cent by 2007.

Financial performance

	2002–03	2003–04
	£ million	
Turnover	1788	787
Operating profit	270	277
Earnings per share (pence)	52	56

In the six months to September 2004, the restaurant division saw comparative sales growth of only 0.7 per cent, while profits there dropped 9.2 per cent.

Strategic objectives

Whitbread's vision is 'to create leisure and hospitality experiences that make people feel better – every time they visit us'. The aim is to grow the business and deliver value to shareholders. The strategy has four elements:

1 operate in markets with high growth potential
2 be the market leader in these markets
3 organic growth
4 targets of 5 per cent like-for-like sales growth, double-digit profit growth and 1 per cent improvement in return on capital employed each year.

Stakeholders

Whitbread has a high reputation for the quality of its human resources (HR). It has won many training awards, and is involved in a Modern Apprenticeship scheme for chefs. In 2004, Travel Inn was placed 72nd in a list of the 100 best UK companies to work for. The Whitbread HR director is a member of the main board. The company aims to become the employer of choice in the UK leisure industry.

Its website sets out its people management philosophy, which is to treat people according to three basic principles:

1 It cares for them.

2 It makes clear what is required from them.

3 It treats people as individuals.

All employees receive a copy of the company's comprehensive code of ethics, which is also available on the company website. The company has an extensive community involvement programme, with the overall aim of 'helping young people achieve their potential'.

ACTIVITY 11.5
Whitbread

Carry out a SWOT analysis of Whitbread.

STRATEGY IN THE BEER INDUSTRY

The beer case studies illustrate a number of different approaches to strategy. The Beer Orders forced strategic change on the industry, as the old model of large brewers with large tied estates was no longer legally possible.

For Scottish & Newcastle, a change of strategy was essential. At the time of the Beer Orders, it was a large brewer, although not the market leader, and its tied estate, and most of its beer market, was concentrated in Scotland and the North of England. It had two strategic imperatives:

1 how to cope with the beer orders

2 how to break out of its regional market and develop nationally.

The strategy chosen was that of market leadership, achieved through the takeover of Courage. This gave S & N national coverage, while the takeover of Kronenbourg gave it international coverage. As the market leader, it enjoyed economies of scale and could pursue a low-cost, efficiency strategy.

Under the Beer Orders, leadership in brewing necessitated a drastic cut-back in pub holdings, and it was logical for S & N to sell off the whole of its retail estate. It could have kept a small retail stake, but this would not have added to its strategic profile.

Greene King was in a very different position. As a medium-sized regional brewer, it had no chance of competing on cost with the market leaders. Some regional brewers decided to follow the pubco strategy, and abandoned brewing. In most cases this was a mistake, as they were quickly gobbled up by the much bigger specialist pubcos (Gibbs Mew, Boddingtons,

Morrells). Greene King opted for focused differentiation, building up both its real ale portfolio and its traditional-style pub estate, with the aim in each case of offering a premium quality product. This strategy had the great merit that it involved differentiation into niches which were of no interest to the big brewers and pubcos, but which were potentially very profitable.

In many ways J D Wetherspoon pursued a very similar strategy, focused differentiation. Its chosen niche was large, low-price but quality pubs, building on the quirky personality of its chairman Tim Martin, the Richard Branson of beer. By opting for organic growth it avoided entering into expensive pub auctions with the big pubcos. To date the strategy has been a successful one, but it may now be reaching its limits. The company may be increasingly vulnerable to takeover.

Whitbread is different again. In the 1990s it was a big brewer with a big pub estate, but in neither case was its position dominant. As number three or four, it was very vulnerable to being squeezed by the more efficient, low-cost market leaders. It opted for a radical strategy of diversification away from beer and into the general leisure industry. This enabled it to achieve the following two strategic objectives:

1   a move into a growth rather than a gently declining industry
2   the opportunity to become the market leader in its chosen segments.

Again the strategy has been successful, but it does have weaknesses. The most important is that the company's three-pronged portfolio of hotels, restaurants and leisure centres has, probably, at least one prong too many. Conglomerates are out of fashion, and the stock market is all in favour of focus.

Bibliography

Chapter 1

JOHNSON, G., SCHOLES, K. and WHITTINGTON, R. (2004) *Exploring corporate strategy.* 7th ed. Harlow: Pearson.

MILES, R.E. and SNOW, C.C. (1978) *Organizational strategy, structure and process.* Maidenhead: McGraw-Hill.

PORTER, M.E. (1980) *Competitive strategy.* New York: Free Press.

Chapter 2

Business Monitor (1990) PA1002.

COHEN, N. (1993) Thurrock, Essex, USA. *The Independent on Sunday*, 31 October.

EAGLESHAM, J. (2004) OFT plans probe of superstore practices. *The Financial Times*, 28 June 2004.

FINCH, J. (2004) Tesco takes more business off rivals. *The Guardian*, 26 August.

GILLAN, A. (2001) US air crews bitter at 'downsizing'. *The Guardian*, 3 October.

HARPER, K. (2000) Bob Ayling's fall from grace. *The Guardian*, 23 May.

HISCOTT, G. (2004) Big chains strengthen hold on Britain's shoppers. *The Independent*, 10 August.

JOYCE, P. and WOODS, A. (1996) *Essential strategic management: from modernism to pragmatism.* Oxford: Butterworth-Heinemann.

KIM, C. and MAUBORGNE, R. (2001) How to earn commitment. *The Financial Times*, 22 October.

LAWTON, A. and ROSE, A. (1994) *Organisation and management in the public sector.* 2nd ed. London: Pitman.

LIPSEY, R. and CHRYSTAL, A. (1999) *Principles of economics.* 9th ed. Oxford: Oxford University Press.

PATON, N. (2002) Store wars. *Personnel Today.* 12 March.

PORTER, M. (1980) *Competitive strategy: techniques for analyzing industries and competition.* London: Macmillan.

PURVIS, A. (2004) Why supermarkets are getting richer and richer. *The Observer,* 25 June.

SCHUMPETER, J. (1950) *Capitalism, socialism and democracy.* 3rd ed. New York: Harper and Rowe.

WALKER, R. (1990) Analysing the business portfolio in Black and Decker Europe. In TAYLOR, B. and HARRISON, J. (eds), *The manager's casebook of business strategy.* Oxford: Butterworth–Heinemann.

WARD, L. (2001) Charities warn Blair about 'cheap service'. *The Guardian*, 22 October.

WEAVER, M. (2001) Labour chooses third way to improve failing services. *The Guardian*, 22 October.

WHEATCROFT, P. (2004) Supermarkets take a convenient route. *The Times*, 17 August.

WINTOUR, P. (2004a) Unions win 'two-tier' victory'. *The Guardian*, 16 July.

WINTOUR, P. (2004b) Unions bury hatchet with Labour. *The Guardian*, 26 July.

Chapter 3

AISBETT, E. (2003) Globalization, poverty and inequality: are the criticisms vague, vested or valid? *NBER Pre-conference on Globalization, Poverty and Inequality*, October.

BARRIENTOS, A. and BARRIENTOS, S. W. (2002) Extending social protection to informal workers in the horticultural global value chain. *Social Protection Discussion Paper Series* No 0216, June. World Bank.

CLENNELL, A. (2004) Call centre switches jobs back from India to Britain. *The Independent*, 23 January.

ELLIOTT, L. (2004) What the WTO needs is a new Reformation. *The Guardian*, 2 August.

FUKUYAMA, F. (2004) Bring back the state. *The Observer*, 4 July.

GHEMAWAT, P. (2003) The forgotten strategy. *Harvard Business Review*. Vol 81, No 11, November.

GRAY, J. (1995) *False dawn*. London: Granta, p6.

JACOBS, M. (2001) Bridging the global divide. *The Observer*, 11 November.

LOEBIS, L. and SCHMITZ, H. (2003) Furniture makers – Winners or losers from globalisation?. *Institute of Development Studies*, September.

LUCAS, C. (2001) Doha spells disaster for development. *The Observer*, 18 November.

MACMULLAN, J. (2004) A sweet deal: sugar in Mozambique. In *Taking liberties: poor people, free trade and trade justice*. Christian Aid.

MADELEY, J. (2001) No end to shackles. *The Observer*, 21 January.

MATHIASON, N. (2003) Debt duties. *The Observer*, 20 April.

MICKLETHWAIT, J. and WOOLDRIDGE, A. (2000) *A future perfect: the challenge and hidden promise of globalization*. London: Heinemann, p7.

MORRIS, H. and WILLEY, B. (1996) *The corporate environment*. London: Pitman, pp197–199.

MULVEY, S. (2004) The EU's eastward drift. *BBC News*. 5 March, news.bbc.co.uk.

OHMAE, K. (1990) *The borderless world*. Glasgow: Collins.

RYLE, S. (2002) Banana war leaves the Caribbean a casualty. *The Observer*, 24 November.

SASSEN, S. (2001) A message from the global south. *The Guardian*, 12 September.

SEGAL-HORN, S. (2002) Global firms – heroes or villains? How and why companies globalise. *European Business Journal*. Vol. 14, Issue 1.

SHAH, S. (2004) India 'losing ground to UK in battle of the call centres'. *The Independent*, 10 April.

STEWART, H. (2002) Africa reinforces debt relief case. *The Guardian*, 2 September.

SWANN, C. (2004) Sixty years on, and still contentious. *The Financial Times*, 29 May.

The Guardian (2004) Leading article, 21 June.

THUROW, L. (1999) *Creating wealth*. London: Nicholas Brealey, p xv.

United Nations Conference on Trade and Development (Unctad) (2001) *World Investment Report*. New York and Geneva: United Nations.

WILLIAMS, F. (2001) Global foreign investment flows 'set to fall to 40 per cent'. *The Financial Times*, 19 September.

WOODS, N. (2000) *The political economy of globalisation*. Basingstoke: Macmillan, pp3–7.

Chapter 4

Bank of England (2003) *Remit for the Monetary Policy Committee of the Bank of England and the New Inflation Target* (www.bankofengland.co.uk).

Bank of England (2004a) The Labour Market (www.bankof england.co.uk/targettwopointzero).

Bank of England (2004b) How do interest rates affect inflation? (www.bankof england.co.uk/targettwopointzero).

BOYCOTT, O. (2004) Transcript reveals doctor's pleas for dying teenager. *The Guardian*, 18 October.

BRINER, R. (2001) Why family-friendly practices can also be performance-friendly. *People Management*, 8 November.

BROWN, K. (2001) Standard that has delivered. *The Financial Times*, 30 October.

DAVIES, M. (2004) Troubled waters?: the economic implications of higher oil prices. *HSBC Economic Review*. Issue 33, July.

DE GRAUWE, P. (2001) Competitiveness and compassion. *The Financial Times*, 8 November.

Department of Trade and Industry (1998) *Building the Knowledge Driven Economy* (www.dti.gov.uk/competitive).

Department of Trade and Industry (2001) *Opportunity for All in a World of Change* (www.dti.gov.uk/opportunity for all).

ECB (2004) *Objective of monetary policy* (www.ecb.int).

ELLIOTT, L. (2004) The outlook is not so Nice when hidden hazards are exposed. *The Guardian*, 18 October.

European Union (2004) *European Performance in Competitiveness and Innovation* (www.europa.eu.int).

FARNHAM, D. (1999) *Managing in a business context*. London: CIPD.

Federal Reserve (2004) *Frequently asked questions: monetary policy* (www.federalreserve.gov).

FORMAN, F.N. and BALDWIN, N.D.J. (1999) *Mastering British politics*. 4th ed. Basingstoke: Macmillan.

FRIEDMAN, M. and SCHWARTZ, R. (1963) *A monetary history of the United States*. Princeton, Princeton University Press.

GOYAL, A. and JHA, A. (2004) Dictatorship, Democracy and Institutions: macro policy in China and India. *Economic and Political Weekly (India)*, 16 October.

HENCKE, D. (2004) Big players lobbying for piece of the action. *The Guardian*, 27 October.

HILTON, I. (2004) A rampaging market, but a long way from global power. *The Guardian*, 13 November.

HUTTON, W. (2004) We must dare to be dynamic. *The Observer*, 7 November.

KEEGAN, W. (2001) The high cost of falling prices. *The Guardian*, 14 November.

KEEGAN, W. (2004a) Erm, there's a danger in paradise. *The Observer*, 17 October.

KEEGAN, W. (2004b) Keeping an eye on the competition. *The Observer*, 31 October.

KEYNES, J.M. (1936) *The General Theory of Employment Interest and Money*. London, Macmillan.

LENNAN, D. (2001) Cartel crooks belong in jail. *The Financial Times*, 2 November.

LIPSEY, R. G. and CHRYSTAL, K. A. (1999) *Principles of economics*. 9th ed. Oxford: Oxford University Press.

MATHIASON, N. (2004) Casino bill derailed by bitter split in Cabinet. *The Observer*, 24 October.

MERRICK, N. (2001) Minority interest. *People Management*, 8 November.

MULVEY, S. (2003) The EU law that rules our lives. *BBC News Online* (www.news.bbc.co.uk).

NELSON, P. (2001) Does IIP still make the grade? *Personnel Today*, 13 November.

PHILLIPS, A.W. (1958) The Rrlation between unemployment and the rate of change of money wage rates in the United Kingdom 1861–1957. *Economica*, 25 November.

PHILPOTT, J. (2002) Productivity and people management. *Perspectives*, Spring 2002, CIPD.

PHILPOTT, J. (2003) Europe. *Perspectives*, Summer 2003, CIPD.

PORTER, M. and KETELS, C. (2003) UK competitiveness: moving to the next stage. *DTI Economics Paper No 3*. DTI/ESRC, May.

STEELE, J. (2001) Food for thought: Amartya Sen. *The Guardian*, 31 March.

World Bank (2000) *Beyond economic growth: meeting the challenges of global development* (www.worldbank/depweb/beyond/global./chapter4).

Chapter 5

CARTWRIGHT, S. and COOPER, S. (1997) *Managing Workplace Stress*. Sage, London.

CURWEN, P. (1997) *Restructuring telecommunications: a study of Europe in a global context*. London: Macmillan.

EARNSHAW, J. and COOPER, C. (1996) *Stress and Employer Liability*. IPD, London.

Electricity Association (1998) Electricity Industry review. HMSO.

FRIEDMAN, M. (1970) The counter-revolution in monetary theory. Institute of Economic Affairs.

HSE (2002) *Tackling Work-related Stress: a Manager's Guide to Improving and Maintaining Employee Health and Well-Being*. HSE.

IRS (2002) Court of Appeal guidelines for stress at work cases. *Employment Law Review 748*, 25 March.

MILLER, S. (1999) Council pays £67,000 for stress injury. *The Guardian*, 6 July, p4.

MARTIN, S. and PARKER, D. (1997) *The impact of privatisation: ownership and corporate performance in the UK*. London: Routledge.

PALMER, B. and QUINN, P. (2004) Protracted Agony, *People Management*, 6 May, p17.

POLLACK, C. (1997) European Union policies. In Lewington, I. (ed.), *Utility regulation 1997*. Centre for the Study of Regulated Industries and Privatisation International.

RICK, J., et al. (1997) *Stress: Big Issue, but what are the problems?* Institute of Employment Studies Report 311, July.

TEHRANI, N. (2002) *Managing Organisational Stress: a CIPD guide to improving and maintaining well-being*, CIPD.

WAINWRIGHT, M. (1994) Mistakes led to chemical plant deaths. *Guardian*, 21 June, p8.

WATKINS, J. (2003) Wellness beats output slump, *People Management*, 18 December, p12.

Chapter 6

BAIRD, R. (2001) Britain's immigrants overstep line as numbers surge to 135,000 a year. *The Express*, November 16.

BRINDLE, D. (1999) Northerners heed south's siren call. *The Guardian*, 27 August, p3.

Business Week (2004) America's bebe boom. 15 March, pp50–52.

CHAMPION, A. (1993) *Population matters: the local dimension*. London: Paul Chapman Publishing.

DICKEN, P. (2003) *Global shift*. London: Sage.

DOWARD, J. (2003) Future imperfect as longer lifespan looms. *The Observer*, 28 December, p9.

Economist (2004) Return of the wrinklies. 17 January, p24.

HASKEY, J. (1993) Trends in the number of one-parent families in Great Britain. *Population Trends*. 71, pp26–33.

JACKSON, S. (1998) *Britain's population*. London: Routledge.

KURTZ, S. (2004) The end of marriage in Scandinavia. *Weekly Standard*, 9, p20.

MARTIN, P. and WIDGREN, J. (1996) International migration: a global challenge. *Population Bulletin*, 51.

MASSEY, D. (1984) *Spatial divisions of labour: social structures and the geography of production*. London: Macmillan.

McCRONE, A. (1999) The pounds and pence of an ageing Britain. *Business Day*, 21 September.

MULLAN, P. (2002) *The imaginary time bomb*. London: Tauris.

NORTON, C. (2002) Japan bribes mothers in bid for baby boom. *Sunday Time,* 15 September.

PEARCE, F. (2002) We need more babies. *Sunday Times*, 17 March.

PERSAUD, J. (2004) Carry on working. *People Management,* 29 July, pp36–37.

SMALLWOOD, T. (2003) People power rings changes. *Sunday Times*, 10 August.

STILLWELL, J., REES, P. and BODEN, P. (1992) *Migration processes and patterns.* Vol. 2. Population Redistribution in the UK. London: Belhaven.

UNITED NATIONS (2005) Report on world fertility rates at 2003. New York: United Nations.

WOODHEAD, M. (2004) Exodus heralds end of Schroder's IT dream. *Sunday Times*, 28 March.

Chapter 7

ADAMSON, L. (2001) It's time to clock off. *The Guardian*, 1 December.

ALDRIDGE, S. (2001) *Social Mobility: a discussion paper*. Cabinet Office, Performance and Innovation Unit.

ALDRIDGE, S. (2004) *Life chances & social mobility: an overview of the evidence*. Cabinet Office, Prime Minister's Strategy Unit.

ATKINSON, J. (1984) Manpower strategies for the flexible organisation. *Personnel Management*, August.

BARBER, B. (1998) Speech to the *New Labour and the Labour Movement* conference, 19/20 June.

BILTON, T., BONNETT, K., JONES, P., SKINNER, D., STANWORTH, M. and WEBSTER, A. (1996) *Introductory sociology.* 3rd ed. Basingstoke: Macmillan.

BRINER, R. (2001) Why family-friendly practices can also be performance-friendly. *People Management*, 8 November.

BRINER, R. and CONWAY, N. (2001) Promises, promises. *People Management*, 25 November.

CIPD (2003a) Managing the psychological contract. *Factsheet.* London: CIPD, May.

CIPD (2003b) Work-life balance. *Factsheet.* London: CIPD, April.

CIPD (2004a) Trade union learning representatives. *The change agenda*. London: CIPD.

CIPD (2004b) Parental rights and other family-friendly provisions. *Frequently asked questions*. London: CIPD.

CLARK, D. (2004) Unto him that hath. *The Guardian*, 6 August.

CLEMENT B, (2001) Honda workers vote for union recognition. *The Independent*, 11 December.

COWAN, R. (2004) Met harnesses its diversity in the war against crime. *The Guardian*, 2 December.

DUNCAN, G. (2001) Pay of business chiefs soars. *The Times*, 26 July.

Focused females forge ahead (2001) *Professional Manager,* November.

FURLONG, A. and CARTMEL, F. (2001) Capitalism without classes. In A. GIDDENS, A. (ed), *Sociology: introductory readings*, revised edn. Cambridge: Polity.

GALL, G. (2001) ISTC wins in recognition vote. *People Management,* 22 November.

GALLIE, D. (2000) The labour force. In *Twentieth century British social trends*, HALSEY, A. and WEBB, J. (eds). Basingstoke: Macmillan.

GEORGE, V. and WILDING, P. (1999) *British society and social welfare: towards a sustainable society*. Basingstoke: Macmillan.

GREEN, A. (2003) Labour market trends, skill needs and the ageing of the workforce: a challenge for employability? *Local Economy*, November.

GUEST, D. and CONWAY, N. (2002) *Pressure at work and the psychological contract*. London: CIPD.

HANDY, C. (1991) *Inside organisations: 21 ideas for managers*. London: BBC Books.

Harlow 2000 Initiative (1993) Harlow District Council.

Harlow Baseline Study 2002 (2002) Harlow District Council.

ISER (2002) Class matters. *ISER Newsletter,* October. Institute for Social and Economic Research.

KANDOLA, R. and FULLERTON, J. (1994) *Managing the mosaic*. London: CIPD.

KIMBERLY, J .and CRAIG, E. (2001) Work as a life experience. *The Financial Times*, 5 November.

MARCHINGTON, M. and WILKINSON, A. (2000) *Core personnel and development*. London: CIPD.

MERRICK, N. (2001) Minority interest. *People Management.* 8 November.

MILBURN, A. (2004) Inequality, mobility and opportunity: the politics of aspiration. Speech to the Institute for Public Policy Research, 9 November.

MOYNAGH, M. and WORSLEY, R. (2001) Prophet sharing. *People Management*, 27 December.

MULLINS, L. (1996) *Management and organisational behaviour*. 4th ed. London: Pitman.

PETERS, T. J. and WATERMAN, R. H. (1982) *In search of excellence: lessons from America's best-run companies*. New York: Harper & Row.

PHILPOTT, J. (2002) *HRH – a work audit*. CIPD Perspectives, Summer.

ROSS, R. and SCHNEIDER, R. (1992) *From equality to diversity – a business case for equal opportunities*. London: Pitman.

Royal Mail recruits excluded groups (2004) *People Management,* 28 October.

RUNCIMAN, W.G. (1990) How many classes are there in contemporary British society? *Sociology*. Vol. 24, No. 2.

Social Trends (2004) Flexible working 2003. Table 4.18, HMSO.

Social Trends (2004) Trade union membership 2002. Table 4.25, HMSO.

TOYNBEE, P. (2004) Going nowhere. *The Guardian*, 2 April.

WALSH, J. (2001) A happy reunion. *People Management*, 8 November.

WILSON, R.M.S., GILLIGAN, C. and PEARSON, D.J. (1992) *Strategic marketing management: planning, implementation and control.* Oxford: Butterworth-Heinemann.

YOUNG, M. (1958) *The rise of the meritocracy.* Harmondsworth: Penguin.

Chapter 8

ARKIN, A. (2002) The package to India. *People Management.* 24 January, pp34–36.

Business Week (2004) Wireless. 21 June, pp62–65.

DICKEN, P. (2003) *Global shift.* 4th ed. London: Sage.

Economist (2000) 23 September.

Economist (2004) Salad days. 6 November, pp38–39.

FREEMAN, C. (1987) *Technology policy and economic performance: lessons from Japan.* London: Pinter Publishers.

GLOVER, C. (2004) Tomorrow's world. *People Management.* 26 February, pp40–41.

HALL, P. and PRESTON, P. (1988) *The carrier wave: new information technology and the geography of innovation, 1846-2003.* London: Unwin Hyman.

KAHN, A. (1967) *The Year 2000.* Macmillan, New York.

People Management (1998) 28 May, p11 (anon).

PRUSACK, L. (1997) *Knowledge in organisations.* London: Butterworth-Heinemann.

REILLY, P. (2000) *HR shared services and the realignment of HR.* Institute of Employment Studies Report 368, IES.

SMITH, D. (2004) Prophet warning. *People Management.* 23 December, pp24–29.

SPARROW, P., BREWSTER, C. and HARRIS, H. (2004) *Globalizing Human Resource Management.* Routledge, London.

STEWART, T. (2001) *The wealth of knowledge: intellectual capital in the 21st century organisation.* London: Nicholas Brearley.

STOREY, J. and QUINTAS, P. (2001) Knowledge management and HRM. In STOREY, J. (ed.), *Human Resource Management: a critical text.* London: Thomson Learning.

STREDWICK, J. and ELLIS, S. (2005) *Flexible working,* 2nd edition. London: CIPD.

SUBRAMANIAN, S. (2004) *Biotechnology and society.* www.chennaionline [accessed Nov 24].

Chapter 9

Accountability Primer: Sustainability (nd) (www.accountability.org.uk).

ARGENTI, J. (1993) *Your organisation, what is it for? Challenging traditional organizational aims.* Maidenhead: McGraw-Hill.

BILLINGTON, R. (2003) *Living Philosophy: an introduction to moral thought.* 3rd ed. London: Routledge, p19.

BITC (2000) Putting your heart into it: purpose and values. *Report of the Business Impact Task Force 2000.* Business in the Community, www.bitc.org.uk.

BITC (2002) *The public's views of corporate responsibility,* www.bitc.org.uk.

BITC (2003) *The business case for corporate responsibility,* www.bitc.org.uk.

BITC (2004) *Awards for excellence 2004.* Business in the Community, www.bitc.org.uk/resources/case_studies.

BRINKMANN, J. and IMS, K. (2003) Good intentions aside: drafting a functionalist look at codes of ethics. *Business ethics: a European review.* Vol. 12, No. 3.

CARROLL, A. B. (1990) Principles of business ethics: their role in decision making and an initial consensus. *Management Review.* Vol. 28, No. 8.

CAULKIN, S. (2003) Ethics and profits do mix. *The Observer,* 20 April.

CAULKIN, S. (2004) Unacceptable face of regulation. *The Observer,* 28 November.

CHARKHAM, J. (1994) *Keeping good company: a study of corporate governance in five countries.* Oxford: OUP.

CIPD (2003a) *Code of professional conduct and disciplinary procedures.* London: CIPD.

CIPD (2003b) *Corporate responsibility and HR's role.* London: CIPD.

COLLINS, C. and PORRAS, J. (2000) *Built to last: successful habits of visionary companies.* 3rd ed. London: Random House.

CONNOCK, S. and JOHNS, T. (1995) *Ethical leadership.* London: CIPD.

COWE, R. (2004) Commanding heights. *The Guardian,* 8 November.

CURTIS, P. (2004) Market graders. *The Guardian,* 17 August.

DEAL, T. and KENNEDY, A. (1990) Values: the core of the culture. In CAMPBELL, A, and TAWADEY, K., *Mission and business philosophy.* Oxford: Butterworth-Heinemann.

DRUCKER, P. (1990) What is 'business ethics'? In CAMPBELL, A. and TAWADY, K., *Mission and business philosophy.* Oxford: Butterworth-Heinemann.

DTI (2002) *Business and society: corporate social responsibility.*

European Commission (2001) *Promoting a European framework for corporate social responsibility.*

Explore Worldwide (2004) *2004–2005 brochure.*

FARNHAM, D. (1999) *Managing in a business context.* London: CIPD.

GOLZEN, G. (2001) What's the big idea? *Global HR.* September.

HARRISON, R. (2002) *Learning and development.* 3rd ed. London: CIPD.

HENDERSON, D. (2001) *Misguided virtue: false notions of corporate social responsibility.* The Institute of Economic Affairs (www.iea.org.uk).

HOFFMAN, M. (1990) What is necessary for corporate moral excellence? In CAMPBELL, A. and TAWADY, K., *Mission and business philosophy.* Oxford: Butterworth-Heinemann.

HOFSTEDE, G. (1980) *Culture's consequences: international differences in work-related values.* London: Sage.

Home Office (1999) *The Stephen Lawrence Inquiry: report of an inquiry by Sir William Macpherson of Cluny.* London: The Stationery Office.

Industrial Relations Services (1999) *IRS Employment Trends* 675, March.

JOHNSON, G. and SCHOLES, K. (1997) *Exploring corporate strategy*. 4th ed. Hemel Hempstead: Prentice Hall.

KEARNS, P. and INGATE, K. (2001) Should the CIPD strike off poor practitioners? *Personnel Today*, 23 October 2001.

LAWTON, A. (1998) *Ethical management for the public services*. Buckingham: OUP.

LEWIS, J. (2002) Testing time. *Personnel Today*, 9 April.

MAITLAND, A. (2003) Profits from the righteous path. *The Financial Times*, 3 April.

MONBIOT, G. (2001) Superstores brand us to ensure we belong to them. *The Guardian,* 31 July.

Personnel Today (2004) CSR help is at hand. *Personnel Today*, 27 July.

REITZ, J., WALL, J. and LOVE, M. S. (1998) Ethics in negotiation: oil and water or good lubrication? *Business Horizons*, May–June.

RICHARDS, D. and GLADWIN,T. (1999) Sustainability metrics for the Business Enterprise. *Environmental Quality Management*, Spring.

SCHWARTZ, M.S. (2001) A code of ethics for corporate codes of ethics. *Journal of Business Ethics,* 41.

SNELL, R. (1999) Managing ethically. In FULOP, L. and LINSTEAD, S., *Management: a critical text*. Basingstoke: Macmillan.

TAIT, N. (2003) A line between protest and persecution. *The Financial Times*, 8 September.

TARGETT, S. (2004) Is good governance good value? *The Financial Times*, 17 April.

WILLIAMS, R. (2001) Under pressure, under pressure, under pressure. *Business Review,* September.

Chapter 10

ANSOFF, H.I. (1965) *Corporate strategy*. Harmondsworth: Penguin.

ARMSTRONG, M. (1999) *Managing activities*. London: CIPD.

BATTERSBY, J. (1999) Nelson Mandela's moral legacy. *Christian Science Monitor*, 10 May.

BBC Online (2003) Potter's potter slides into the red.

BBC2 (1990) *Troubleshooter*.

BLACKWELL, D. (2004) Sales surge helps Churchill China. *The Financial Times*, 1 September.

BOROUGHS, D. (1999) Proving that one man can make a difference. *US News and World Report*, 24 May.

BOWMAN, C. and FAULKNER, D. (1996) *Competitive and corporate strategy*. Homewood, Ill: Irwin.

BRIDGES, W. (1995) Breaking with the past. *Human Resources*, September–October.

BRIDGES, W. and MITCHELL, S. (2000) Leading transition: a new model for change. *Leader to Leader* 16, Spring.

BURNES, B. (1996) *Managing change: a strategic approach to organisational dynamics*. 2nd ed. London: Pitman.

Churchill China Plc (2004) Corporate summary and five-year record. Churchill China website (www..churchillchina.plc.uk).

CIPD (2004) *Factsheet*. Change management (www.cipd.co.uk).

Dilbert website (www.dilbert.com).

FELSTEAD, A. (2001) Falling US demand takes toll on Churchill China. *The Financial Times*, 10 November.

FINCH, J. (2004) Morrisons' duo determined to deliver. *The Guardian*, 8 September.

FURNHAM, A. and GUNTER, B. (1993) *Corporate assessment*. London: Routledge.

HAMEL, G. and PRAHALAD, C. K. (1994) *Competing for the future*. Boston: Harvard Business School Press.

HAMEL, G. (1996) Strategy as revolution. *Harvard Business Review*, July–August

JOHNSON, G., SCHOLES, K. and WHITTINGTON, R. (2004) *Exploring corporate strategy*. 7th ed. Harlow: Pearson.

Key Note (2004a) *Market report: bookselling*.

Key Note (2004b) *Market report plus: china and earthenware*.

KOTTER, J. (1995) Leading change – why transformation efforts fail. *Harvard Business Review*, March–April.

McCARTHY, B. (2004) How to manage organisational change. *People Management*, 9 December.

MESURE, S. (2004) Morrisons keen to show it hasn't lost its magic touch. *The Independent*, 8 September.

MINTZBERG, H. (1994) *The rise and fall of strategic planning*. Hemel Hempstead: Prentice-Hall.

MINTZBERG, H. (1998) Five Ps for strategy. In MINTZBERG, H., QUINN, J. B. and GHOSHAL, S. *The strategy process*, revised European edition. Hemel Hempstead: Prentice-Hall.

Ottakar's Plc (2004a) About Ottakar's: a brief history. Ottakar's website (www.ottakars.com).

Ottakar's Plc (2004b) Ottakar's today. Ottakar's website (www.ottakars.com).

Ottakar's Plc (2004c). *Annual report* 2004.

PETERS, T. and WATERMAN, R. (1982) *In Search of excellence*. New York: Harper & Row.

PETERS, T. (1985) *Thriving on chaos*. New York: Macmillan.

PORTER, M. (2004) *Competitive strategy: techniques for analysing industries and competition*. New York: The Free Press.

PORTER, M. (1985) *Competitive advantage: creating and sustaining superior performance*. New York: The Free Press.

PORTER, M. (1999) *On competition*. New York: The Free Press.

PRAHALAD, C. K. and HAMEL, G. (1990) The core competence of the corporation. *Harvard Business Review*, May–June.

Press Association (2004) WH Smith shares fall after profit warning. *The Guardian*, 2 January.

QUINN, J. (1980) *Strategies for change: logical incrementalism.* Homewood, Ill: Irwin.

RIDGEWAY, C. and WALLACE, B. (1994) Empowering change: the role of people management. London: CIPD.

RYLE, S. and WACHMAN, R. (2005) Morrisons faces investor revolt over Safeway. *The Observer*, 20 March.

SEBAG-MONTEFIORE, H. (1993) Who's who at the Zoo? *Management Today*, July.

SENGE, P. (1990) *The fifth discipline.* London: Century Business.

STACEY, R. (1991) *The chaos frontier: creative strategic control for business.* Oxford: Butterworth-Heinemann.

STACEY, R. (1993) *Strategic management and organisational dynamics,* London: Pitman.

STEVENSON, H.H. (1989) Defining corporate strengths and weaknesses. In BOWMAN, C. and ASCH, D. (eds), *Readings in strategic management.* Basingstoke: Macmillan.

TOMLINSON, H. (2001) Stop me and buy a Ben & Jerry's. *The Independent on Sunday*, 9 December.

TOMLINSON, H. (2004) Richard and Judy show boosts Ottakar's. *The Guardian*, 24 September.

TOWNSEND, A. and WEBB, T. (2004) A City memo to Morrisons: you're not a little firm up north now. *The Independent on Sunday*, 12 September.

WALTON, J. (1999) *Strategic human resource development.* London: FT/Prentice-Hall.

WH Smith Plc (2003) *Annual Report and Accounts.*

WH Smith Plc (2004a) Our company. WH Smith website, (www.whsmithplc.com).

WH Smith Plc (2004b) What we do. WH Smith website (www.whsmithplc.com).

Workers' Educational Association (WEA) in Northern Ireland (nd). *Mission Statement and WEA Values* (www.wea-ni.com).

Zoological Society of London (nd) *ZSL Mission Statement* (www.zsl.org).

Zoological Society of London (2003) *Annual Review.*

Chapter 11

BBC (2004) The Money Programme. *The booze business: trouble brewing*, 3 November.

CAULKIN, S. (2003) Brewing up taste for success. *The Observer*, 26 October.

Greene King Plc Report and Accounts 2003–2004.

Greene King Company Profile 2004. Datamonitor.

GWYTHER, M. (2001) Whitbread on the wagon. *Management Today*, September.

JACOBS, T. and STEELE, M. (1997) The European brewing industry. In JOHNSON, G. and SCHOLES, K., *Exploring corporate strategy: text and cases.* 4th ed. Hemel Hempstead: Prentice Hall.

J D Wetherspoon website (www.jdwetherspoon.co.uk).

J D Wetherspoon Company Profile 2004. Datamonitor.

JOHN, P. (2004) Tradition that goes back to the mash tun. *The Financial Times*, 10 July.

MILLAR, M. (2004) Whitbread gets HR on board to drive agenda. *Personnel Today*, 4 May.

PROTZ, R. (ed.) (2004) *Good beer guide 2004*. St Albans: CAMRA.

Scottish & Newcastle website (www.scottish-newcastle.com).

Scottish & Newcastle Company Profile 2004. Datamonitor.

STEVENSON, R. (2004) S&N cheers end of supermarket bloodbath. *The Independent*, 24 June.

The Publican (2002) Beer Orders to be revoked, 20 February.

Whitbread website (www.whitbread.co.uk).

Whitbread Company Profile 2004. Datamonitor.

WRAY, R. (2004) Whitbread seeks £800m in series of sell-offs. *The Guardian*, 29 October.

Index

Also from CIPD Publishing . . .

Becoming an Employer of Choice

Judith Leary-Joyce

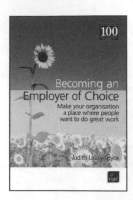

Being an 'employer of choice' can make a huge difference to your organisation's performance. If you create a great working environment, not only do great people want to work for you but everyone will strive to deliver their very best.

But how do you become an employer of choice? The companies that the Sunday Times has listed as the 'best places to work' can tell you. From ASDA and Microsoft to Timpson and Bromford Housing Association, all these organisations have one thing in common. They have created an environment in which employees feel valued and respected; in which they feel so connected to the company that they willingly give the effort required to deliver great results.

Judith Leary-Joyce has spoken to leaders, managers and employees within those companies and others to discover the secrets that have made them fantastic places to work. Her book will help you assess your organisation's current claim to greatness and make the business case for creating the sort of truly great company atmosphere that will attract great people who will deliver great results. It will help your organisation become an employer of choice.

Order your copy now online at www.cipd.co.uk/bookstore or call us on 0870 800 3366

Judith Leary-Joyce is an expert in leadership and management. She is CEO of Great Companies Consulting, which she established in 2002 after spending the previous year working on the Sunday Times' '100 Best Companies to Work For' list. She is a board member of the Servent Leadership Centre and, from 1979–1990, was MD of the Gestalt Centre, a psychotherapy training insititute.

| Published 2004 | 1 84398 057 6 | Paperback | 224 pages |

The Chartered Institute of Personnel and Development is the leading publisher of books and reports for personnel and training professionals, students and all those concerned with the effective management and development of people at work.

Also from CIPD Publishing . . .

Everyone Needs a Mentor:

Fostering talent in your organisation

4th Edition

David Clutterbuck

Mentoring is the most cost-efficient and sustainable method of fostering and developing talent within your organisation.

Mentoring can be used to:
- stretch talented employees to perform even better by exposure to high performing colleagues;
- ensure that experience is passed and kept within your organisation; and
- power your diversity programme by supporting employees from groups that are under-represented in your organisation by having them talk with others who have overcome similar barriers.

It is the ultimate win-win business tool. The employee gets a helping hand to fast-track their career and the mentor gets the satisfaction of helping others develop, while the organisation gains from improved performance and employee retention.

This text explains what mentoring is and how it differs from coaching. It shows you how to make the business case for mentoring and then how to set up, run and maintain your own mentoring programme – everything from selecting and matching mentors and mentees to measuring the results.

Order your copy now online at www.cipd.co.uk/bookstore or call us on 0870 800 3366

David Clutterbuck is one of Europe's most prolific and well-known management writers and thinkers. He has written more than 40 books, including *Managing Work–Life Balance* and *Learning Alliances*. *Everyone Needs a Mentor* is now the classic book on the subject and he is recognised as the UK's leading expert on mentoring and co-founder of the European Mentoring and Coaching Council. He is Visiting Professor at Sheffield Hallam University.

| Published 2004 | 1 84398 054 1 | Paperback | 200 pages |

The Chartered Institute of Personnel and Development is the leading publisher of books and reports for personnel and training professionals, students and all those concerned with the effective management and development of people at work.

Also from CIPD Publishing . . .

Managing Performance:

Performance management in action
2nd Edition

Michael Armstrong and Angela Baron

Managing performance is a critical focus of HR activity. Well-designed strategies to recognise and improve performance and focus individual effort can have a dramatic effect on bottom-line results. The problem is to determine what the processes, tools and delivery mechanisms are that will improve performance in your organisation, as well as determine which ones are best avoided.

The authors have tracked performance management processes over the past seven years, and their comprehensive survey reveals what leading organisations are doing to manage their employees' performance and how they are delivering results.

With detailed illustrations from the real world, and clear practical advice, this text shows you how to improve the management of your employees' performance.

Managing Performance will help you:
- design performance management processes that reflect the context and nature of the organisation;
- create supportive delivery mechanisms for performance management; and
- evaluate and continuously develop performance management strategies to reflect the changing business environment.

Order your copy now online at www.cipd.co.uk/bookstore or call us on 0870 800 3366

Michael Armstrong is a Fellow of the Chartered Institute of Personnel and Development, and a Fellow of the Institute of Management Consultants. He has over 25 years experience in personnel management, including 12 as a personnel director. He has also been a management consultant for many years and is a former Chief Examiner, Employee Reward, for the CIPD. He has written a number of successful management books, including *The Job Evaluation Handbook* (1995) and *Strategic HRM* (2002), both co-written with Angela Baron; *Employee Reward* (third edition 2002); *Rewarding Teams* (2000); and *New Dimensions in Pay Management* (2001). All are published by the CIPD.

Angela Baron has been Advisor, Organisational and Resourcing at the Chartered Institute of Personnel and Development since 1990. Her other books, *The Job Evaluation Handbook* and *Strategic HRM* were both co-written with Michael Armstrong.

Published 2004	1 84398 101 7	Paperback	192 pages

The Chartered Institute of Personnel and Development is the leading publisher of books and reports for personnel and training professionals, students and all those concerned with the effective management and development of people at work.

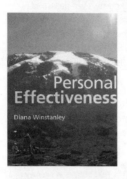

CIPD Policies and Procedures for People Managers

Sign Up for Your FREE 28-Day Trial Now and Save!

As a subscriber to *CIPD Employment Law for People Managers* you are entitled to an extra **10%** discount off the usual price of **CIPD Policies and Procedures for People Managers.**

Do you have time to create good practice policies compliant with the law?

Do you know what policies you ought to have in place?

Do you need resources to manage the HR function in your organisation?

Well, now help is at hand!

At the CIPD we are ideally placed to offer you example policies and procedures along with expert commentary.

In *Policies and Procedures for People Managers* you will find policies, procedures and documents covering every aspect of employment from recruitment to termination. Policies and procedures for every work scenario.

As part of your subscription all these documents are also *available free online* for you to download and adapt to your organisation's requirements.

What will I receive?

CIPD Policies and Procedures for People Managers is built around a loose-leaf volume including:

The manual – a comprehensive resource contained within an A4 binder

Updates – issued four times a year, these comprise the latest developments and legislative changes to keep the manual completely up to date, making sure you avoid problems in the future by ensuring that your policies and procedures are current now

Internet access – providing searchable unlimited access to the full service, including downloadable policies and procedures for you to adapt

Free book – a best-selling title from CIPD Publishing's portfolio, giving you further vital information.

To find out more, visit www.cipd.co.uk/ppfpm

CIPD Members	Non-members
Usual price £270	Usual price £300
You pay £245	You pay £270

Call 0870 442 1020 quoting media code EL1004 to get these special rates

Remember, you pay nothing for 28 days. If you are not entirely satisfied with *CIPD Policies and Procedures for People Managers*, you can return it with no further obligation.

Request your free 28-day trial of *CIPD Policies and Procedures for People Managers* today! Call 0870 442 1020 quoting media code EL1004

Also from CIPD Publishing . . .

The New Rules of Engagement:

Life–work balance and employee commitment

Mike Johnson

How many of your employees care enough about their work, or organisation, to do anything more than the bare minimum? How many would stay if they were offered another job?

Highly-engaged employees are six times less likely to be planning to leave their employer than the disengaged. How much could you save on recruitment costs by improving engagement? How about the 'discretionary effort' that highly engaged employees put in?

This text argues that there are ways to develop a new psychological contract between employer and employee. Start by recognising that talk of a 'work–life balance' is the wrong way round as far as employees are concerned – they are much more interested in a 'life–work balance'.

The advice in this book will:
- help to convince senior management that employee engagement matters;
- help to improve your employees' productivity and willingness to try out new ideas and work practices;
- help to retain key employees; and
- make it easier to attract a higher calibre of employee.

Order your copy now online at www.cipd.co.uk/bookstore or call us on 0870 800 3366

Mike Johnson is a consultant, author and Managing Partner of Johnson Associates Limited, a coprorate communications consultancy. The firm's main activities are internal communications strategy, researching and writing on world-of-work issues, and management education strategy for major corporations and institutions.

| Published 2004 | 1 84398 072 X | Paperback | 192 pages |

The Chartered Institute of Personnel and Development is the leading publisher of books and reports for personnel and training professionals, students and all those concerned with the effective management and development of people at work.